UNTANGLING THE MIDDLE EAST

UNTANGLING THE MIDDLE EAST

A Guide to the Past, Present, and Future
of the World's Most Chaotic Region

ORI Z. SOLTES

Skyhorse Publishing

*In loving memory
of my mother-in-law, Judith,
who never stopped inquiring
into this web,
among so many others.*

CONTENTS

PREFACE

Let me begin by saying what the reader of this volume will not walk away with: a solution to all the problems of the Middle East. Some suggestions that point in that direction are offered, but no unequivocal road map. On the other hand, what you will come away with is a sense of *why* there are no simple answers; of how extraordinarily complex the region is—and has been, for millennia. And as a bonus, you will understand that any politician or pundit who offers a simple solution—"If X only did this!" or "If Y only did that!"—either has no idea what s/he is talking about, or is simply lying.

All too often, the Middle East is considered from too narrow a viewpoint, even by those not trying to be political or clever. Many are the experts and authorities who understand the ins and outs of Arab culture or of Islam or of the Israelis or the Iraqis or the Egyptians. But rarely does one encounter a discussion that encompasses the extraordinary array of complications that interweave one another to yield an answer to two essential questions: why is this region so riven by conflict and why is it so difficult to understand for outsiders? The intention of this volume is to make accessible to an intelligent reader an answer to these intertwined questions.

In so doing, its goal is primarily to make its readers wary of any "authority" —academic, journalistic, or political—who glibly asserts that the problem is simply this or the solution simply that. Thus, its intention is to function as a primer: each of the areas encompassed can be studied in much greater detail in other works mentioned in the endnotes and bibliography.[1] Its goal is not to propose a given solution, in fact, but to follow the lead offered in Athens more than twenty-four centuries ago by Plato's Socrates. In dialogue after dialogue he asserted that, if the truth on any given matter were not easily attainable, the only hope for even coming close to it would be through *elengkhos*—cross-examination. Socratic-Platonic *elengkhos* is a close and continuous multilayered dialogue engaged in by determined intellectual explorers. What follows is also an *elengkhos* of sorts.

Moreover, I must stress that the focus of this volume is to explore a very complex *past* history that is full of paradoxes and contradictions—as opposed to emphasizing the present and the future. While I do bring the discussion up to the "present" day and even offer a few ideas for dealing with some of the issues in the region that look toward the future, (such as a *three*-state Israel-Palestine solution), the reader and I must recognize two absolutes in the discussion that follows. The first is that my primary goal is to approach the present-future with a solid grounding in the layers and intertwinings that define the past, so much of which is typically ignored as the politicians and pundits hold forth.

The second is that the region is so extraordinarily volatile that changes can and do occur—and certainly have occurred—with breathtaking speed. A situation that I might discuss in these pages as part of the present may well have been superseded by the time this volume hits the light of day and ends up in the reader's hands. Thus, the concluding parts of my discussion are intended to be understood as tentative and temporary, even as the verities of the past encompassed in most of my chapters are so painfully enduring.

To this I must add that I began writing this narrative in 2004, when Ariel Sharon was still physically healthy and serving as the prime minster of Israel, and Yassir Arafat was alive and in charge of the Palestinian Authority. A good deal of water has passed under the myriad bridges of this discussion since then, from the eclipse of these two figures and the concomitant changes—multiple changes—in the leadership structures of those they once led, to the Israel-Gaza explosion; from the advent of ISIS to the so-called "Arab spring" to shifts in Iran's position in the world, to say nothing of the expanding number of real and imagined, potential and actual flash points, from Afghanistan and Pakistan to Iraq and Syria and Turkey to Yemen and the Sudan.

I have continued to update in accordance with new developments, even as current events continue to corroborate the essential themes and issues that I discuss through the majority of the text. By the time these words are being read there will have been further events and changes that will shift current nuances and perhaps future consequences but will further validate the time spent trying to understand the layered and interwoven past that has fed into the layered and interwoven array of presents in which we find the region and ourselves.

ACKNOWLEDGMENTS

I t is my pleasure to acknowledge several individuals who were essential to the writing of this narrative. My first explorations of this topic were limited to the Arab-Israeli Conflict, which was the name of a course I was given the opportunity to teach many times in the 1980s at Siegel College (then known as the Cleveland College of Jewish Studies), for which opportunity I am grateful to David S. Ariel, then-president of the college. My colleagues, Moshe Berger and Bernie Steinberg, and my students were invaluable in helping me to think more clearly and hone my ideas. It was in preparing that course for the first time that I realized that one could not understand the Arab-Israeli conflict without understanding the much larger arena of the Middle East in which such a range of conflicts was taking place—and had been taking place for centuries. I also began to realize that the vast array of materials on the topic always seemed to include parts of it and exclude other parts.

In the 1990s, I was privileged to lecture on the broader aspects of the Middle East and its complexities under the umbrella of a number of organizations, particularly Hadassah, the Conference on Alternatives in Jewish Education, and Washington and Lee University's Summer Alumni College, which provided further opportunities to research and think about this subject. I thank their leaders (particularly Rob Fure of W&L) for such enriching opportunities.

Most significantly, my good friend Mark A. Smith, more forceful than others in the past had been, pushed me to write things down, and read and commented on the first draft of the manuscript. His encouragement and more importantly his astuteness were essentials for turning verbal observations into written ones. Another good friend, Allison Archambault read the next draft with her usual sensitivity to nuance of both style and content. I am extremely grateful to both of them: to Mark for pushing me to the starting line and to Allison for pulling me toward the finish line.

Finally, I am grateful to Jeremy Kay, both for his editorial acumen and for his decision to get me *to* the finish line by entering a very crowded arena with this publication in its first iteration, in 2009; and to Jerrod MacFarlane, for his pulling it into the astonishing realm of Skyhorse Publishing in this second, expanded version of my narrative, to say nothing of his extremely astute editorial recommendations.

Summer, 2016
Washington, DC

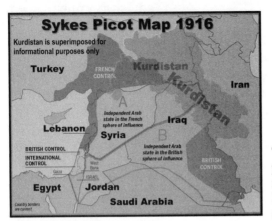

The Sykes-Picot agreement projecting a division of the region between British and French spheres of influence after World War I.

The 1947 UN proposal—one of half a dozen between 1930 and 1947—for dividing Western Palestine into two states: one Jewish and one Muslim/Christian Arab.

Sunni Arab, Shi'i Arab, and Kurdish population areas in Iraq and its environs; since 2003, the strife among these three groups has been constant.

TIMELINE

BCE

ca. 2000	Abraham the Hebrew and the first *muslim*.
ca. 1450	Moses, leader of the Israelites.
ca. 1000–965	Reign of Israelite King David.
ca. 965–30	Reign of Israelite King Solomon; building of the First Temple.
ca. 925	Division of Israelite Kingdom into Israelite North and Judaean South.
853	Reference to Prince Gindibu Arabi in Assyrian inscription of Shalmaneser III.
ca. 720	Swallowing up of Northern Israelite kingdom by Assyrians.
586	Destruction of First Temple by the Babylonians (Chaldaeans); exile of uppercrust Judaeans.
538	Return of Judaeans (not all) from exile under Achaemenid Medo-Persian patronage.
ca. 530	*Arabaya* referenced in Achaemenid Persian documents.
ca. 490	Reference to *Magos Arabos* in Greek playwright Aeschylu's *The Persians*.
444	Traditional date for redaction (final written form) of the Torah.
ca. 330	Fall of Achaemenid Persian Empire to Alexander the Great, whose rule extends from Libya to India.
323	Death of Alexander the Great; beginning of "Hellenistic" period.
ca. 300	Seleucids in power in Syria and beyond, Ptolemies in Egypt and beyond, Judaea in between, sometimes subject to or allied with one or the other.

168–5	Successful revolt of Hasmonaean-led Judaeans against Seleucid rule.
37	Death of last Hasmonaean ruler.
37–4	Rule of Idumaean-born King Herod "the Great" over Judaea.
4	Loss of Judaean independence; establishment of Roman procuratorial system.

CE

26–36	Procuratorship of Pontius Pilate.
70	Destruction of Second Temple.
ca. 100	Definitive schism within Judaeanism, birth of Judaism and Christianity.
132–5	Bar Kokhba Revolt against the Romans.
140	Canonization of Hebrew Bible.
325	Council of Nicaea under Emperor Constantine; official embrace of Triune Christian as *religio*; Arian Christianity termed heretical.
354–428	St. Augustine, shaping of key Christian concepts.
ca. 390	Under Emperor Theodosius, Christianity becomes official religion of the Empire.
397	Synod of Hippo approves canon of New Testament.
476	Romulus Augustulus deposed; end of Western Roman Empire.
517–25	Dhu Nuwas, Jewish king in Yemen.
570–1	Birth of Muhammad.
610	Muhammad experiences his first revelations.
622	Muhammad's *hijra* from Makka to Yathrib/al-Madina.
624	Muslim victory over the Makkans at Badr; expulsion of the Jewish Banu Qaynuqa tribe from Madina.
627	Muslims repel Makkans at the Battle of the Trench; extermination of the Jewish Banu Qurayza tribe.
628	Muhammad's successful attack, siege, and subjugation of the Jewish oasis of Khaybar.
630	Makka submits to Muhammad.
632	Death of Muhammad; Abu Bakr first caliph.
633–8	Arab Muslim conquest of Syria and Mesopotamia (Iraq).
634–44	Caliphate of Umar.
639–42	Arab Muslim conquest of Egypt.
644–56	Caliphate of 'Uthman.
653	'Uthman establishes standard version of the Qur'an.

656	Murder of Caliph 'Uthman; first civil war in Islam.
656–61	Caliphate of Ali. Parts of the Dar al-Islam are controlled by Muawiyah I; Ali moves his capital to Kufa (in Iraq), where he is eventually assassinated.
661–750	Umayyad Caliphate in Damascus.
680	Battle of Karbala; martyrdom of Ali's son, Hussein.
ca. 685–91	Construction of Dome of the Rock in Jerusalem.
711–18	Muslim Berber/Arab conquest of Spain with widespread Jewish support.
750–1258	Abbasid Caliphate in Baghdad.
813–33	Caliphate of al-Ma'amun; beginning of Muslim cultural Golden Age.
929	Umayyad ruler of Spain assumes title of Caliph, asserts equality with Abbasid Caliphate in Baghdad.
969	Fatimid conquest of Egypt.
1007–19	Persecution of Christians by Fatimid Caliph al-Hakim; destruction of church of Holy Sepulchre in Jerusalem (rebuilt by Hakim's successor).
1012–19	Persecution of Jews by al-Hakim.
1054	Great Schism between Eastern (Orthodox) and Western (Catholic) churches.
1061–91	Normans take Sicily from the Muslims.
1071	Battle of Manzikert: victory of Seljuk Turks over Byzantine Christians.
1085	Christians recapture Toledo (Spain) during *reconquista*.
1090	Almoravids conquer Muslim Spain.
1096–99	First Crusade led by Count Raymond IV of Toulouse.
1099–1187	Latin Kingdom of Jerusalem.
1147–60	Almohads conquer Maghrib (Northwest Africa) and much of Islamic Spain; heavy persecution of Jews.
1147–9	Second Crusade led by Holy Roman (German) Emperor Conrad III and French King Louis VII.
1171–1250	Ayyubid dynasty established in Egypt and Syria by Salah ad-Din (Saladin).
1187	Salah ad-Din defeats Christian Crusaders at the Horns of Hattin.
1187–92	Third Crusade led by English King Richard Lionheart, French King Philip II and Holy Roman Emperor Frederick I.
1193	Death of Salah ad-Din.
1202–4	Fourth Crusade; Sacking of Constantinople.

1215–21	Fifth Crusade led by King Andrew II of Hungary, Duke Leopold VI of Austria, and John of Brienne.
1220	Founding of Templar Knights organization.
1228–9	Sixth Crusade led by Holy Roman Emperor Frederick II.
1248–54	Seventh Crusade led by King Louis IX (Saint Louis) of France.
1250–1517	Mamluk empire in Egypt, Syria and Palestine.
1258	Baghdad captured by Mongols, end of Abbasid caliphate and beginning of Ilkhanid dynasty; no distinction between Muslims and *dhimmi*s.
1260	Mamluks turn back Mongols at Ayn Jalut.
1270	Eighth Crusade led by Louis IX.
1271–2	Ninth Crusade led by English Prince Edward, (later King Edward I).
1291	Sultan Khalil retakes Acre, ending French presence and era of the "Great Crusades".
1380–1405	Timur Leng (Tamerlane)'s conquests across Middle East and India.
1391	Jewish refugees from Spanish Catalonia and Majorca arrive in Tunisia and Algeria.
1405–1506	Timurid dynasty in eastern Persia and Afghanistan.
1438	First *mellah* (Jewish quarter) established in Fez, Morocco.
1453	Ottoman Turks capture Constantinople; end of Byzantine Empire.
1492	Expulsion of Jews from Spain; many Jews take refuge in Ottoman lands.
1497	Expulsion of Jews from Portugal.
1501–1614	Expulsions of Muslims from various parts of Spain.
1501–1722	Safavid Shi'i (Shi'ite) Dynasty in Persia (Iran).
1517	Ottomans conquer Mamluk Empire; Jewish cultural and economic revival throughout Middle East.
1526–1857	Mughal (Moghul) Dynasty in India.
1529	First Ottoman Siege of Vienna.
1571	Battle of Lepanto: stunning naval defeat inflicted on Ottomans by European allies.
1574–95	Reign of Ottoman Sultan Murad III: reintroduction of the sumptuary restrictions for *dhimmi*s.
1683	Failed Ottoman siege of Vienna, first of several key Ottoman defeats in Europe.
1738	John Wesley founds Methodist Church as breakaway from Episcopal Church.

ca 1750	Wahhabi movement begins in the *hijaz*.
1768–74	Russo-Turkish War; Ottoman Turks defeated.
1785	John Lamb conducts first American diplomatic mission to the Middle East.
1788	John Ledyard, first American to explore the Middle East, arrives in Egypt.
1798–1801	Napoleon occupies Egypt.
1801–4	Wahhabis capture Makka and Madina.
1805–48	Mehmet (Muhammad) Ali independent ruler of Egypt under nominal Ottoman Suzerainty, but first shaper of concerted Arab political nationalism.
1810	British annex the Ionian Islands.
1817–18	Mehmet Ali turns on his erstwhile Wahhabi allies.
1819	First American missionaries to the Middle East: Levi Parsons and Pliny Fisk.
1821–29	Greek War of Independence from Ottoman Turkey.
1822	Massacre of Greeks of Chios by Turks (twenty-five thousand killed, fifty thousand enslaved of total population of one hundred thousand).
1823	Pliny Fisk establishes first American school in the Middle East.
1830	France invades Algeria.
1831	First American Ambassador to the Middle East, David Porter, arrives in Istanbul.
1831–40	Egyptian occupation of Syria and Palestine.
1837	American evangelist Harriet Livermore sets sail for Palestine.
1839	*Khatt-i Sherif* improves civil status of *dhimmi*s in Ottoman Empire.
1842	Cyrus Hamlin opens a school just outside Istanbul, later evolves as Robert College.
1844	Restorationist and US Consul Warder Cresson sets sail for Palestine.
1851	Clorinda Minor arrives in Palestine to establish an agricultural school to provide Jews with the skills necessary for statehood.
1853–56	Crimean (Russo-Turkish) War; French and British troops occupy Greece.
1856	*Khatt-i Humayan* grants equality to non-Muslims in Ottoman Empire.
1860–1904	Theodor Herzl, founder of modern Zionism.

1862	Daniel Bliss offers proposal to open the Arab world's first modern university: the Syrian Protestant College (later American University in Beirut).
1866	George Adams recruits 166 Americans to form a colony in Palestine.
1866–69	Unsuccessful revolt of Greeks on Crete against Ottoman Turks.
1868	Egyptian leader Isma'il recruits American Civil War vets to modernize his army and strengthen Egyptian-American ties.
1869	Suez Canal opened.
1873	Persian Shah offers and later revokes Reuter concession to British company for railway and mining activities.
1881	French occupation of Tunisia.
1882	Britain occupies Egypt; first European (mostly Russian) and Yemenite Jewish agricultural colonists in Palestine.
1883	Tunisia declared a protectorate of France; Samuel Benjamin heads first US official mission to Persia (Iran).
1886–1973	David Ben-Gurion, first prime minister of the State of Israel.
1890	Persian shah sells tobacco concession to British company.
1897	First Zionist Congress in Basel, Switzerland.
1902	American naval theorist Alfred Mahan coins the phrase, "Middle East"; Ottoman Sultan Abdul Hamid II engages Prussian firm to build Baghdad railway.
1904–14	Second Aliyah of Jews, mainly from Russia and Poland, to Palestine.
1908–9	"Young Turks"—Ottoman Turkish army officers—depose Abdul Hamid II.
1909	American State Department creates a Division of Near Eastern Affairs (NEA).
1912	Henrietta Szold founds the women's Zionist organization, Haddasah.
1913	First Arab Nationalist Congress in Paris.
1914–18	World War I.
1915	British High Commissioner in Cairo, Sir H. Mcmahon, asserts British support of Arab independence to Hussein, Sharif of Makka.
1916	Sykes-Picot Agreement articulates British and French vision of dividing political administration of the Middle East after World War I.
1917	The Russian Revolution; assertion by Lord Balfour of British embrace of the concept of a Jewish state in Palestine.

1919	At the postwar Paris Peace Conference, American President Wilson tries vainly to secure independent national self-determination across Middle East.
1919–22	Greco-Turkish War.
1920	Post–World War I Paris, London, and San Remo Conferences establish French and British Mandates, confirmed by League of Nations in 1922.
1921	Iraq becomes independent kingdom; becomes republic in 1958.
1922	Egypt becomes an independent kingdom (ending 1914 British protectorate status). Final collapse of Ottoman Empire; founding of secular State of Turkey by Atatürk the following year.
1924	American and European oil companies form the Iraq Petroleum Company (IPC); the United States recognizes British mandate over Palestine; Ibn Sa'ud takes *hijaz* from Hashimites.
1927	Saudi Arabia becomes independent kingdom.
1928	Conclusion of the Red Line agreement, specifying areas for IPC oil exploration in the Middle East.
1929	Anti-Jewish riots in Jerusalem, Hebron, and six other locations.
1933	Saudi Arabia grants the right to prospect for oil to American companies.
1933–45	Hitler in power in Germany (and eventually elsewhere).
1939–45	World War II.
1941–5	Holocaust of European Jewry.
1937	Peel Commission Palestine Partition Plan; escalating attacks by Arabs against Jews and reprisals by Jews against Arabs; these would expand the following two years, as would conflicts between the British and the Arabs and of Arabs against Arabs; three major Jewish terrorist attacks against Arabs took place in 1938, in which year there were two further Palestine partition proposals, one British and one Jewish.
1938	American engineers strike oil in Damman, Saudi Arabia.
1939	British White Paper limits Jewish immigration to Palestine to fifteen thousand per year for following five years.
1943	Syria becomes independent republic (ending 1920 French Mandate); United States and Britain compel France to respect Lebanon's independence.
1944	Lebanon becomes independent republic (ending 1920 French Mandate).
1945	Establishment of the Arab League.

1946	Transjordan becomes independent kingdom (ending 1920 British Mandate); Jewish Agency's Palestine Partition proposal; the United States, working through the UN, succeeds in pressing the USSR to withdraw from Iran.
1947	United Nations' Palestine Partition Plan; escalation of Arab attacks on Jews.
1948	Establishment of the State of Israel (ending 1920 British Mandate), followed by War with neighboring Arab states; Arabs leave Israel from Haifa-Acre, Beersheba, Jaffa-Ramallah areas: 100,000 to Lebanon, 75,000 to Syria, 4,000 to Iraq, 70,000 to Transjordan, 7,000 to Egypt, 190,000 to Gaza Strip and 280,000 to West Bank; Egypt occupies the Gaza Strip; Transjordan occupies the West Bank; war continues into 1949 and Rhodes Armistice.
1948–72	Jewish refugees from Arab lands include 260,000 from Morocco, 14,000 from Algeria, 56,000 from Tunisia, 35,666 from Libya, 29,525 from Egypt, 6,000 from Lebanon, 4,500 from Syria, 129,290 from Iraq and 50,552 from Yemen and Aden.
1950	Transjordan annexes the West Bank, renaming the totality under its control the Hashimite Kingdom of Jordan.
1951	Libya becomes independent kingdom (ending 1912 Italian, 1945 joint Anglo-French rule).
1951–56	Arab Fedayeen attacks into Israel from Egypt and Jordan (and some from Syria and Lebanon) leave 967 Israelis dead.
1953	Egypt becomes a republic. MI6 (Britain's Foreign Intelligence Service) and CIA together engineer a coup that deposes Iran's elected Prime Minister Mossadeq, restoring Muhammad Reza Pahlavi to the throne as Shah of Iran.
1955	Formation of the Baghdad Pact, an American-backed anti-communist coalition; Egyptian blockade of the Straits of Tiran and Gulf of Aqaba to ships seeking ingress to and egress from Israeli port city of Eilat.
1956	Israeli military attack into Sinai; French and British attack on Port Said; Morocco becomes independent kingdom (ending 1912 French and Spanish protectorate status).
1957	American pressure causes full Israeli withdrawal from Sinai
1962	Algeria becomes independent republic (ending 1842 French colonial governance).
1967	Six-day June war between Israel and her Arab neighbors.

1967–73	Sixteen Israeli settlements founded in the West Bank, with total civilian population of 1,150; 44,000 Arabs who fled the West bank in 1967 return there by 1972.
1969–70	Egypt's War of Attrition against Israel.
1970	"Black September" campaign of Jordanian King Hussein against PLO after the latter culminates a two-year-long campaign of autonomy within Jordan with an attempt to seize political control; thousands of mostly Palestinians are killed between September 1970 and July 1971; relocation of PLO command center to southern Lebanon.
1971	Creation of the United Arab Emirates (UAE).
1973	October "Yom Kippur" War between Israel and her Arab neighbors; Saudi Arabia spearheads an oil boycott against the United States because of its support of Israel.
1974	Coup in Cyprus is followed by Turkish invasion.
1975–90	Lebanese Civil War.
1977	Egyptian President Anwar Sadat speaks before Israeli Knesset at invitation of Israeli Prime Minister Menahem Begin.
1978–9	Iranian Revolution deposes Muhammad Reza Shah and brings from exile and into power Ayatollah Ruhallah Khomeini; Iran becomes an Islamic republic.
1979	Camp David and Israeli-Egyptian Peace agreement; fifty-two Americans taken hostage in Iran; an American rescue attempt the following year fails; Saddam Hussein becomes president of Iraq.
1979–89	Soviet occupation of Afghanistan.
1980–88	Iran-Iraq War.
1981	Hosni Mubarak becomes president of Egypt after assassination of Anwar Sadat.
1982	Israeli War in Lebanon against PLO; relocation of PLO command center to Tunisia.
1983	Terrorist attack on military installation in Tyre, Lebanon, leaves 241 US Marines and 30 Israeli soldiers dead.
1986	In response to terror attack on American servicemen in a Berlin nightclub, US President Reagan bombs Tripoli, Libya.
1987–91	First Intifada of Palestinian Arabs in Gaza and West Bank against Israeli Occupation forces.
1989	Death of Ayatollah Khomeini in Iran.
1990	Iraq invades Kuwait.

1991	First Gulf War; thirty of the Scud missiles fired by Iraq make it to Israel; post-conflict, the United States convenes a Peace Conference in Madrid, seeking a comprehensive Arab-Israeli peace accord; population of Jewish settlers in West Bank and Gaza reaches 103,855; 137th Jewish settlement established on West Bank on August 5.
1993	The Oslo Accords, following secret Israeli-Palestinian negotiations, are signed on the White House Lawn; over the next four years negotiations continue, leading, among other things, to the creation of a Palestinian National Authority (PA) and the extension of its administration to most of the West Bank and Gaza Strip.
1994	Peace Treaty between Israel and Jordan.
1995	Jewish extremist assassinates Yitzhak Rabin.
1996	Nineteen American soldiers killed in a terrorist attack on Khobar Towers housing complex in Saudi Arabia; the Taliban establish rule over most of Afghanistan.
1997	Election of reformer Muhammad Khatami as president of Iranian republic.
1998	President Clinton brokers interim Palestinian-Israeli peace agreement at Wye River Plantation; responding to al-Qaeda attacks in East Africa, the US bombs presumed terrorist targets in Sudan.
1999	Abd'Allah II becomes king of Jordan after death of Hussein; Ehud Barak becomes Israeli Prime Minister, pushes Israeli-Palestinian negotiations ahead.
2000	A suicide bomber kills seventeen sailors aboard the USS *Cole* near the Yemen coast; beginning of Second (al-Aqsa) Intifada; Bashar al-Assad becomes president of Syria after death of his father, Hafiz al-Assad.
2000–1	Collapse of final Israeli-Palestinian negotiations at Camp David and in Taba.
2001	Usama bin Ladin and al-Qaeda orchestrate terrorist attacks on World Trade Center in New York City, the Pentagon outside Washington, DC, and an unspecified target for which the intended plane went down in Pennsylvania, killing nearly three thousand people altogether; Ariel Sharon elected Israeli prime minister.
2001–2	The United States declares war on the Taliban and topples the regime in Afghanistan; President Bush's strategists coin the phrase "axis of evil" to refer to Iran, Iraq, and North Korea; Sharon sends tanks into West Bank cities, killing between 500

and 1,500 Palestinians; Palestinian suicide bombers become increasingly active in Israel; Israel begins building a security fence, cutting off much of the West Bank, to end terrorist attacks.

2003   Islamist/Modernist Recep Tayyip Erdogan is elected prime minister of Turkey. President Bush announces a "road map" for resumption of Israeli-Palestinian negotiations, but with no follow-up (he subsequently refuses to receive Arafat at the White House). Claiming that Saddam Hussein had been associated with the al-Qaeda terrorists and possessed Weapons of Mass Destruction, President Bush and a handful of allies invade Iraq to topple Saddam's regime; over the next six years the regime collapses, Saddam is captured, tried by an Iraqi court, and executed; Iraq is reduced to internecine chaos involving Sunni and Shi'i Arab Muslims and Kurdish Muslims; by 2009 well over four thousand Americans had been killed and countless Iraqis.

2004   Formation of a Mesopotamian branch of al-Qaeda in Sunni-dominated area of former Iraq; prelude to the eventual shaping of ISIS/ISIL. Israeli Prime Minister Ariel Sharon announces a plan to unilaterally withdraw from Gaza Strip, also announcing construction of new houses in West Bank settlements (violating "road map"); Palestinian chairman Yassir Arafat dies in Paris.

2005   Palestinians elect Mahmud Abbas to succeed Arafat in presidential election; Sharon offers to evacuate troops and Jewish settlers from Gaza Strip, and to reopen peace talks, if Abbas closes down *Hamas* and other groups accused of terrorist activity against Israel; *Hamas* and *Islamic Jihad* verbally support Abbas's plea to Palestinians for a cease-fire; Sharon effects Israeli withdrawal from Gaza and dismantling of Jewish settlements; Iraqi Shi'is and Kurds form a new government after long negotiations; former Lebanese prime minister Rafiq Hariri assassinated in Beirut; Egyptians demand that President Mubarak open scheduled presidential elections to opposition candidates; United States begins to put pressure on Iran to end its nuclear research program.

2006   Sharon has a stroke and falls into a coma; Ehud Olmert becomes Israeli prime minister; Gazan Palestinians overwhelmingly vote *Hamas* in as new leadership of Palestinian Authority; Abbas and *Fatah* are reduced to clinging to power in the West Bank Territories.

2007   Civil War primarily in Gaza Strip between *Fatah* and *Hamas*;
            beginning of steady stream of rocket attacks into southern
            Israel from Gaza Strip, which, apart from a brief period of
            cease-fire, continues through the end of 2008.

2008–9   Monthlong Israeli military attack on Gaza Strip to decimate
            Hamas; hundreds of Palestinian civilians among those who are
            killed.

2009   Binyamin (Bibi) Netanyahu is elected Israeli Prime Minister,
            with a stated perspective that does not favor Palestinian state-
            hood; newly elected US President Barack Obama visits Middle
            East in June, speaking publicly in Cairo.

2010   In late May, six small ships, largely from Turkey, try to break
            the Israeli blockade of Gaza and are intercepted by the Israeli
            navy. One ship violently resists being boarded; in the ensuing
            fight, nine activists are killed and seven Israeli commandos are
            wounded. Turkish-Israeli relations are strained but the Arab
            media response, as with the Israeli attack on Gaza the previ-
            ous year, is muted. In the fall, American-sponsored peace talks
            resume between Israel and the Palestinians without positive
            outcome; controversy continues regarding expanding or lim-
            iting Jewish settlements around Jerusalem. Questions expand
            regarding Iran's actual or potential nuclear arsenal: concern
            is raised by both Israel and a number of key Arab states; a
            report emerges in November asserting that claims regarding
            the arsenal are fraudulent as other reports doubt the truth of
            this report. Al-Qaeda emerges in Yemen, provoking concern
            that "Yemen may be the next Afghanistan." Iraq appears to
            move toward stability; US troops continue their presence, in
            lesser numbers, in Iraq; they have now spent as much time in
            Afghanistan as did Soviet troops three decades earlier.

2011   The so-called Arab Spring begins with the deposing of Tunisia's
            long-term president, Zine El Abidine Ben Ali; includes a
            range of developments in eighteen different countries from
            Mauretania to Iraq, over the following three years, that extend
            from the overthrow of leaders (Tunisia, Libya, Egypt, Yemen)
            to government reforms (Saudi Arabia, Bahrain, Kuwait,
            Morocco) to major protests (Algeria, Iraq, Jordan, Sudan) and
            minor protests (Mauretania, Oman, Saudi Arabia, Djibouti,
            Palestine) to ongoing—through the present, 2016—civil war
            (Syria, Libya, Yemen). The Syrian civil war, between adherents

of Bashar al'Assad and diverse groups of rebels is joined by al-Qaeda and other Sunnis from former Iraq, shaping ISIS. As the United States gradually pulls out most of its troops from Iraq, members of ISIS/ISIL will return to Iraq, seeking to form a unified "caliphate" that straddles Syria and Iraq. President Mahmud Abbas submits an application on behalf of Palestine to become the 194th member of the UN General Assembly. The Security Council does not vote on the proposal.

2012   Election of Muhammad Morsi, candidate from the *Muslim Brotherhood's* political wing, as president of Egypt. Attack on the American Consulate in Benghazi, Libya that leaves American Ambassador Christopher Stevens dead, among others. With the Security Council failing to vote on the Palestine application for full state representation in the UN, Abbas submits a draft resolution to accord Palestinian status as a nonmember observer state, to which the General Assembly votes in the affirmative.

2013   Reformist-backed cleric, Hassan Rouhani, elected president of Iran; three months after his election he asserts to an American news reporter that Iran would never build nuclear weapons and in an address to the UN General Assembly extends an offer for serious talks with key nations to assure this. Gezi Park protests in Istanbul; definitive shift in Erdogan's leadership from forward-looking leader to demagogue. Egyptian president Muhammad Morsi deposed by a coup led by the Minister of Defense, General Abdul Fattah Al-Sisi, who is elected President in 2014.

2015   Videotaped beheading of twenty-one Egyptian Coptic Christians by Libyan-based branch of ISIS/ISIL. US Congress approves deal that will eliminate economic sanctions against and freezing of assets of Iran in exchange for wide-ranging assurances that nuclear weaponry is not being developed by Iran. Municipal elections in Saudi Arabia for the first time include female candidates, allow female voters and yield female victors.

2016   Alleged coup against Erdogan regime leads to massive purging of any and all perceived opposition to Turkey's president; witch-hunt-style aftermath in particular targets those associated with the *hizmet* movement inspired by Fethullah Gülen. Kurds gain autonomy over Hasaka province in northeast Syria through treaty with Assad, adding a second area to that in former Iraq over which they have unofficial autonomy. The struggles between Kurds in Turkey and Erdogan's government continue. Turkey ramps up attacks on ISIS/ISIL positions in Syria. Saudi Arabia ramps up heavy bombing of Houthi strongholds in Yemen.

2017   Donald Trump is sworn in as president of the United States; among the cabinet and other appointments proposed within the first month of being in office is David Friedman as ambassador to Israel, a bankruptcy lawyer with an unequivocal history of alignment with the Israeli far right.

INTRODUCTION

It has become fashionable, particularly as the months after September 11, 2001, have evolved into years, to focus on the Israeli-Palestinian issue as the key to a solution to the problems of the Middle East. There is no question that this is a crux—perhaps the crux—issue. At the very least, within the Arab and Muslim worlds, this issue has, particularly in the last few years, been repeatedly referred to as the most pressing one with respect both to the Middle East and with respect to the relationship between the region and the United States.[2] And the narrative that follows expends a disproportionate volume of energy on the Israeli-Palestinian issue.

But to imagine that, even were this problem to be solved, the region would shift into a calm and forward-looking mood is not to understand its history, its culture, and its multiple-dimensioned personality. The elimination of Saddam Hussein has not solved the problem of terrorism, much less the larger problem of the Middle East, nor will it. The elimination of Usama Bin Ladin has not solved it. A change in the nature of the Saudi regime won't. All of these and a large group of other issues play roles, but no single one among them is by itself the key, and the same is true for Israel-Palestine. Indeed, *had Israel never come into existence* or were it to disappear utterly, the Middle East would still be a hotbed of tensions and conflict. So while Israel-Palestine is a key, it is only part of the larger regional dynamic.

One might liken the Middle East to a tangled web, in which threads of two sorts interweave each other: those which, running from center to periphery we might call "parallel," but are actually intermingled rather than separate; and those which, in concentric waves and parallel to the center and periphery, are similarly intermingled with each other. In turn these two sorts of threads, instead of running at more or less right angles to each other are also inter-mingled in a snarl that, in sum, appears nearly impossible to disentangle. The threads that run one way (we might mix our metaphor and call them warp threads of a tapestry) are religion, ethnicity, politics, culture, nationality, and economics. Those that run counter to these (let us call them weft threads) are conflicting and confusing definitions, aspirations, and interferences.

The pages that follow seek to unravel that tangled web—that is, to isolate and elucidate the many threads that make up the web, as opposed to reorga-nizing them into a nice, neat tapestry. Neatness is hardly possible, as I hope the discussion will make clear. But clarity is possible, even in a relatively brief compass. Clarity does not mean simplicity. The most we can hope for is a clear delineation of the threads.

With this in mind, I have indulged in what, while it remains merely the tip of the iceberg of detail, is a good deal to absorb in so few pages. My purpose will become obvious as one reads on: all of the details and each of the little complications are important to some faction or factor within the Middle East in its geography and its history. To ignore any one of them is to ignore what, to some group, is important and therefore to miss one of the reasons that the region is a tangled web. To ignore the massive volume of historical detail is to forget how tangled the web is and to be deluded into imagining that it can be easily disentangled. And even at that, what follows is only the tip of the iceberg. A reader consulting even a mere handful of the books offered in the bibliography will recognize this instantly.

At the end of this volume, I shall repeat the following mantra: *the key to understanding—and possibly to solving—the problems of the Middle East is developing the capacity to remember all of its historical complications (not just to cherry-pick the ones that are convenient for one's own point of view) and at the same time to forget all of the region's history.* To move forward toward resolu-tion and peace, if it is possible, will only be realized when the protagonists can both keep in mind other protagonists' histories—there are Jews who still retain the house keys taken by their ancestors when they were forced to leave Spain in 1492, and there are Palestinians who still retain the house keys taken by their grandparents or great-grandparents when they were forced to leave what was becoming Israel in 1948, and there are Kurds who never achieved state-hood and were massacred by Sadam Hussein's chemical warfare, and there are Darfurians who were and are still being slaughtered by Arab and non-Arab Sudanese—and who abandon, in part at least, the pain of their own; when they can clear the slate without erasing it and ask: where do we go from *here*?

PART ONE
DEFINITIONS

1

SEMITES AND ARABS

It is important to begin any discussion of the Middle East with an accounting of terminology. Terms are often used either inaccurately or in a falsely
interchangeable manner when the region is discussed.[3] Important terms
in that discussion include but are not limited to: "Semite," "Arab," "Muslim,"
"Jew," "Israeli," "Palestinian." The term "Semite" grows out of the changing academic landscape of nineteenth-century Europe. In that landscape, as the Bible
was increasingly subject to secularized analysis and discussion, and as, at the
same time, the colonial urge brought with it an increasing interest in how to
understand and categorize the world in its entirety, the term "Semite" grew
out of a web spun out of the book of Genesis. There, Noah's three sons include
"Shem." As the discipline of anthropology evolved, the human race came to be
understood as falling into three categories derived—actually or symbolically—
from those three sons. Those descended from Shem were labeled Shemites,
or Semites. In turn, the emerging field of comparative historical linguistics
appropriated the term sometime between the 1780s and the 1830s to refer to a
group of languages spoken by Semites. Thus Hebrew and Arabic, for example,
came to be called Semitic languages, whereas English, say, or Turkish or Farsi
are not.

There is a paradox and an irony in the shaping of this biblically based racial
and linguistic category. The biblical Shem is represented in Genesis 9:23–27 as
the wisest and most responsible of Noah's sons, and both Jewish and Christian
medieval biblical commentators had already interpreted the statement that
he would have dominion over his brothers as a divinely ordained authority accorded to the descendants of Shem over the other races on the planet.
But by the late nineteenth century, the twisting of the linguistic term back

toward racial category gave it a reversed, pejorative connotation. Thus when Wilhelm Marr, seeking election to the Prussian Reichstag in 1879 used the term "Semite," he applied it specifically to the Jews. His intention was to marginalize them as a group. By presenting the Jews to Prussian voters as a racial category, and by implication a group apart from the non-Semitic Europeans, he could assert the legitimacy and the importance of his vow to protect his fellow Prussians from such dangerous outsider-interlopers.

The racialization of Jews by Marr and others, utilizing terminology that had been disconnected from its language-associative roots, was intended to suggest a direct connection between all Jews and the Near East, regardless of the fact that, historically, such a direct connection could neither be so clear and direct nor in any case expressible in pure racial terms.[4] It also ignored others who—assuming that the term "Semite" might refer to various groups inhabiting the Near East and speaking certain languages—should have been included in its purview. Among these other groups certainly the Arabic-speakers—i.e., Arabs—should be included. But that term, "Arab," itself refers not to speakers of Arabic (although most or all Arabs may be Arabic-speakers) but to those whose ancestry is traceable back to a geographic location. The *'arav* is the western, central part of the peninsula that bears the same name (the Arabian peninsula). All those who are called Arabs, in theory, trace their ancestry to that part of the peninsula in that corner of our planet, even as, based on the language category into which they all fit, they might also be labeled "Semites."

But understanding the roots and evolution of the term is not that simple. "*'Arav*" is cognate with the linguistically Semitic Hebrew term "*'aravah*," referring to steppe-like wilderness. The connotation of the Arabic term is of an association with nomadism—that is, Bedouin, as opposed to town dwellers. A form of the term appears early in the history of the region at large, on an 853 BCE Assyrian inscription (Assyrian being another member of the family of Semitic languages) of Shalmaneser III in which, in boasting of his defeat of a series of princelings he includes in the list of those he conquered one Gindibu Arabi, together with his army of one thousand camels. Both Assyrian and Babylonian inscriptions of the next two hundred years refer variously to *Aribi*, *Arabu* and *Urbi*; by about 530 BCE Achaemenid Persian documents begin to refer to *Arabaya*.

Not long thereafter, the Greek playwright, Aeschylus, in his play, *The Persians* mentions a *Magos Arabos* as one of the commanders in Xerxes's army; perhaps he was an Arab. In *Prometheus Bound*, Aeschylus refers to Arabia as a distant place from which come warriors with sharp-pointed spears. Other Greek writers, like Herodotos, and subsequently, Roman writers, extend the use of terms such as "Arab" and "Arabia" to include the entire peninsula between the Red

Sea and the Indian Ocean and its inhabitants. It is in such literature as well that the term "Saracen" first appears. While the word appears originally to have referred to a particular desert tribe in the Sinai region, it continued in use into the medieval period to refer to nomads generally. Indeed, in the era of the Crusades that began at the end of the eleventh century, Christian writers began using the term "Arab" to offer a nomadic, Bedouin, piratical connotation, while using the term "Saracen" to refer to the Muslim population at large.

The first *Arab* use of some version of the term "Arab" is in south Arabian inscriptions where the term seems to refer once again to Bedouins or raiders—i.e., nomadic tribes that are different from (and pose a threat to) sedentary groups. Such tribes are distinguished from dwellers in key centers such as Makka and Madina, yet the term "Arabic" comfortably refers to the language used by both the Bedouin and the dwellers in those centers, and ultimately "Arabic" will refer to the language in which the Qur'an will be written. In other words, a term with pejorative connotations in one context reverses its connotation to be emphatically positive (the Qur'an, after all, is no less than God's word, dictated through the Prophet Muhammad, and that it was dictated in Arabic offers a powerful statement of the positive quality associated with the language called by that name). For that matter, Muhammad himself is an Arab in the following specific sense contemporary with his early life: while ostensibly from Makka, he was orphaned early and, impoverished, was raised most likely by his grandfather away from the city. Thus, he would have been called an "Arab" in the non-sedentary, away-from-the-city-and-its-culture sense. This would also help account for the illiteracy ascribed to him by most scholars.

But Muhammad would grow up to bring out of the desert a form of faith that would sweep half the world. Within the context of terms that we have been reviewing, Islam, a religion, swept out of the *'arav*, carried by *Semitic Arabs*, in the seventh century. It is important for this discussion that we keep in mind that Islam *is* a religion—a Muslim is someone who defines him/herself by the religious principles of Islam—and specifically one of the three faiths which, like Judaism and Christianity, see their point of spiritual origin in the figure of Abraham.

It is a truism of the Abrahamic religions (as with most forms of faith) that they begin with revelation: the constituents of Judaism or Christianity or Islam, or any of the other forms of faith that may be seen as offshoots of these, all believe that their founders were prophets to whom and through whom God spoke directly. So, too, all of these faiths continue forward in history by means of two modes of interpretation. The first generations after the founding prophets are gone argue as to whether (t)he(y) said *this* or *that* (i.e., *what* was said). Subsequent generations devote most of their energy—for the obvious reason: God's word is at issue—to clarifying what the prophet(s) *meant* by the words that are finally agreed upon and written down.

So Jews vary as to whether they believe that Moses brought down a mere ten commandments from Sinai (ca. 1400 BCE) or the entirety of the Torah's 613 commandments; whether he wrote all of the Torah or whether it was written down over time and whether Ezra merely fine-tuned the text into its definitive form—the traditionally understood date for Ezra's redaction is 444 BCE—or substantially edited constituent parts written down at different times and places, which were then woven together by him. (For the purposes of this discussion, I am ignoring those who question whether or not Moses existed.) And Jewish history is gloriously rampant with argument over every word in the Torah, whether in the fanciful discussions over whether God created the heavens or the earth first or over what, precisely "thou shall not seethe a kid in its mother's milk" (in Exodus 23:19, among other places) means. How that phrase ends up meaning that a traditional Jew may not consume a cheeseburger is overrun with interpretive discussion.

Mainstream Christianity begins with no less than four variants on the theme of Jesus's life, times, and words, none of which was written down earlier than forty years after the Crucifixion. The patristic and scholastic students of those words, from Augustine to Aquinas, pour rivers of ink into the question of how ultimately to understand what lies beneath them. And Islam is no different from Judaism and Christianity in this respect: if it begins with Muhammad, viewed as the final prophet whose words are the ultimate expression of God's wishes for how we should be, its history is fraught with disagreement and argumentation as to how to *understand* the prophet's words—or rather, God's words spoken *through* the Prophet. Those words are recorded in nonchronological sequence in the Qur'an, a text written down a generation after Muhammad's death and to which a second text—with words not universally accepted as coming from him and sometimes merely speaking *about* him—is, as it were, appended, as we shall see.

2

MUHAMMAD AND THE BIRTH OF ISLAM

Muhammad was born in 570 CE in Makka, a city in the central-western Arabian Peninsula—an area called the *hijaz*.⁵ Makka was an important trading center because it was both coastal and central. It could mediate between traders from East and North Africa and those of the Persian Gulf, and between those coming from the southern tip of the peninsula and those coming from the north: Egypt on the one hand and Syro-Palestine (and beyond it, both Anatolia and Mesopotamia) on the other. A central point between very different economic trade worlds, Makka was a cosmopolitan city and also a largely pagan city.

We have fairly good evidence of the spirituality of the Makkans. They seem to have centered their cults in a shrine the central element of which was a black stone that had fallen from the sky—perhaps a meteorite. That shrine was called the *Ka'ba* and was, together with the images around it, associated with gods of nature. Ritual defined the sacred area around the *Ka'ba*. Makkans consecrated other spaces as well. They made an annual spring pilgrimage—a *hajj*—to a site two miles east of the city, where three mounds of stone (*jamras*) were piled. There they left cuttings of hair and made animal sacrifices. These elements formed part of the rich religious tradition of the Makka of Muhammad's youth. Other parts probably included Christianity and certainly Judaism. The Judaism of Muhammad's time had developed in various directions and was an archipelago of spiritual and cultural islands within seas of other faiths, which themselves were not monolithic, but diverse in their sensibilities and spiritualities—and Makka was one of the places in which an island of Jews could be found.

The Prophet had a proclivity for wandering outside the city in the surrounding hills. At the age of forty, in the year 610, according to the preponderant tradition, during a spring pilgrimage out to those hills, a common custom of the pagan community of which he was part, he experienced the first of a series of visions in a cave on Mount Hira outside Makka; these visions would continue for the rest of his life. He was inspired by the angel Gabriel who spoke the words of God—the Arabic word for which is "Allah"—directly to him.[6]

According to Muslim tradition, Gabriel had communicated God's word to Abraham, Moses, the prophets of the Hebrew Bible, and to John the Baptist and Jesus, among twenty-eight major and scores of lesser prophetic figures—twenty-four of which, from the Hebrew Bible and New Testament, are mentioned by name in the Qur'an. All, including Jesus, are understood to be prophets, then, forerunners of Muhammad.

After his vision, Muhammad returned into Makka preaching repentance and an Armageddon accompanied by judgment to be meted out against those who do not repent. Those who did repent would form a group who submitted to the will of God. Thus, the faith that Muhammad was beginning to articulate is called in Arabic, *Islam*, commonly translated as meaning "submission" (some misrender it as "commitment" or "commission"): submission to the will of God. Its followers are called *Muslims*—those who submit themselves to God's will.[7]

Muhammad preached in Makka for about a dozen years, gathering a small group of followers. Ultimately the authorities came to perceive his preaching as a threat; by the year 620 he began to plan a strategy that included a departure from the city of his birth. In 622, he and his followers went to—were invited to—an oasis town some 210 miles (ca. 340 kilometers) to the north, called Yathrib. The tribal conflicts within Yathrib and Muhammad's reputation as an adjudicator and peacemaker combined to make him welcome there. The year of the migration—the *Hijra*, as it is called in Arabic—marks the beginning of the Muslim calendar. Yathrib would later be known as *al'Madina* (more commonly rendered simply as Madina)—"the City"—because of the importance that it would assume in the life of the Prophet.[8]

Madina/Yathrib, at the time of Muhammad's arrival, was inhabited not only by pagans but also by Christians and Jews—to be specific, three Christian and five Jewish tribes are known by name to have resided there. Some have argued that the Jews actually dominated the town numerically.[9] These Jewish tribes were distant from the Jewish mainstream, but were apparently familiar with the rabbinic traditions of commentary on the Torah and adjudication of everyday issues and problems by means of referring to the Torah and other parts of the Hebrew Bible, known as *Midrash* (Torah commentary) and *Talmud* (adjudication of issues). In the course of Muhammad's years in Madina, as he developed both a political organization and a more systematic spiritual foundation for Islam, he seems to have had a good deal of contact with the Jews as well as with their Christian counterparts.

If Muhammad arrived as a peacemaker, he seems to have unified the divergent groups in Yathrib by about 627/8—which was also the time when a powerful force of Makkans, outnumbering the Prophet's followers nearly five-to-one, attacked and nearly destroyed the small Muslim community of Yathrib. But after nearly three years of conflict marked by three crucial and unexpected, zeal-and-inspiration-driven victories, Muhammad not only defeated them, he entered Makka in triumph. Contrary to the expected norm, he did not destroy his conquered enemies, but embraced them as they embraced his faith. He did destroy the idols that are said to have festooned the *Ka'ba*—but not the central stone itself. In other words, he didn't completely sever the connection between the Makkans and their ancestors.

He adopted and adapted the cult centered in the *Ka'ba*, suggesting that the rock from heaven symbolized 'Allah's abiding interest in and relationship with us—and moreover associating it with Abraham and Ishmael, as related in the second *Sura* (chapter) of the Qur'an,[10] where we read that Abraham and Ishmael established the *Ka'ba* together, making it the first shrine in the Abrahamic tradition. The spiritual and the secular, the religious and the political, intermingled as Muhammad's form of faith completed its beginnings.

With the political power signified by control of both Madina and Makka, the consolidation of Islam's internal world began, and the term *'umma* (cognate with the Hebrew word *'am*, and meaning "people/nation" defined by a spiritual bloodline connection) came into use for his Muslim constituents. The tribal-based, ethnically driven self-definition endemic to the two cities was superseded by the faith-based spiritually driven reality that Muhammad's revolution had brought about.

Muhammad articulated to his followers the marriage between the practical—political organization—and the spiritual: divine election and support. To paraphrase *suwar* 3 and 21, Muhammad in effect said that "the Yathribians asked me to come; but it was divine agency that caused them to seek me out. And my consolidation of Madina was a function not of conquest as much as acquiescence: acquiescence to 'Allah on my part meant acquiescence to me on their part, all of which reflects divine agency and not just human action."[11] For Muhammad's followers his understanding of his role in history is unequivocal; it is important to note that, over the centuries, ongoing interpretation can sometimes yield directly opposite views even of the Prophet's self-conception.

I know at least one contemporary Muslim scholar who maintains that Muhammad misunderstood the *means* according to which he was to take

Makka: the word, rather than the sword was 'Allah's intended instrument, which is why the prophet died only a few years later—analogous to Moses's death before the final crossing of the Jordan, which has been construed by the rabbinic tradition as punishment for his moments of doubt and anger through the course of his forty years of leading the Israelites through the wilderness.[12]

When he died in 632 CE, Muhammad left behind a legacy of principles set forth in ongoing discourses and sermons. These were based on the revelations to Muhammad from 'Allah, and they were recorded—probably written down in its definitive form within about twenty years of the prophet's death, by a member of his inner circle and one of his successors, Uthman—in the Qur'an. That these are oral teachings is underscored by the meaning of the word Qur'an: "recitation."[13] Most scholars assume that the prophet was illiterate—but even if he wasn't, he spoke rather than wrote the thoughts that divinely inspired him. It was some of the companions, fearful that the ideas would be lost with his death, who are said to have written down whatever they could on whatever was available, including camel bone and saddle leather.

The Qur'an is not a chronologically systematic and linear narrative as the Torah is and as each of the Gospels is.[14] It is not the story of Muhammad's life and that of his companions, as the Gospels and Acts of the Apostles tell the story of Jesus's life and of those around him and as much of the Hebrew Bible is the story of dozens of lives from Adam and Eve to the last king of Judah. The Qur'an is an assemblage of speeches and discourses from Muhammad to his followers in which he is the mouthpiece through which God speaks, analogous to those parts of the Torah where Moses sermonizes, or to the words of Isaiah and the other Hebrew biblical prophets, or to those parts of the Gospels in which Jesus offers sermons and declaratory statements—it is filled with parables and narrative fragments.

The Qur'an's 6,200 verses are organized into 114 chapters—*sura* in the singular; *suwar* in the plural. They are ordered from longest to shortest, with the exception of the first, which is an affirmation of faith, and a few others. In other words, the organization is strictly aesthetic, with absolutely no story line connecting one *sura* to the next—and no way of knowing for certain which sermons came earlier and which later. Thus, if one seeks to chart the development of Muhammad's thinking, one will need significant powers of interpretation. This also means that ideas that appear to contradict each other—an aspect of every religious tradition—require extensive discussion. And given the fact that we cannot even know if it was all written down before or after Muhammad's death, and what may have been added, subtracted, or interpolated, we are confronted with analogous questions to those we face in seeking an explanation for the different names of God used in different parts of the Torah or for the variant versions of Jesus's life and death found in the different Gospels.

The difficulty of apprehending the absolute truth manifests itself soon after the Prophet's death—specifically with regard to the choice of a successor. For Muhammad designated no one, unlike Moses—who, after all, is said to have known the hour of his death in advance, and who designated Joshua the son of Nun as his successor. His key companions were divided. A minority thought that it should be 'Ali, nephew and son-in-law of Muhammad, and therefore, they agreed, both part of his bloodline and also most privy of them all to the prophet's innermost thoughts and ideas. The majority—for reasons unknown to us—preferred to follow Abu Bakr, Muhammad's father-in-law as well as his earliest follower and closest friend.

The first group's belief system, as expounded by 'Ali, was called the Shi'a, meaning "sect"; more fully, Shi'at 'Ali: "the sect of Ali." And that minority group within the schismatic Muslim world continues to be called Shi'i to the present day. The majority called—and still call—themselves Sunnis. The term Sunna might be translated as "custom" by which is meant that Abu Bakr and his followers agreed that Muhammad preached an acceptance of many customs and traditions from among those whom Islam would come to embrace, adopting and adapting new customs and traditions in accordance with the needs of the people and thus maintaining a certain degree of flexibility for the Faith. He had exemplified this himself in his transformation of the focus on the Ka'ba, as we have noted: rather than destroying it, he re-angled the understanding of its significance.

By the 640s, in any case, the Muslims had swept up out of the hijaz and beyond the 'arav into the Middle East. Islam swallowed the Sassanian Empire to the East and Egypt and North Africa to the West. By the year 718, the new Faith extended westward as far as the Pyrenees and eastward as far as India. Needless to say, whereas the initial Muslim conquerors were Arabs—from the 'arav—the chain reaction of expansion, the further it got from that geographic source, was less and less an Arab expansion. A handful of Arab chieftains, for instance, led Berber armies into Spain between 711 and 718. Indeed, when five and seven centuries later, Turkic (not remotely Arab) peoples, first Seljuks and then Ottomans, swept from south central Asia westward into the world of the Middle East, they embraced the Islam of those they conquered.

Thus, when the Christian Byzantine Empire finally fell, its capital at Constantinople sacked in 1453, the Ottoman conquerors were Muslim conquerors but by no means Arab conquerors. On the contrary, political and even cultural nationalism would evolve in the Arab world later on, in the nineteenth century, initially as a desire to throw off their Turkish masters—the Arabic word for "throwing off" is intifada.

The Pillars and Edifice of Islam

The Qur'an is the foundational text of Islam: God's words to humanity through the conduit of Muhammad as seal of the prophets and messengers of God. It teaches that there is one God—omnipotent, omniscient, the creator of all that exists, beneficent and merciful but stern in judgment. Man's primary duty is to submit to the will of God; those who rebel against 'Allah and His prophets will be punished both in this world and in the next. The Qur'an teaches that after death there is a Heaven and a Hell. Submitters to God's will—*muslims*—will experience paradise (its terms are very physical and male oriented: delightful food, drink, and beautiful maidens); rebels against it will experience Hell (a decidedly unhappy fate, although the concept of Hell is not elaborated with nearly the vehement detail that one finds in Christian thought).

At the end of time there will be a resurrection of the dead and a final judgment, an eternal disposition of soul and body. The Qur'an also teaches that there is predetermination toward good and evil within the world, even as we are ultimately judged and thus are assumed to have free will in the matter of our behavioral patterns. Thus an important issue throughout Islamic history has been whether or not we can change anything if everything is predetermined (the same issue assails Christianity and Judaism).[15] Recognizing this tension is important not only for grasping Islam but for understanding some of the socioeconomic fabric of the Middle Eastern world dominated by Islam.

The Qur'an is viewed as the last in a *series* of revelations; it follows the Torah, understood as revealed to Moses; the Psalms, understood as revealed to David; and the Gospels, understood as revealed to Jesus. Islam thus understands the Gospels not as texts written about Jesus by others but as revelations by God to Jesus—it is not exactly understood, then, how clear Muhammad's understanding of Judaism and Christianity was, or to what extent he believed their own understandings of their own texts to be in error. He developed *his* understanding, presumably, during the time he spent in Madina conversing with spiritual leaders within the Jewish and Christian communities, listening to their sermons, and perhaps deriving a kind of "midrashic" sense of both Judaism and Christianity.

Within the vast seas of beliefs that surrounded him, Muhammad swam with an auditory, not a written, life preserver—supplemented, of course, by what 'Allah Itself revealed directly to him. This revelatory component cannot be overemphasized and perhaps needs to be restated, eliminating the term "supplemented." For Jews and Christians would necessarily discount this material as the direct "word of God"; whereas from a Muslim viewpoint, since the Qur'an was in its entirety revealed to and through Muhammad, then the many contact points among passages in the Qur'an and those within the Jewish or Christian literary and oral traditions are solely a function of *God's* relationship to all three bodies of literature, and not at all a function of Muhammad's relationship to the *people* around him.

As the Qur'an is the last of the revealed texts, Muhammad is the last prophet: the *Seal of the Prophets*. But the Qur'an is supplemented, as Islam moves forward beyond the prophet's life and death, by *Hadith*. These are sayings and narrative sequences that are not in their entirety universally embraced by Muslims and in any case are not recognized as divine in origin—and are therefore not worthy of inclusion in the Qur'an. They offer both words ascribed to Muhammad—the words of the Prophet, as opposed to the words of God *through* the Prophet—and accounts of him, which have in many cases acquired a stature near, but by no means equal, to that of the Qur'an. If the Torah and the Gospels are the heart of the Hebrew Bible and New Testament, respectively, and the Qur'an is the equivalent of the Torah and Gospels, the *Hadith* are not quite the equivalent of the other parts of the Hebrew Bible or New Testament but far more important than, say, the rabbinic or patristic literatures are.[16]

Together, the Qur'an and the *Hadith* comprise the beginning of "the way" in Islam. The Arabic word summarizing this is *shari'a*—"highway"—the conceptual analogue of the Hebrew word *halakhah* (the "way to go"). *Shari'a* may also be understood as based on the Qur'an on the one hand and on the *sunna* (tradition) arrived at through the careful study and *'ijma* (consensus) of the *ulama* (leading legal minds) within a given sect of Islam.

Shari'a more specifically means a path to water. Since water is essential to survival—the more so in a desert environment such as that in which Islam was born—then one may recognize how essential commitment to *shari'a* is for traditional Islam, for survival in both the here and now and the hereafter. Moreover, the term also puns on the Arabic word *shar*, meaning water source, for the *shari'a*, the legal system that guides the life of a Muslim is as much the spiritual, emotional, psychological, and intellectual source of life as water is its physical source.

The building blocks of Islam are two: *din* ("law") and *iman* ("belief").[17] What belief? That there is no God but 'Allah and that Muhammad is the Seal of the Prophets; that there are twenty-eight other important prophets: eighteen Hebrew biblical ones, three figures from the Gospels, and seven from other sources, including diverse historical and legendary figures such as Alexander the Great; belief in angels and *shaitanin* (evil spirits); belief in the divine inspiration of the scriptures; belief in a last day, the day of judgment; and belief in the predetermination of good and evil in this world.

Belief together with law *are* Islam. There are five pillars that have been erected on these two foundation stones. First, a testimony of faith, the *shahada*, is similar in the intention of its opening words ("there is no God but God") to the *sh'ma* in the Jewish tradition: "Hear (*sh'ma*) O Israel, the Lord is our God the Lord is One"—and also, in form if not substance, to the Nicene creed for Christianity, which expresses belief in the co-substantiality of the Father, Son, and Holy Spirit. The second pillar is prayer. *Salat*, formal prayer, takes place five times daily at sunrise, noon, mid-afternoon, sunset, and evening, although informal prayer—*du'a*—can take place anytime.

During the *salat*, Muslims face Makka and engage in a process that involves the entire body: going down on the knees, placing the forehead on the ground twice, coming back up, going down again, and then rising again—while reciting passages from the Qur'an at each stage. To pray, the individual must be ritually pure: the hands, feet, eyes, ears, and neck must be washed. And one must perform the *salat* in a ritually clean place. The praying space must be separated from the surrounding, profane space; this might be accomplished by using a prayer rug but also simply by laying down newspapers or paper towels on the ground. Further, praying together as a community once a week at the mosque—Friday (*juma*) at noon—though not absolutely obligatory, is regarded as desirable.

The third pillar is *zakat*, charity for pious purposes. The term *sadakah*—freewill offerings—is also used (a Jewish reader might recognize the cognate in word as well as concept with Hebrew *tzedakah*). The terms seem more or less interchangeable, referring to helping those in need, although *sadakah* also refers to gifts offered as acts of expiation, so it might be directed at, say, a relative whom I've offended, whereas *zakat* is the term more strictly in use with regard to charitable acts toward those such as the poor. Perhaps the highest form of *zakat* would be to enable someone without the necessary resources to make the *hajj*.

The fourth pillar is *sawm*—fasting—during Ramadan, the ninth month of the Muslim year. Devout Muslims fast from sunrise to sunset each day of this month. Those who cannot fast, either due to illness or because of other conditions, such as travel, are obligated to "make up" those days as soon as they are able. As the Islamic calendar is a 355-day purely lunar calendar and doesn't adjust to the solar calendar, Ramadan shifts each year ten to eleven days back relative to the Gregorian calendar used in the West.[18]

The fifth pillar is *hajj*: pilgrimage. Pagan Makkans of Muhammad's day had used the word *hajj* to refer to a two-mile periodic visit to a sacred site outside Makka. Muhammad may have absorbed this concept into the development of his faith, just as he may have been aware of the pilgrimage traditions in Judaism and Christianity. After his death, *hajj* came to refer to a journey to Makka and Madina, the locations central to the prophet's life. If possible, every devout Muslim makes an annual *hajj*—or at least once in his/her lifetime—to Makka, from there to Madina and back to Makka, repeating the route that Muhammad followed from the time of the *hijra*. The central focus of this is of course the *Ka'ba*, around which the pilgrim walks seven times, but includes other sacred sites in and around the Muslim spiritual capital.

There is a sixth element, not a pillar of Islam, yet a term more familiar than perhaps any other to non-Muslims: *jihad*. The word means "struggle" and contrary to the understanding of it by many Muslims as well as most non-Muslims, *jihad* need have no military connotation whatsoever. The first level of struggle is within one's self, to render one's self as purely and fully a Muslim—a submitter and committer to God's will—as possible. The second level is the struggle within the *dar al'Islam* (the realm of Islam)—the *'umma*—to render it as purely *muslim* (submitted to God's will) as possible. This is most obviously expressed in the centuries' long struggle between *shi'i* (commonly anglicized as "*shi'ite*") and *sunni*: what originated as a difference regarding leaders (*Khalifat*) evolved as a series of doctrinal differences over which many words and, ultimately, a good deal of blood have often been spilt.[19]

It is fair to say that the *shi'a* tends to take the narrower, strictly textual view and the *sunna* the broader view—which includes orally transmitted customs—of a given religious issue, athough there are plenty of exceptions to this rule.[20] There are specific later echoes of the original basis for the schism, as well. Thus, there are those who believe in the future coming of the *mahdi*, a quasi-messianic figure, the "rightly guided one," who will effect the final victory of Islam by means of a divine catastrophe. Shi'is argue that he will be a descendant of the house of 'Ali, but Sunnis dispute that assertion. The majority of Shi'is, in fact, called "Twelvers," believe that he will be the twelfth spiritual leader in succession from 'Ali, who disappeared and is being held in abeyance by God until the proper moment arrives for his return.

The understanding of *jihad* shared by most non-Muslims is only its tertiary focus: to make those outside the *dar al'Islam*—in the *dar al'Harb*—recognize the ultimate truth from God that was preached by Muhammad. While that certainly can be and has been understood by any number of Muslims throughout much of history to mean a Holy War in the military sense of that phrase, even this aspect of *jihad* can be construed otherwise: that the struggle must be with the word and not the sword. It is with this idea in mind that Muhammad himself is said by some interpreters to have erred in the manner in which he conquered Makka.[21]

Moreover, the Qur'an can be and is very specific—most famously in *Sura* 2:256, which reads "There is no compulsion in religion"—that God disfavors violent attempts to force Muslim faith on those whose faith is otherwise. There are more than a dozen other passages, as well as half a dozen *hadith*s that distinctly militate against violent behavior toward non-Muslims in general.[22] The few passages in the Qur'an that might, in isolation, be seen to embrace violent *jihad* against non-Muslims (specifically, 8:12, 9:5, and 47:4) may be seen rather readily not to offer that embrace when read in their historical (8:12 and 47:4) and literary/textual (9:5) contexts.

As there are pillars of Islamic belief, there are gradations of practical observance. The first category includes *obligatory* actions, such as praying five times daily. Second are *desirable* and *recommended* actions, such as the *hajj*; one who is genuinely without the resources to make the pilgrimage will not be deprived of his place in paradise as a consequence of that omission—but woe unto the one who could and did not. The third category is religiously *neutral*—such as the gray area of how to relate to non-Muslims. This is by definition the category most open to discussion and differences of interpretation.

The fourth category includes actions that are *objectionable* but not forbidden. Some foods fall in this category, such as donkey's milk and meat. Similarly, for a man to take more than one wife, unless he has the economic means to insure the prosperity of the entire household—and can also insure the overall happiness of more than one wife—is objectionable, but not forbidden. The fifth category includes that which is absolutely *forbidden*, such as the consumption of pork or alcohol.

Moreover, as Islam developed over the centuries, a series of different schools of interpretation emerged. Three variations of Sunni orthodoxy might be called primary. The *Hanafi* School, founded by Abu Hanifa, who died in 767, is based on patterns of belief that developed in Mesopotamia. The *Maliki* School, which developed in Madina, is associated with the name of Malik Ibn Anas (who died in 795). A third school, the *Al Shafi'i* school, based on the teachings of a ninth-century disciple of Malik Ibn Anas, combined Malik's and Hanifa's teachings. I mention these without the space to expand on their thought patterns; I merely wish to underscore the diverse, non-monolithic quality of Islam over time and across space.[23]

Indeed, many additional schools beyond these three developed between the ninth and eleventh centuries, in both the Sunni and the Shi'i communities. Thus an ongoing body of discourse has continued to evolve—the analogue of the rabbinic and patristic-scholastic traditions. As Judaism doesn't end with the Torah, nor with the *mishnah* or the *gemara*—discourse within Judaism continues to the present day; and as Christianity doesn't end with the New Testament but evolves in the hands of generations of patristic and scholastic discussants; Islam moves from the Qur'an and *Hadith* and their synthesis with *sunna* (varied customs and traditions), to commentaries and discussions of specific issues adjudicated by *Muftis*—"expounders," the analogues of the *rabbanim* of medieval and post-medieval Judaism and of commentators like St. Augustine, St. Anselm, Peter Abelard, and St. Thomas Aquinas in the late ancient and medieval Christian tradition.

The *Muftis* have, over the centuries, recorded their opinions as *fatwas*—pronouncements ("expositions") on legal issues—like Jewish *responsa* literature and papal bulls. Entire collections of *fatwas* have been produced over time, focusing on how to live a life according to *shari'a*.

Islam, Judaism, and Christianity: Theories and Practices

Islam is a complex religion, beginning with a mixture of political and spiritual elements recorded in mixed oral and written traditions, which in turn bred a series of divergent sects, extending over a long history and a vast geography—from the Pyrenees to Southeast Asia. In each of the different parts of the Islamic world—Syria, Iraq, Spain, North Africa, Turkey, India, Indonesia—and in different eras, there arose different political structures and dynasties, which often exercised differing interpretations of religious principles. While one can reduce the foundations of Islam to five pillars as a matter of convenience, the conceptual and historical edifice is really far more complicated.

The complication is twofold. First: how to understand the foundations in their context—the political and spiritual interweave in which Muhammad himself managed to engage is distinctly different from that in which Jesus is said to have noted that one should separate what one renders unto Caesar from what one renders unto God, and that the sword should be put away, for "those who live by the sword die by the sword." It extends beyond even where Moses stood when, with arms upheld, he encouraged the Israelites in their bloody struggle with the Amalekites (Exodus 7:8–16). Second: how to continually reshape aspects of those foundations without undermining them in changing contexts across time and space.

For Jews and Christians, a particularly interesting facet of this issue is the degree to which Muslim customs, practices, and beliefs are rooted in aspects of the two older Abrahamic faiths. Prophecy as an idea, of course, goes back to the Bible, whereas angels and *shaitanin* are far more a part of Christian than Jewish theology.[24] In certain respects, the prayer structure of Islam may be seen to have derived from that of Judaism, but Muhammad enlarged on Jewish practices. Rather than merely three times a day, he came to prescribe prayer five times and included the very body language of obeisance to 'Allah that Judaism eschews. Though not always: interestingly, Abraham Maimuni, son of Maimonides and his successor as *Nagid*—spiritual and political leader—of

Egyptian Jewry, sought to introduce prostration into the synagogue service in the early thirteenth century, inspired to do so, in fact, by the Muslim custom. Originally, Muslims prayed toward Jerusalem, as Jews and some Christians do, but after his break with the Jewish tribes of Yathrib who had initially supported him—possibly even before Makka became his capital, with the *Ka'ba* as the central shrine of Islam (some scholars argue that his break with Yathrib's Jews came as early as 624 CE)—the Prophet redirected Muslims to pray toward Makka.

Muslims initially fasted on the tenth day of Ramadan; the fast was called *'Ashura*, cognate with the Hebrew *'esser*, meaning "ten." According to a *Hadith*, when it was pointed out to Muhammad that the Jews fasted on the tenth day of their month Tishri, he changed the Muslim fast to the ninth day; the eleventh was preferred by some; the idea was expanded to encompass the first ten days of the month until finally the entire month, from sunrise to sunset, was prescribed. The Jewish-Muslim interface is further evidenced by the fact that, whereas Jewish tradition came to connect Yom Kippur with the giving of the second set of the Decalogue to Moses, Muslim tradition speaks of the *tanzil*—the sending down of the Qur'an from Heaven through Gabriel to Muhammad—as having taken place during the *'Ashura* fast.

So, too, *kashrut*, absorbed from Judaism, while in part eventually rejected by Muhammad, it was retained to the extent that pork, blood, and carcasses are forbidden foods; and ritual slaughter—*halal*—was decreed by the Prophet for all animals intended for human consumption. Just as Judaism and Christianity diverged radically with respect to what the Second Temple period concept of *mashiah* means, the Muslim concept of the *mahdi* can be traced back to the same source but represents another variant on that theme.

Where for Christianity the *mashiah* arrived specifically in the person of Jesus and it is Jesus who will return at the end of time as we know it, for Judaism a vaguer concept prevails. This is, in part, because according to the Jewish view, the messianic arrival has not yet taken place and thus whom—or for that matter, what—precisely Jews are awaiting is unclear.

The Islamic concept is specific, in that the *mahdi* will come from a particular family, to complete the work of perfecting the world begun by Muhammad—but there is disagreement, as we have observed, as to which family, and not all Muslims accept the idea at all. As in the history of Judaism there has been a number of self-proclaimed messianic figures, so within Islam there has been a number of *mahdis* proclaimed by diverse groups of followers.[25]

The five Jewish tribes of Yathrib with whom Muhammad was initially allied did not unite against Muhammad as he was both growing stronger and turning against them—because they were involved in struggles with each other.

They apparently failed to notice that Muhammad was becoming a dangerous enemy. In the end, he defeated them one by one.[26] Toward the end of the 620s, just prior to his final assault on Makka, he attacked the Oasis of Khaybar, which had become the refuge of one of the Jewish tribes that he had ousted from Yathrib/Madina.

Upon defeating them after a siege of forty-five days, he is said to have come to an agreement—a *dhimma*, or "pact"—which included a series of injunctions, such as a requirement that Jews cede half their produce to Muslims, and decreeing Muhammad's right to break the agreement and expel the Jews at will, which reduced the Jews but at the same time extended a certain amount of protection to them and the right to practice their faith more or less freely.

The official version of the *dhimma* was eventually called the *Pact of Umar*— but it is not clear whether the Umar who may be called the author of the definitive written version was the Umayyad *Khalif* Umar of the mid-seventh century, or the Abbasid *Khalif* Umar of the mid-eighth century. We possess no version from Muhammad's own time, and therefore, no documentary proof that the *dhimma* as we have it stemmed in the *form* in which we have it from the Prophet himself. But the Jews came to be called *dhimmi*—"people of the pact."

That term, over time, came to refer also to Christians, Zoroastrians, Samaritans, and Sabaeans—peoples with a text at the center of their faiths. It was Muhammad, indeed, who coined the phrase "People of the Book" in referring to the Jews. Peoples of the Pact were entitled to better treatment than pagans and other non-Muslims without books as the basis of their faith, in part because the Prophet recognized Judaism and Christianity as older sibling forerunners, albeit misguided forerunners, of Islam.

In retrospect, it is clear, indeed, that as with Jesus, Muhammad initially saw himself as a reformer, not as the originator of a new faith. But whereas the vocabulary of Jesus was specifically Judaean-Jewish, and his followers would eventually see him as an incarnation of God Itself, Muhammad's terms were more generally those of Islam (by which I mean that Abraham and Moses, for example, were viewed as *muslims* in that they submitted to the will of God)— and his followers never view him as any more than the ultimate Messenger of God's word to those who seek to submit themselves to God.

To summarize: each of the edifices of Judaism, Christianity, and Islam stands on four "foundation stones." They share a common belief in an all-powerful, all-knowing, all-good, all-merciful God that has historically been interested and involved in human history. They share a belief in the notion of a people that is unique in its commitment and devotion to and relationship with that God, as well as a belief in a key text—or texts—that offers an umbilical connection between God and that people. They share a sense that there are particular places on the planet that stand out in being extraordinarily conducive to carrying out that relationship.

They differ from one another with respect to how each of these four elements is interpreted: Jews and Muslims maintain the certainty that God never assumes physical form; for Christians, a physical God in the person of Jesus is central to their faith. For Jews, the Hebrew Bible, with the Torah as its ultimate core is the central umbilical text; for Christians, the Hebrew Bible is called the Old Testament and is viewed as a prelude to the more central New Testament, of which the ultimate core comprises the Gospels.[27] For Muslims, all of these texts, divinely given, have become corrupted by error over time; the Qur'an offers the definitive Divine word in which all issues are correctly presented.

While all three Abrahamic denominations consider Jerusalem to be extremely important, their primary reasons differ. For Jews, the centrality of Jerusalem derives from the conviction that Abraham offered up his son Isaac to God on the hill (described in Genesis 22)[28] where, a millennium later, Solomon built the Israelite Temple (described in I Kings 6) with its Holy of Holies on that very site. For Christians, while these are significant issues, the primary importance pertains to Jesus, to the Crucifixion, to Golgotha, and the Holy Sepulcher—and there are other similarly important sites, such as Nazareth and Bethlehem, that, like Jerusalem, are significant for their connections to the life of Jesus and his circle, rather than for Hebrew Biblical connections.

So, too, for Muslims, Jerusalem is less significant than Makka and Madina, and its primary importance derives from the *Hadiths* that speak of the Rock in Jerusalem that marks a particular connecting point between heaven and earth: it is the place from which the Prophet ascended to heaven and to which he returned thence during his miraculous *'isra* (night ride), culminating with his ascent, *mir'aj*, to the throne of God—rather than due to its Hebrew Biblical or New Testament connotations.[29]

Finally, the messianic idea that takes full and specific form in Christianity as God-become-human remains unspecified and vague in Judaism, and in Islam the concept is variously held but with the exception of the followers of al-Hakim, whom most Muslims consider heretical, the concept of *mahdi* never includes the assertion that God assumed human form.

3

ARAB, MUSLIM, AND JEW; ISRAELI AND PALESTINIAN

While Islam was founded in the *'arav*, and its first adherents were therefore Semitic Arabs, as a religion its rapid sweep not only up into the Middle East and East Mediterranean but west as far as Spain by the early eighth century, and east as far as India by that time—and eventually as far as Indonesia—encompassed increasing numbers of non-Arab, non-Semitic peoples. Most of the Muslims who invaded Spain in 711–718 were non-Arab, non-Semitic Berbers from northwest Africa, for example. The Iranians are neither Arabs nor Semites; the language they speak, Farsi, a direct descendant of Old Persian, is much closer to English than to Arabic, even if it so happens that, for reasons beyond this discussion, Farsi uses Arabic *writing* to express itself nonverbally. Not a single native Filipino or Indonesian who practices Islam is an Arab or a Semite.

To make matters more complicated, both the terminology and the historical infrastructure of Islam itself carry the term "Islam" beyond the simply *faith*-bound category into which one might place it. The term *'umma*, used to refer to members of the Muslim community, has a broader connotation than "faith." It suggests a comprehensive realm in which faith interacts with education, economics, commerce, and culture, affecting aspects of lifestyle that extend from gastronomy to symbols in art. At the same time, Islam—like Christianity and Judaism—has been schismatic almost from the outset, as we have observed above. Thus Sunni-Shi'i antagonism, and antagonism *within* each of these two groups among varied sects and/or schools of thought, has been nearly as much of a factor in preventing cohesion in the Middle East as have extra-Islamic antagonisms.

Nor is this small array of definitional complications simplified when one turns to the word "Jew" and its correlates. Between the destruction of the

Second Temple in the year 70 CE and the time of Wilhelm Marr's 1879 coinage, "Semite," to refer to Jews, the term most prominently carried a religious connotation. To the extent that Jews actively associated themselves in their minds or were associated by others in *their* minds with Jerusalem, the site of the Temple, and its surrounding real estate, the term might be understood to have also had a nationalist connotation. For Judaism—albeit in a far-flung diasporic manner, rather than across a far-flung contiguous area, as is the case for Islam—the self-defining Hebrew term, *'am*, is cognate with the Arabic term *'umma*. The Jewish use of the term *'am*, even during those eighteen centuries of dispersion, intended a comprehensive reference to the same sort of elements as those that define the Muslim *'umma*. But Marr's designation of Jews as Semites, to repeat, was intended to recategorize them as a *race*—a race apart from the "Caucasian" Christian "race" of Europeans to whom he wanted to present Jews as dangerous interlopers.

A century and a quarter after the era of Wilhelm Marr's racialization of Jews, the question of how to define a Jew, Jewishness, or Judaism is nowhere close to having found an answer. In the United States, Judaism is perceived by most Jews and non-Jews alike as a religion. In most of Europe, Judaism is perceived as a nationality. In the former Soviet Union, this was explicit: one's internal passport indicated one's nationality as Russian or Azeri or Ukrainian or Georgian or Jewish—among others. But even in the West, in Germany, for example, when Jewish-Christian dialogue in the aftermath of the Holocaust is a discussion point, the phraseology that one encounters more often than not is "Germans and Jews"—not "German Christians and German Jews."

Beyond this distinction, between Judaism as a religion and Judaism as a nationality, is the fact that there are many Jews who don't believe in God, and who do not practice the religion of Judaism at all, but who understand themselves to be culturally Jewish—or in some cases, ethnically Jewish, but in any case *historically* connected to their Jewish forebears. Add to this the notion first articulated in the early 1930s by Mordecai M. Kaplan, that Judaism is best understood not as a religion or a culture, not as a nationality or a race, not as a body of customs and traditions, but as a civilization, and one begins to understand how this simple term refuses a simple definition.

To the extent that a given Jew can trace his lineage to the Semitic-speaking parts of the Middle East, and to the extent that Hebrew as the primary language of the Jews is classifiable as Semitic, Jews might be labeled Semites. For that matter, by the time Muhammad was born in the *'arav*, Jews had been resident there for at least half a millennium, which means that, like Muhammad and those who embraced the form of faith that he was shaping, the Jews with whom he had such intense contact and eventually conflict were also *Arabs*.

That is, if the term is used in the historical sense that I have noted earlier to refer to those who trace their ancestry to the *'arav*, there are certainly Arab Jews.

On the other hand, if we reuse the term "Arab" to refer to a political, rather than ethno-linguistic group, and therefore use it as in the phrase "The Arab World," then we broaden it to refer to peoples from Morocco to the border of Iran—and Jews would be excluded by definition, regardless of whether or not any of them originated in the *'arav*. The same might be said, of course, of Christians. In fact, the Christian role in Pan-Arab Nationalism in general and in Palestinian Arab identity in particular is significant.

We shall also observe, in considering Jewish Nationalism, that the matter of how to define a Jew would be rendered exponentially more complicated by the advent of a Jewish nationalist movement in general and also the particular sense of Jewish nationalism that came to be articulated in Zionism by the late nineteenth century.[30] Both for the non-Jewish European world, wrestling with how far to identify itself as *Christian* and as *secular*, and for the Jews themselves, the question arose: are Jews most properly and purely understood as adherents to a religion, or does the advent of Zionism, in recasting Jews as a nation with a homeland—with a language, literature, music, art, and all the other concomitants of Romantic Nationalism—separate them from a religion-based definition? This question and the varied responses to it would have practical consequences both for shaping the Zionist movement and for shaping the State of Israel over the decades following its independence.

What *of* Israelis? And what of Israelis and Palestinians? Definitional complications apply here, as well. Israel is so often simply referred to as "The Jewish State" that one might assume that all Israelis are Jews. Indeed, the government and its infrastructure—from the makeup of the *Knesset* (Israeli parliament) to regulations governing public transportation on the Sabbath—have from the outset been a wrestling match between the will to be governed by Jewish law and the will to be a secular democracy. Israel is both a Jewish theocracy and a secular democracy and as such, its citizenship is composed not only of Jews but of Christians, Muslims, and other religious groups. While it is true that the majority of Israelis are Jews—many of whom define themselves as Jews by culture and history and not by their religious beliefs—a substantial minority are not. An Israeli is a citizen of the polity, Israel.

Some of those citizens might also be called Arabs and most of the latter might also be called Palestinians. Anyone who lives in Palestine, or who traces an ancestry to inhabitants of Palestine would be called a Palestinian. But where *is* Palestine? It is where Israel, Jordan, and the parts between and around them, otherwise known as Gaza and the West Bank are currently located. The latter is also known as Judaea and Samaria; one's choice of terminology will depend largely upon one's political and/or religious point of view. Much of this area was called Judaea two millennia ago. Even then, though, the inhabitants of the polity Judaea distinguished it in the larger geopolitical sense, from Judaea in the narrower sense, as separate from Samaria and the Galilee.[31]

In the wake of the failed but—from the Roman point of view—frustrating (because it took three years to suppress) Bar Kokhba revolt of 132–35, the Roman Emperor Hadrian astutely deduced that if he could undercut the religion of the Jews, he might be able to undercut the Jewish nationalist aspirations that had led to three major uprisings within the Empire and/or against Roman rule in seventy years. As another part of his program to suppress Jewish nationalism, he renamed Judaea *"Palestina"*—apparently appropriating and adapting the Semitic designation, *Philistia*, formerly applied to that corner of Judaea that we now call "Gaza." The name *Palestina* remained in use in the Western vocabulary (but not the Hebrew language, Jewish vocabulary) for the next nineteen centuries.

So a Palestinian would be anyone living in Palestine during those centuries—be that individual Muslim, Christian, Jewish, or an adherent of any other sort of faith system, for that matter. That would be simple enough were it not for the history of the past hundred years or so. For reasons that will be explored shortly, the British and the French carved up the Middle East in the aftermath of World War I, and the area designated as Palestine fell under a British colonial administration, so that one reads and speaks of Britain's Palestinian Mandate. From that Mandate three entities would be further carved out over the following thirty years. That part of Palestine east of the Jordan River, which would also supply it with its name, became the postwar Emirate of Jordan; in 1946 it became the Hashimite Kingdom of Transjordan. Part of the area west of the Jordan River would become the State of Israel in 1948. The part of western Palestine that did not become Israel—Gaza and the "West Bank"—continued to be called Palestine, although these areas were governed by Jordan and Egypt respectively until 1967. Thus, if one's understanding of that term is informed by a post-World War II perspective, rather than a post-Bar Kokhba/Hadrianic perspective, the term "Palestinian" refers only to someone dwelling in one of these two last-mentioned areas as opposed to those inhabiting either Israel or Jordan.

Those who assert that there already exists a Palestinian state east of the Jordan are right. But those who insist that, over the decades since 1946–48, the continued separation between communities east and west of the Jordan has reshaped those to the east as functionally Jordanians, so that those to the west remain the only true Palestinians and their desire for political identity and statehood is legitimate, are *also* right. Those Israelis who, descendants of generations of dwellers in this area assert that they are Palestinians are also right, although few individuals in common parlance would be likely to recognize the cogency of that historical datum. And the non-Jewish—i.e., Muslim and Christian Arab—population that inhabits Israel? They are certainly Israeli and also, to repeat, Arab, but particularly in the post-Oslo world since 1993 or so, many of them have reidentified themselves as Palestinians. Many, but not all.

Or perhaps better put: since 1993—the year of the Oslo Accords between Israelis and Palestinians—there exists a new layer to the tensions felt by Israeli Arabs for which the tightness increased exponentially after the advent of the most recent *Intifada* that began in 2000, regarding how to identify themselves, as Israelis or as Palestinians. As with every self- definitional choice available to a given group, its constituent members vary as to which one they select. This issue can be seen to apply along various religious and ethnic lines in varying degrees throughout the Middle East, and not only in the context of Israel-Jordan-Palestine, as we shall see in more detail in subsequent chapters of this narrative.

PART TWO
HISTORICAL ASSOCIATIONS AND ASPIRATIONS

4

THE ERA OF THE CRUSADES

The issues of carving up Palestine and the conflict between forms of self-definition prove to be part of the larger matter of the conflicting and often confusing aspirations throughout the region during the past two hundred years. The reference in the previous chapter to the British and the French and their role in redefining "Palestine" in the first half of the twentieth century reminds us that the third weft thread in this tangled web, along with definition and aspiration, is *interference*.

Interference arrives into the complications of the Middle East in two related but different forms before we arrive into the modern era. The first interference by outside forces is from the European Christian world, specifically in the form of the Crusades that dominate Christian-Muslim relations between the end of the eleventh century and the middle of the fifteenth. The second form of interference will come from the opposite spiritual and geographic direction, taking the shape of a succession of Turkic and Mongol conquerors whose faith is animist. The most significant of these, for this discussion, are the Seljuk and Ottoman Turks.[32]

The two forms of interference interface on several levels. In the first place, it is the arrival of the Seljuks that most directly gave the impetus to the first Crusade. The Seljuk victory over the Byzantine—Eastern Christian—army at the Battle of Manzikert in 1071 and the subsequent Seljuk obstruction of the Christian pilgrims' route to Jerusalem was the most immediate reason for the call for a Crusade by Pope Urban II, in 1095, to liberate those routes.

Of course there was an array of other issues as well. Christians would later look back and retrofit onto the call for Crusade as its first cause the burning of the Church of the Holy Sepulchre by the crazed Fatimid Shi'i Egyptian overseer of Jerusalem, al-Hakim (985/996–1021(?)), in 1009.[33] Nobody is quite certain why he did it, but al-Hakim himself disappeared into the desert a few years later never to be heard from again, and his successor promptly rebuilt this most important of Christian structures.[34] Nonetheless the burning of the Church would later be referred to as the first cause for the Crusade.

More significant surely were intra-Christian issues. These ranged from the great schism that separated the Eastern and the Western Churches in 1054 to the great conflict between Pope Gregory VII and the young German King Henry IV that culminated with Henry's arrival to Canossa, a mountain stronghold in northern Italy, in 1077, where he stood in the snow barefoot for several days before gaining an audience with the Pope in which he begged forgiveness for his audacious opposition to the Holy Father. Intra-Christian issues included the emergence of Cluniac reforms that revitalized the troubled monastic orders in Western Christendom and with the reforms a renewed zeal for pilgrimages by the second half of the eleventh century.

They included the fact that Urban, successor and disciple of Gregory, was himself a Cluniac and was already engaged in a struggle against secular feudal Christian lords who opposed his leadership of Western Christendom. This last issue would both inspire the Pope to think beyond the bounds of Christendom with regard to spiritual hegemony and offer a channel for the energy of such feudal lords, redirecting it away from—and reshaping it to function on behalf of—the Papacy. In other words, the promotion of a Crusade to the Holy Land against the Muslims would serve a range of papal needs.

On the other hand, the formerly "barbarian," pagan Normans and Magyars had recently come into the fold of "civilized" Christianity, which offered both an encouraging sense of how violent enemies could be made to enter the fold in peace and an instrument to be directed toward the *Dar al'Islam* as the ultimate enemy. Moreover, in Spain the Umayyad dynasty with its great capital at Cordoba had collapsed by 1031, reducing Islamic Spain to a series of petty kingdoms, called in Arabic *ta'ifas*. This development enabled the *reconquista*—the Christian reconquest of Spain—to move forward for the first time since the Muslim takeover of the early eighth century. Half of formerly Muslim Spain fell into Christian hands over the next half century, culminating with the conquest of Toledo in 1085. Similarly, in the central Mediterranean, Norman Christians wrested Mahdia (Tunisia) from the Muslims in 1087 and by 1091 had established a new, Christian kingdom in a Sicily that had been governed in part or totally by Muslims for 260 years.

Add to this array of issues the fact that in 1055 the Seljuk Tughrul Bey forced the Abbasid Caliph to make him Sultan, and we understand that an astute observer of the Muslim world would have recognized that the dismantling of traditional infrastructures that had been in place within it for three centuries meant that the time to strike had arrived. Urban called together a Council at Piacenza, Italy, in early 1095 and another at Clermont later in the year. Ostensibly, he sought to restore unity to the church; to heal the rift of 1054 by responding to the request of the Byzantine Emperor Alexios I for recruits for an army that could reclaim what had been lost in the Battle of Manzikert. In the end, though, the Pope instead sent his own army, under his own knightly leadership. Raymond IV, Count of Toulouse, accompanied by the Bishop of Le Puy, led volunteers from Southern France. Those from Northern France were led by Robert II, Duke of Normandy; Robert II, Count of Flanders; and Godfrey of Bouillon, Duke of Lower Lorraine—among others. And from Apuleia, in Southern Italy, came an essentially Norman contingent led by Bohemond, son of Robert Guiscard.

This disparate array of crusaders—"Franks" as they were called by the Muslim world—all converged on Constantinople between July 1096 and July 1097. It was an undisciplined horde, including pilgrims and clergy as well as a range of less spiritually directed participants, rather than a well-organized group of recruits. Negotiations immediately began with Emperor Alexios: Bohemand demanded that he be granted the office of the Grand Domestic of the East in the presumed-to-be-inevitable event of a victory, which would have made him the Imperial Viceroy for the conquered lands. Alexios, in turn, asked that any of his territories that were conquered by the Franks be returned to his jurisdiction. By late 1097, the group had taken Nicaea, in what is now Turkey. There, Alexios soon installed a contingent of Byzantine soldiers to limit the looting being accomplished by the Franks, which naturally raised the level of hostility between the two groups of Christian fighters.

Between October 1097 and June 1098, the Crusaders besieged and finally took Antioch, in what is now Syria; had there been less disunity among them, the process would probably have been much quicker. Alexius began, rather late in the siege, to send reinforcements, but he got word that the Seljuk *atabeg* (regent) Kerbogha of Mosul was advancing with a large relieving force and he turned back in fear. Indeed, the *atabeg* did arrive at Antioch with his army shortly after the Crusaders took the city on June 3: the besiegers now found themselves besieged, but on June 28, Bohemand took on and defeated Kerbogha in a pitched battle outside the city. Almost immediately, arguments ensued between Bohemand and Raymond as to who should be put in charge of the city.

The argument remained unresolved when the two set out with their combined forces toward Jerusalem in November. En route, just before Christmas, Bohemand turned back and took control of Antioch on his own. Raymond and his forces arrived at the walls of the Sacred City in June 1099, where he encountered much stiffer resistance than he might have anticipated given the very light opposition he had encountered along the way. But the Shi'i Fatimids, who had taken control of the city from Sunni Seljuks the previous year, understood both the symbolic and the strategic significance of Jerusalem as a key to the region. Nonetheless, the Franks took Jerusalem on July 15. A massacre ensued; one Christian writer, reporting to the Pope, described the Crusaders as wading in blood up to the thighs of their horses. When the smoke cleared, and Godfrey of Bouillon had been appointed *advocatus*—defender—of the Church of the Holy Sepulchre (underscoring the retrofitting of the destruction of that edifice eighty-five years earlier as the cause for the Crusade in the first place), four Latin Crusader kingdoms had been put into place. As such, Jerusalem would remain a state between 1099 and 1243. Up the coast toward the Lebanon, Tripoli would take three years of further campaigning to be solidly in Crusader hands, and the Kingdom of that name would last from 1102 to 1289. Antioch, having been put under the charge of Bohemand, survived as a Crusader kingdom until 1268. Edessa, further north and east, and also having been taken in 1098, would last as a Crusader kingdom only until 1144.

The attempt at an Islamic counter-conquest—followed by the counter-counter-conquest of the Second Crusade—would not be that far in coming. In the first place, Zanji, the latest *atabeg* of Mosul, seized Aleppo in 1128, and from there offered a clear threat to the Burdis in control of Damascus. The latter maintained positive commercial and cultural relations with the Crusader states, but didn't receive the assistance they should have from those states in the face of that common threat. In 1144, Zanji took the northernmost of the Crusader states, Edessa, but he died two years later. His son, Nurredin, declared a *jihad* against the three remaining Crusader states. But even had he not done so, the fall of Edessa shocked the Europeans and set quickly in motion the decision of Pope Eugenius III to declare a second Crusade. Among the respondents to that call were the French king Louis VII and the German king Conrad III—the latter inspired, in part, by Bernard of Clairvaux, the monastic reformer known otherwise for his destruction of the Christian scholar, Peter Abelard.

Disaster met the two monarchs every step of the way. Conrad was defeated at Dorylaeum on October 25, 1147, by the Turks, and Louis was defeated by them at Laodicea in January 1148. The siege of Damascus that they undertook with their remaining forces in late June proved disastrous, and the prestige of the Franks as warriors—so high after the first Crusade, imposing fear on the Muslim inhabitants of the Middle East—was severely damaged. Shortly thereafter, Nurredin defeated Raymond of Antioch at Inab in 1149. He sent his lieutenant, the Kurd, Shirquh, to Egypt where, in spite of his being a Sunni, he was accepted as a vizier to the Fatimid Caliph. Upon Shirquh's death, his nephew Salah ad-Din Yusuf Ibn Ayub—better known to the West as Salah ad-Din, or Saladin—assumed that position as vizier, but by 1171, nominally still as lieutenant to Nurredin, he declared that Egypt now would answer to the Abbasid caliphate, effectively ending the Fatimid control of that region.[35] Saladin's military and political success had resulted—by 1183—in his control not only of Egypt but of the larger region that encompassed Antioch and Tripoli; Jerusalem fell to his sword on October 2, 1187. It is worthy of note that *no bloodbath followed that conquest,* and that Christians, Jews, and others were permitted to continue to live their lives without much interference from their Muslim overlords in the years of Saladin's control.

Nonetheless, the new dominance of the Muslims provoked a new response on the part of new Popes: Gregory VIII and Clement III declared a third Crusade in 1189. The key respondents this time were the English king Richard "Coeur-de-Lion" and the Holy Roman Emperor, Frederick Barbarossa. The most serious tangible result of the campaigns of Richard were the reclamation of the coastal cities south of Acre that gave to the truncated Kingdom of Jerusalem the wherewithal to survive for another century; so, too, by 1192 Richard gained the right by treaty for Christian pilgrims to visit the Church of the Holy Sepulchre. One might note, as a reminder of how confusingly divided both the Christian and Muslim worlds remained within themselves and not only with regard to each other, that on his way home Richard was waylaid and held for ransom by the Viennese, who demanded and received a substantial supply of silver from the English in exchange for his release.

On a similar note, the fourth Crusade began shortly thereafter, in 1199, instigated by Thibaut III, Count of Champagne, with the blessing of Pope Innocent III and with the assistance of the Venetians under Doge Enrico Dandolo. This Crusade yielded as *its* most tangible consequence the enriching of Western Christendom and Venice in particular, to whom the French and other Crusaders owed a good deal of money. This came about through the plundering of Eastern Christendom; the Crusaders never got further east and south than Constantinople, which they sacked in 1204, and from which they sent or brought back an extraordinary range and volume of precious material. Thus, to the massacre of Muslims in Jerusalem and elsewhere during this era, and the massacres and expulsions of Jews both there and back in the Rhineland on the way to the Holy Land, may be added the massacre of their Christian brethren by these champions of the God of Love.

They established a new Latin dynasty in Constantinople which, although it lasted only until 1261, would assure that Byzantium would never become the sort of power it had once been. In retrospect, one might argue that this helped make the Empire vulnerable to the Ottomans when they arrived on the scene. Indeed, when Constantinople itself was under siege in the mid-fifteenth century, the memory of the cruelty of their Western brethren was profound enough that the Greek Orthodox citizens of the city preferred conquest by the Turks to submission to the Papacy as the price for its assistance.

Innocent III and his successor to the Papal tiara, Honorius III, pushed for the fifth Crusade that finally arrived in 1218. Honorius was the same Pope who, in part in response to the unresolved problems of corrupted monasticism and heresy within Christendom—and to the challenge to Papal authority afforded by far-flung and materially successful monastic organizations such as the Cluniac order—sanctioned two new monastic orders. The Franciscans and Dominicans were distinguished from their monastic predecessors in being mendicant (wandering beggar) orders that, it could be expected, would never set down the kind of land-based permanent roots that might lead to material power and with it antipapal behavior. Moreover, the Dominicans in particular would evolve as servants of the Papacy who in the course of the century became famous for their rooting out of heretics. They developed Boards of Inquiry—known in the vernacular as the Inquisition—into the faith of believing Christians, first in northern Italy and southern France and eventually in southern Italy and Sicily; and finally, by the fifteenth century, in Spain.

As for the Crusade sponsored by Honorius, its direct spiritual leader, the Papal legate Cardinal Pelagius of Albano, wrested defeat from the jaws of victory by his stubborn refusal to accept rather favorable terms offered to him by his Muslim counterpart. Pelagius might have regained full control of Jerusalem. The sacred city had remained in Muslim hands since the time of Saladin, even if the "Kingdom" continued to have nominal Christian "rulers" essentially limited to the Church of the Holy Sepulchre and its immediate environs. But through his hunger to conquer all of Egypt, Pelagius lost the chance to regain full control of Jerusalem. And so Frederick II—who had taken the cross in 1215 but never sailed off and was crowned by Pope Honorius III as Holy Roman Emperor in 1220—responded to the call for a sixth Crusade by Pope Gregory IX in 1227.

Frederick turned back shortly after setting sail in September on the grounds of being seasick. The turnaround earned him excommunication, but in the summer of 1228 he set forth once more, and with more diplomacy than warfare, he concluded a treaty with the Egyptian Sultan al-Kamil that gained Jerusalem and other sites within its ambit and a promise of peace for ten years. But the Pope condemned his having negotiated with, rather than warring with, Muslim infidels, and declared a "crusade" against Frederick's own lands in Italy. In the decades that followed, the Franks were more involved in fights with each other than against Muslim foes, except when they fought as allies with one Muslim force against another. It was in the course of such inter-change that Jerusalem was captured by an army of Khwarizmian Turks in July 1244 working as mercenaries for the Egyptians.[35]

In December of that year, the French king Louis IX took the cross, and by 1248 he had set off on the seventh Crusade. The aftermath of six years of that debacle—the most significant moment of which was the capture of Louis himself in 1250; and the most interesting fact that in the aftermath of Louis's ransom his hopes for reinforcements from the Papacy were disap-pointed because Innocent IV was too busy with a "crusade" against Conrad IV, son of Frederick II—was a return home by the French king with the grow-ing conviction on his part and those of others that God is simply indifferent to crusades! But meanwhile, in the very year of Louis's capture, the Mamluks of Cairo, war-loving slave troops in the service of the Seljuks, asserted their own rule in Egypt.

Other developments shaped the following decade. In 1258, Hulagu the Mongol sacked Baghdad, ending the Abbasid rule of that city and an Empire which had lasted, at least nominally, since 750. Two years later, the Mongols took Aleppo and Damascus. In the same year, the Nestorian Christian general of the Mongols, Kitbugha, was defeated and killed at 'Ayn Jalut, near Nazareth, by the Mamluk Sultan Qutuz of Egypt and his general, Baybars. The primary significance of that moment was that the pagan Mongols embraced Islam, con-vinced that it was a stronger faith than that of Christianity. This would have repercussions into the next century, when the successors to the Mongols, the Ottomans, arrived onto the scene.

In any case, the continued depredations of the waning Latin kingdoms by Baybars, who soon became Sultan himself, brought a response from Europe in the form of an eighth Crusade, in which once again Louis IX, despite pre-viously expressed doubts, took up the sword. He began his new enterprise in 1267. Within three years, though, Louis was diverted to Tunisia by his brother, Charles of Anjou, King of Sicily, since the latter did not want a Crusade to distract Western Christendom from the war he was contemplating against the Byzantine Christians—and besides, he was on good terms with Baybars. With Louis's death of dysentery in Tunisia that same year, Baybars was able to take the last of the inland Crusader fortresses. One might say, in the for-mal historiographic sense, that the Crusades were at an end, leaving behind a legacy of increased intolerance in Christian Europe, whether against the Muslim world or against non-Western Christians or against Jews or against heretics: the thirteenth century saw, among other God-inspired events, the virtual extermination of the heretical Albigensians, also known as the Cathars, burned in their hill towns in the south of France by the Dominican inquisitors.

On the other hand, the increased and intensified intercourse between Europe and the Middle East brought new commercial interests and directions back into Europe, together with new tastes in food and new thinking with regard to long-distance commerce effected by the abstraction of a banking system that used *checks* (from the Arabic *sak*). The development of a money economy and with it, a rising merchant class, affected nobles and serfs alike. So, too, the Crusaders brought back to Europe an interest in and understanding of massive stone masonry construction; it is no accident that the thirteenth century marks a precipitous increase in the size of churches, cathedrals, and castles. The developments of heraldic emblems, of chivalric codes, and of heroic narratives, are also part of that legacy.

Nor did the Crusades really end when they ended. Chivalric orders continued a presence in and around the region. Thus the Templars held out on the small island of Arwad, two miles off Tortosa, until 1303. Their brother knights, the Hospitaliers, would make their way to the island of Rhodes, whence they would finally be forcibly removed in 1522 by a massive Ottoman effort; they would reestablish themselves on Malta before slowly fading toward the backstage of history by the Napoleonic era. But with the arrival of the Ottoman (Osmanli) Turks into Anatolia by about 1350, and ultimately with their taking of Constantinople in 1453—bringing to an end Byzantine history that had played out for a thousand years after the collapse of the Western Roman Empire—the zeal to Crusade, while nominally pointed toward the Holy Land, more often directed itself toward some other site that served more generally as a symbol of Christian-Muslim hostility.

Historically, one of the more interesting interfaces between religion and politics is when the Ottoman Turks, as conquerors of a substantial portion of the Muslim world, embraced the Muslim faith rather than imposing the Turks' own form of animist paganism upon those they conquered. Unusual, but not entirely surprising, if one considers the inherent logic in seeking a faith dominated by a single God for a group that evolved from a nomadic sweep of tribes to a dominating, sedentary empire governed by one all-powerful leader. That said, in retrospect the preference of Islam rather than Christianity may ultimately be traced to the choice made by the Ottomans' predecessors in the wake of that previously mentioned critical moment: the defeat of the Christian-led Mongols by the Muslims in 1260 at 'Ayn Jalut.

In any case, it was against the Ottomans that efforts were mounted in the fourteenth and subsequent centuries, from an attack on Smyrna on the western coast of Turkey in 1344 to the crusade called by Pope Pius II that remained stillborn in 1464: the Pope waited in vain that summer on the eastern coast of Italy for the ships promised from various quarters to arrive and set sail. In the end they never showed up and he contracted dysentery and died on the way back to Rome. But the interface between the Ottomans—as the ongoing representative of Islam—and Christendom continued along a handful of significant paths as the decades and then centuries moved forward. A generation after the death of Pius II, the Jews were expelled, in 1492, from a newly unified Christian Spain—and from Portugal in 1496–97—and one of the places where many of them took refuge was the Ottoman Empire. Sultan Beyezit II is said by some traditions not merely to have invited them but to have sent ships to transport them from the coastal cities of Barcelona and Malaga.

Beyezit was not merely being gracious or simply Judaeophilic. The Sephardic Jews brought with them something of an international trade network and considerable experience at intermediating commercially and culturally between the Muslim and Christian worlds. They also brought with them knowledge of movable type. The first books printed in the Muslim world—in Instanbul—as Constantinople had come to be called, were—ironically enough, given subsequent history—Hebrew books. Mostly, the Jews brought with them from Christendom knowledge of gunpowder and cannonry, which would transform the Ottoman Empire into a spectacular military machine. In the following century, a Jew known as Joseph HaNassi, or Joseph the Prince, would rise to the position of vizier to Beyezit's successor's successor, Suleiman the Magnificent. HaNassi would be honored with a Dukedom and granted permission to establish a semiautonomous Jewish community in the northern Palestine area of Safed and Tiberias. This would mark the first activated non-messianic attempt on the part of Jews to return to the Holy Land since the fourth century.

Suleiman the Magnificent would extend the Ottoman presence into the heart of Europe and offer a weight equal in historical significance to that offered at the other end of the Mediterranean by Charles I of Spain and Francis I of France, as well as Henry VIII of distant England. In retrospect, the unanticipated defeat of the Ottoman navy of Suleiman's successor, Selim II, by a combined Christian force at the 1571 Battle of Lepanto marked the beginning of a long swoon that would finally bring the Empire to its end three and a half centuries later, during World War I. Much, though, would transpire in the course of those centuries, including the near-taking of Vienna in 1683—the second time an Ottoman army had stood beneath the walls of that city, which Suleiman had unsuccessfully besieged more than 150 years earlier.

Three serendipitous factors saved the city and, with it, central Europe: the arrival of a relieving army under the Polish leader John Sobieski; the arrogance of the Ottoman generals in being so entirely focused on the siege that they ignored what was happening at their rear, assuming either that no relieving army would arrive or that it would pose no threat; and dysentery that ran rampantly through the Ottoman army at virtually the same time, helping to necessitate the withdrawal of the Turkish forces.

In the century that followed the last Ottoman siege of Vienna, Europe began to seethe with a series of revolutions. Thus, in the period between about 1760 and World War I, the Christian world made spectacular progress in industrial, technological, and scientific—as well as political and secular intellectual—thinking, while the Ottoman and Muslim worlds did not. By the nineteenth century, as Ottoman power was shrinking back toward the Middle East, European colonial ambition and imperial rapaciousness were beginning to encircle the globe and, in the Mediterranean world, to swallow piece after piece of Ottoman-held North Africa.

The culmination of that process for the purposes of this discussion was the entrance of the Prussians into the Near East at the behest of the last somewhat significant Ottoman Sultan, Abdul Hamid II, who arrived onto the imperial throne in 1876. The invitation to Kaiser Wilhelm was extended with the hope that the Prussians would replenish Abdul Hamid's empty coffers and build railroads connecting Istanbul to the Persian Gulf on the one hand (the more efficiently to move troops back and forth between the Ottoman capital and the gulf) and from Damascus to the *hijaz* on the other, all the way to Makka.[36] This was not only in order to be able to move troops back and forth, but to add more weight to the Sultan's claim to be the Caliph of Islam as the protector of its primary holy sites. Most significantly, Abdul Hamid wanted the Prussians to modernize his army by shaping new officers' training schools.

This last issue would have important consequences with respect to the final dismantling of the Ottoman Empire. It would also have important consequences for the evolution of nationalism among the Arabs. For one thing, some of their leadership would be developed—and gain new military and general organizational skills—in those training academies. For another, the dismantling of the Empire from within, due to an uprising of modernist Turkish officers against the Sultan in 1908, would turn its back on the modernist Arab officers who participated in the uprising.[37] This would leave that well-trained Arab leadership frustrated and eager to find a different outlet for national self-expression.

5

NATIONALISM AMONG THE ARABS

That the range of confusing and conflicting definitions cuts across complicated, confusing, and conflicting religious and political lines should be clear at this point. But the complexities cut across the issues of ethnicity and nationalism as well, particularly as we turn our focus from the category of definitions and interferences to that of aspirations. This last word, as it applies to the history of the region in the last two and a half centuries or so, refers primarily to nationalist aspirations, on the part of various groups among the Arab and non-Arab Muslim and Arab Christian peoples as well as among the (primarily but not exclusively non-Arab) Jews. The first effort toward fulfilling what might be called Arab Nationalist aspirations came in the early nineteenth century, but drew on a religious issue for some of its early strength and ultimately foundered in large part on an ethnic issue. These efforts were led by Mehmet and Ibrahim Ali to create a pan-Arab state between about 1805 and 1848. Mehmet was an Albanian Ottoman of putative Arab descent—albeit who spoke no Arabic—and who served under the Ottomans as an army officer against Napoleon. It was Napoleon, we may recall, who effected the final demise of the Hospitalier Knights and in 1798 mounted the first European invasion of the Middle East since the Crusades.

The reported success of Napoleon's invasion reinforced the growing European Christian notion that had gradually evolved from the time of the Battle of Lepanto in 1571 through the failed Ottoman siege of Vienna in 1683 and the subsequent erosion of Ottoman power in Hungary and central Europe, that the Muslim foe was not nearly as fierce as had once been the case. This set the stage not only for an expansion of archaeological interest in the Near East (one recalls that it was Napoleon's expedition that yielded the Rosetta Stone, which led to the decipherment of Egyptian Hieroglyphs by 1820) but also for the effort to colonize it.

Conversely, the reshaped forces that would eventually oppose such colonization also began their development in the context of Napoleon's invasion. When Napoleon eventually departed, Mehmet decided that, rather than continuing to answer to a weak administration in faraway Istanbul, he might establish himself as an independent ruler. He sought to break up the old feudal structure not only in Egypt but in Syria and to unify that entire region under his command as an Arab state. That state would not only be separate from the shrinking Ottoman Turkish state, but use the extensive cultivation of cotton in Egypt to develop closer economic ties with Christian Europe, in particular England, Napoleon's implacable foe.

In spite of the rather profound impediment of speaking virtually no Arabic—although, to repeat, he referred to himself as an Arab by way of his parentage—Mehmet[38] managed to initiate the unifying process, in which he was strongly assisted by his son, Ibrahim—who at least spoke the language of those they were seeking to unify. One of the keys to Mehmet's success was his astute turn south toward the *hijaz*, where he gave support to the spiritual revolution then in progress led by followers of the Hanbali scholar, Muhammad Ibn 'Abd al-Wahhab. Ibn 'Abd al-Wahhab had made a pact in 1744 with Muhammad Ibn Sa'ud, prince of the market town oasis, Dar'iya, to enforce purer Islamic doctrines than had prevailed during the previous centuries.

Specifically, the doctrines preferred by the Wahhabi movement were those that had been articulated in the early fourteenth century by Taqi al-Din Ibn Taymiyyah of Damascus (d. 1328), doctrines which were anti-innovational in general and opposed, in particular, to the veneration of saints (Taqi has been called the "Martin Luther of Islam") and even to excessive veneration of the Prophet Muhammad. Taqi and Ibn 'Abd al-Wahhab were not afraid to say that *'ijma*—consensus—is not always right, or even emphatically to declare it wrong: in other words, the Wahhabi movement, as a purist movement, may be understood as a descendant not only of Taqi's teachings, but ultimately, conceptually, of the Kharajite branch of Shi'i Islam.

Mehmet Ali threw his support to the Wahhabis, who in turn supported him and helped position him as a champion of independent Arab Islam after centuries of subjugation to Turkish and other rulers. When the situation had stabilized under his control, Mehmet turned his back on the Wahhabis, ignoring their religious hopes and aspirations and indeed crushing them as a force in 1818. The same hostile stance toward Wahhabism remained in place under the rule of his son, who successfully expanded this new Arab state from Egypt to the edge of the Tigris-Euphrates valley. Mehmet's motives and accomplishments were not merely political but cultural as well. He founded new schools and training colleges and made use of a battery of new printing presses that he imported into his state to publish some 243 books in Turkish and Arabic between 1822 and 1843. But ultimately, the state collapsed because neither Mehmet nor Ibrahim was able, in the long run, to engender a sufficiency of enthusiasm for a unified Arab identity to compete with the familial and tribal loyalties that continued to define that region. Islam, at least at the outset of its own history, was able to offer itself in place of such loyalties, but within two generations of its birth was already being torn apart in part by tribal strife, and the echo of that issue on a more purely political front came twelve centuries later with the first failure of a politically pan-Arab movement.[39]

By the time of the demise of that movement, another means of shaping pan-Arab identity was beginning to emerge from an unexpected source. American Protestant and French Catholic missionaries arrived into Syro-Palestine and its environs by the 1830s and, through the end of the 1860s, established a series of schools throughout the region.[40] Their intention was simple: if they could educate Arab Muslim children from an early age along the Christian path that such schools offered, they could in the end convert them to Christianity. Not only schools but printing presses were established.[41] The consequence of this process was twofold. The number of Christian Arabs was significantly multiplied to supplement the earlier Christian Arab communities, such as the Maronites in Lebanon. Moreover, in introducing young Arabs among other things to their own language as a writing instrument and vehicle for literature, the mission schools not only created a literate community, but a yearning to further Arabic writing and literature. This, in turn, produced not only a revival and extension of such literature but, more broadly, an Arab cultural nationalism movement.

By 1860, there were thirty-three schools in operation—with a pupil population that included among its constituents about 20 percent girls—and by 1866, the Syrian Protestant College in Beirut was fully operative. By the end of the 1860s, developments regarding specific Arab leaders were manifesting themselves. Thus Nasif al-Yazigi (1800–1871), a Christian Lebanese, for instance, became a key literary figure, producing books on Arabic grammar as well as on rhetoric and logic. His writing inspired both Christian and Muslim Arabs to think in expansive terms of Arabic language and literature. Similarly, Butrus al-Bustani (1819–1883), also a Christian from Lebanon, spent ten years translating the Bible into Arabic and created the first modern dictionary of the Arabic language in 1870 as well as an Arab Encyclopedia, of which he had completed six volumes by the time of his death.

Al-Bustani also produced what may be construed as the first political journal in Syria, the *Clarion of Syria*, which, in the aftermath of the massacre of five thousand Christian Arabs in Damascus in 1860, sought to douse the flames of religious hatred that prevailed, arguing for a primacy of Arab ethno-cultural sensibility over Muslim or Christian religious sensibility, and also preaching that knowledge is the key to ending discord among diverse religions within the Arab ambit. Al-Bustani founded a "National School" to promote Arab thought, ideas, and ideals in 1863, in which al-Yazigi was the principal teacher of Arabic language. Seven years later, al-Bustani began publishing another journal, *Al-Jenan*, a political and literary review which, like its predecessor journal, strove to fight against religious fanaticism and to preach Arab unity and a broad-based concern for Arab national welfare.

Earlier in their careers, both al-Yazigi and al-Bustani had established a *Society of Arts and Sciences* in Beirut, together with the American, Eli Smith, and other missionaries. There were no Muslim or Druze members in the original group of about fifty members, but this was the first society in the Arab world of its kind; the first organized collective effort not based on traditional ethnic, tribal, or religious considerations. Three years later, no doubt inspired by this largely Protestant effort, the *Oriental Society* was founded by French Jesuits. Both organizations disbanded around 1852, but many of the principals in both entities reorganized themselves as the *Syrian Scientific Society* five years later, with about 150 members, including Muslim and Druze as well as Christian Arabs. By 1868, the *Syrian Scientific Society* had been officially recognized by the Ottoman authorities; it extended membership to those outside Syro-Palestine, reaching as far afield as Istanbul and Cairo.

It was in the context of the *Syrian Scientific Society* and its symbolic presence as the first outward manifestation of a collective Arab national consciousness that Ibrahim al-Yazigi—the son of Nasif—was inspired to write a patriotic poem speaking of an Arab resurgence and calling for an Arab insurgence against the Ottoman rulers. The poem spread by word of mouth. One might see this as the first act of purely indigenous political, as opposed to merely cultural, nationalism among Arabs.[42]

The era of the poem coincided with the penultimate phase of the petering out of Ottoman leadership: Abdul Aziz (Sultan, 1861–76) was erratic and extravagant and draining the Ottoman coffers of their already-shrunken funds. His nephew, Murad V, succeeded him but lasted only three months on the throne. He was in turn succeeded on August 31, 1876, by Abdul Hamid II. Cultural nationalism had bred political nationalism in the course of the middle decades of the century. The notion of an *intifada*—a movement of "throwing off" the Turkish presence from the Arab world—was in part inspired, ironically enough, by European nationalism, which in its colonialist aspect saw the

French eliminating the Turkish presence in Algeria by 1830 and in Tunisia by 1881, and the British effecting the same result in Egypt in 1882.

The consequent unrest was sufficient so that shortly after his accession to the throne, Sultan Abdul Hamid II offered a new Constitution on December 23, 1876, for the inhabitants of his now-truncated realms. The Constitution included full rights for the Arab peoples under his governance with respect to cultural autonomy. The following year, the Ottomans found themselves buried in a war with Russia that ended in 1878 with the Treaty of Berlin, which complication gave Abdul Hamid II the excuse to eliminate the constitution that he had trumpeted two years earlier.

6

JEWISH NATIONALISM

In the aftermath of Abdul Hamid II's new Constitution, which having never been put it into force failed to fulfill its promises of cultural and linguistic respect for the Arabs, the Arab leadership inevitably became more politicized. Meanwhile, the Jews were in the midst of shaping their own nationalist aspirations. Indeed, Jewish hopes were, in retrospect, moving on a course that made collision with part of the Muslim and Christian Arab aspirations almost inevitable.

In the period following the industrial and political revolutions that would so radically reshape western and central Europe between the 1750s and the early nineteenth century that followed the era of intra-Christian (Reformation/Counter-Reformation) crisis and questioning of the sixteenth and seventeenth centuries and the secularizing movements eventually derived from Descartes, Spinoza, Leibnitz, Bacon, and others, the western and central European world began to open up for Jews. From the "Jew Bill" in England in 1753;[43] to the decrees of Hapsburg Emperor Joseph II in 1764 granting a range of socio-economic rights to "the Jewish nation" and subsequent decrees permitting Jewish participation in the Hapsburg armies and in medicine and law throughout the Hapsburg domains in the 1780s; to the decree of the new French government on September 28, 1791, that recognized Jews as fully French; to the granting of a new range of socioeconomic rights to the Jews of Prussia in 1812—over the course of four decades, Emancipation began to shift Jews from the periphery toward the center of European cultural, social, economic, and eventually even political life.[44]

Concomitant with this era was the double development of European Romanticism and European Nationalism. The former saw a powerful, even mysterious, emotion-governed relationship between individuals and the land in which they and their ancestors were born, lived, and died, the language that they spoke, the literature and folk songs of which that language is the key instrument, and the visual art and dances that are endemic to the land and its inhabitants. The latter supplemented the former not only in articulating the relationship between a people and its land in political terms, but in inspiring a desire to expand into and/or reclaim more land, often thought of as having been wrested from one's ancestors at some distant or more recent time in the past. That movement, taking shape between about 1780 and 1850, would yield the fragmentation of the Hapsburg Empire, the urge to spread out on the part of the Prussians and the conviction on the part of the English that a world-encircling British Empire was divinely ordained and part of their morally superior "White Man's Burden."

Among the many groups inspired along Nationalist lines were the Italians, whose land had—virtually since the late fifth century and the collapse of the Western Roman Empire—been a crazy quilt of city-states and kingdoms in constant conflict and kaleidoscopically shifting alliances or dis-alliances with each other. The articulator of the notion that Italy could and should become reunited and that ultimately it could reclaim the imperial glory that belonged to Rome in antiquity was Giuseppe Mazzini. He and his discussion of the *Risorgimento* in turn inspired a German Jewish writer, Moses Hess, to pen the work, *Rome and Jerusalem*, in 1862. With that treatise, Hess might be said to have given birth to Jewish nationalism in the modern European sense just described.

Meanwhile, European attitudes toward Jews were moving steadily backwards from where they had been by the end of the previous century—away from acceptance toward a new intolerance. Wilhelm Marr was creating the terminology of modern political anti-Semitism referred to above and, with it, the marginalizing racialization of Jews in 1879, and other politicians and journalists soon picked up the idea. An anti-Semitic professor at Berlin University—Eugen Duehring—published a book in 1881 entitled *The Jewish Question as a Racial, Moral and Cultural Question*, inspired by and extending Marr's political ideas.[45]

In France—regarded since 1791 as the paragon of tolerance and secular modernity in Europe where Jews were concerned—the journalist Edouard Drumont, publisher of a feuilleton, *La Libre Parole* ("Free Speech") authored a book that appeared in 1886, called *La France Juive* (*Jewish France*). In it, he warned his fellow Frenchmen of the powerful threat to their country: its takeover by Jews and Jewish influences. The world in general and Jews in particular were shocked not only by the appearance of the book but also by its embrace by the French readership. Between the time of Marr's coinage and Drumont's publication and in the aftermath of the pogroms of Russian Jews sponsored by the Tsarist regime after the assassination of Alexander II in 1881, two developments of particular interest for this discussion are observable.

First, literary leaders like Mendele Mocher Seforim and after him, Y. L. Peretz and then Shalom Aleichem—the European Jewish equivalent of Nasif al-Yazigi and Butrus al-Bustani—were engaged in reviving the Hebrew language as a functional profane literary instrument (as opposed to one limited to prayer and sacred scholarship) that would ultimately yield Hebrew as an everyday spoken street instrument. The culmination of this process in pure linguistic terms would be the work accomplished by Eliezer Ben-Yehudah to organize a modern Hebrew language dictionary—and the effort he and his wife made to bring up their children as the first native speakers of Hebrew since mid-antiquity.

Second, a Jewish physician by the name of Leo Pinsker led what was a growing discussion of the problem of anti-Semitism in his 1882 work *Auto-Emanzipation (Self-Emancipation)*. Pinsker was the first among several thinkers to refer to anti-Semitism as an incurable disease process. The spreading ugliness of that disease seemed confirmed in the next decade, when in so-called liberal France a Jewish army captain was framed by his commanding officers and charged with having engaged in espionage on behalf of Prussia. The French army, still smarting a generation after its defeat by the Prussians in the Franco-Prussian War of 1870–71, and unwilling to admit that its armaments had been archaic and those of the Prussians modern, and still seeking a scapegoat to account for its defeat, found it in the Jew, Alfred Dreyfus, who was accused of having passed secrets to the enemy.

More significant, perhaps, than the framing of Dreyfus by the conservative army or the fanning of flames of anti-Semitism by the Catholic Church and the French Press, such as Drumont—so that not Dreyfus, but "Dreyfus the Jew," was excoriated—was the vociferous embrace of this propaganda by the French masses. The Dreyfus trial became *l'Affaire Dreyfus*, and precisely a century after Emancipation, French Jews found themselves subject to the intense heat of unprecedented hostility from their Catholic neighbors.

Among those dispatched from other lands to report on the trial, who were struck by this turn of events, was a Jewish reporter for the *Neue Freie Press* in Vienna by the name of Theodor Herzl. Herzl was an upper middle-class, highly assimilated Jew who grew up thinking of himself as an Austrian who happened, by descent and cultural continuity, to be Jewish—rather than as a Jew living in Austro-Hungary or, for that matter, a Hungarian in Austro-Hungary. In 1882, he read with shock Eugen Duehring's anti-Semitic volume.[46]

That shock marked the beginning of a turning point in his life and his thinking that completed its first twist the following year. Herzl was a member of an exclusive student fencing fraternity, *Albia*, which helped sponsor festivities on March 5, 1883, honoring Richard Wagner's memory, several weeks after the composer's death. But when those festivities became an extended anti-Semitic outburst (Wagner himself had been virulently anti-Semitic), and that outburst included among its protagonists vociferous members of *Albia*—who were close friends, or so Herzl had thought—he not only withdrew from the fraternity, but he became suddenly more conscious of himself *as* a Jew and suddenly more intensely aware of "the Jewish Problem."

Within the following decade, Herzl wrote a popular play, *The New Ghetto* (1894), among other works. In the play, he represented assimilated Jews (like himself) as caged in an invisible ghetto both by their own mentality and by the mentality of their secular Christian neighbors. In that play the hero, a Jewish physician, plays what may easily be construed as the role of a secular messiah to his Jewish neighbors—and one recognizes in him Herzl's self-image.

Arriving into the City of Light in 1891 as the Paris correspondent for the *Neue Freie Press,* Herzl became fairly quickly aware of the anti-Semitism rampant in the French capital spearheaded by Édouard Drumont. Thus when the playwright–journalist covered *l'Affaire Dreyfus* in 1894, all of these mental paths converged. The result was a pamphlet that he wrote in a white heat, and which was actually published in 1896: *Der Judenstaat—The Jewish State.* In it, he offered his radical solution to the Jewish problem: the creation of an independent Jewish polity. Herzl's contention was that given an opportunity to develop as an autonomous entity with its own economy, no longer as a minority of "guests" "hosted" by one Christian state or another, Jews would be able for the first time in nearly two millennia to stand on equal ground with their Christian neighbors.

They would be dealing government to government with those neighbors, be it economically or be it politically, militarily or otherwise. Moreover, the departure of Jews from Christian communities would eliminate Jews as competitors for slots in the socioeconomic infrastructure, undercutting the antagonism toward Jews which, he argued, derived from that competition and its uneven playing surface. "There will be an inner migration of Christian citizens into the positions relinquished by Jews," he wrote. His plan was not limited to theoretical thinking; he suggested practical ways in which the plan that he conceived could be implemented. Thus the entire project would be placed in the hands of a corporation formed to fulfill this mission. A "Jewish Company" would define Jews in the legal sense, "to conduct economic activities," and a "Society of Jews" would "deal with all but property rights" and thus function on behalf of the Jews as a "moral person." "The Jewish Company will be the liquidating agent for the business interests of departing Jews, and will organize trade and commerce in the new country . . . The Society of Jews will treat with the present authorities in the land, under the sponsorship of the European powers, if they prove friendly to the plan."[47]

"We shall not dwell in mud huts; we shall build new, more beautiful and more modern houses, and possess them in safety. We shall not lose our acquired possessions; we shall realize them. We shall surrender our well-earned rights for better ones.[48] We shall relinquish none of our cherished customs; we shall find them again . . . The very creation of the Jewish State would be beneficial to neighboring lands, since the cultivation of a strip of land increases the value of its surrounding districts."[49] Furthermore, "anti-Semitism will cease at once and everywhere . . . a wondrous breed of Jews will spring up from the earth . . . The world will be liberated by our freedom, enriched by our wealth, magnified by our greatness. And whatever we attempt there for our own benefit will redound mightily and beneficially to the good of all mankind."[50]

In the passages from which I have quoted there are at least four issues that might interest us. The first is his absolute conviction that the Christian states of Europe will applaud and assist with this plan; concomitantly, the second is that anti-Semitism will cease. It is interesting to note that there was Christian interest—particularly among the groups called the Restorationists, in America—in seeing Jewish "exiles" ingathered into the Holy Land. This group sent emissaries to Palestine in the 1840s through 1860s to teach indigenous and incoming Jews to farm.[51] This effort may be seen as somewhat parallel to the American religious interest in creating schools throughout the Middle East with the ultimate goal of converting Arab Muslims. For the conviction of the Restorationists was that ultimately the ingathered Jews would see the light of Christianity and turn to it.

The third aspect of Herzl's plan of particular interest to our discussion—apropos of Arab Muslims—is his certainty that the new State will benefit its neighbors, who might be expected to embrace it as much as the Europeans will; indeed the whole world will benefit. The fourth issue has two elements worth consideration. The first is that Herzl seems to assume that the land that will be devoted to the new state will be previously uncultivated, concerning which none of the indigenous neighbors will have a prior claim; second, that in fact the two places he discusses as possibilities are Palestine and Argentina, although he prefers Palestine because it "is our unforgettable historic homeland," and while he suggests that "the holy places of Christendom could be placed under some sort of international extraterritoriality," Islam's concerns or those of the Arab world in general (to the extent that such a settlement specifically in Palestine was countenanced) are nowhere to be found in his narrative. This is hardly surprising: he is a child of his Victorian-Edwardian era and its Eurocentric prejudices.

Herzl's modestly bold proposal caught fire more quickly than his friends expected: by August 1897, the First Zionist Congress, as it was called, was held in Basel, Switzerland, with 205 delegates from all over the world in attendance. Between that year and the year of Herzl's sudden death at the age of forty-four in 1904, a succession of Zionist congresses met and with them a growing array of questions with regard to how to concretize the theoretical plan set forth by Herzl in his 1896 treatise and in more poetic form in his work, *Alt-Neu Land* (Old–New Land), of 1902.

Herzl became increasingly concerned about the future of Eastern European Jewry during this period. The unrelenting progress of pogroms in the Tsarist Russia of the Romanovs as the nineteenth century spilled into the twentieth and his personal visit to some of the communities in the East pushed him to emphasize the importance of the Zionist idea as offering salvation for a beleaguered people. Thus, his vision focused on physical survival and sought a political means to effect that survival—he was willing to negotiate with almost any relevant power.[52]

By contrast, there emerged Zionist leaders like Asher Ginzberg, writing under the pen name Ahad Ha'Am, meaning "one of the people" who, coming out of the Eastern European pogrom-ridden milieu, argued that no threat of physical extermination had yet succeeded in destroying the Jews, and that what was needed was, on the contrary, a key to spiritual survival. For those like Ahad Ha'Am, the Zionist idea offered a means of spiritual rejuvenation, not physical salvation. This meant focusing itself on *Eretz Yisrael* and no other place.

While a concomitant of this was the continued goal of fulfilling specifically *Eretz Yisrael*-directed national aspirations, those aspirations did not necessarily require full political fulfillment. In other words, spiritually based *nation*hood, perhaps under Ottoman governance, not politically based independent *state*hood. A subset of the spiritual side of Zionism was *cultural* Zionism. The most obvious concrete manifestation of this was the decision to establish an arts school in Jerusalem that opened under the directorship of Boris Schatz in 1906. Schatz had been court painter and sculptor to the Bulgarian King Ferdinand III at a time when, in the early 1890s, having established its independence from the Ottoman Empire, Bulgaria was seeking to define its identity along the lines of Romantic Nationalism that had been percolating all over Europe for the previous century. Schatz had been a key figure in synthesizing different visual ideas in order to create what could be recognized as a distinctive Bulgarian national art.

With the support of the Zionist leadership and important Jewish figures such as the philosopher and theologian Martin Buber, Schatz set out to create a Jewish National visual art at the Jerusalem art school and museum named for Bezalel, the ancient Israelite artisan whose efforts at devising the Tabernacle in the Sinai wilderness are described at the end of the Book of Exodus. Bezalel arts and crafts, as they evolved during the next twenty-five years, may be understood in both aesthetic and political terms.

The use of specific symbols was promoted. Thus, for example, the image of the rising sun appears again and again to suggest renascent Jewish nationalism. The recently internationally recognized six-pointed star—made international and specifically "Jewish" by its appearance in 1897 on the cover of Herzl's publication *Die Welt* (*The World*)—as a Star or Shield of *David* suggested a connection back to ancient Israel at the Davidic beginning of its Golden Age. The older and more familiar symbol found for centuries in Jewish art, the seven-branched candelabrum, offered a doubly relevant implication. Not only does it symbolize the ancient Temple in Jerusalem. In its seven-ness, it offers connotations of that moment at the foot of Mount Sinai—between servitude and freedom, Egypt and the Promised Land—of the Covenant between God and the Israelites. That Covenant insisted, among the other commandments, that the Israelites must keep the *seventh* day holy.

So, too, the subject matter of Bezalel art. Individuals either from the heroic Hebrew-Israelite-Judaean past, such as Abraham, Moses, David, or Judah the Maccabee; or heroic figures from the present, such as Theodor Herzl, were endemic to the vocabulary of Bezalel art. These might be synthesized, as when the image of Moses in a woodcut by Ephraim Lilien, one of the school's master teachers, offered Herzl's familiar black-bearded face as the image of the leader of the Israelites out of slavery. Or landscapes—both the divinely wrought hills, rocks, trees, and wildernesses of Palestine or the man-made buildings, the familiar dome-on-cube architecture and its variants—became stereotypical in Bezalel imagery.

At this time in Europe, various arts and crafts movements were elevating the importance of objects beside drawings, paintings, and sculptures to the status of art: an ashtray could be as invested with aesthetic significance as a canvas. Variously, the *art nouveau* and *jugendstil* movements of France, Belgium, Germany, and Austria were championing the swirling curlicues and repeating geometric forms coupled with vegetal and floral elements found in Arabo-Islamic art—coining the term "arabesque," in fact, to describe this stylistic proclivity. Schatz and Bezalel pushed both in the arts and crafts direction and in the stylistic direction of the Arabo-Islamic world, to further underscore the Middle Eastern origins of Jewish nationalist identity.

Even the substance of much of Bezalel art and craft was connected to The Land. Thus the objects produced in the school frequently were shaped with materials such as olive wood from the hills of Galilee, stones and rocks from the Negev Desert, copper and silver metals associated with the legendary mines of King Solomon in that heroic Israelite age of the distant past. The goal of Bezalel art and craft was to form a concomitant of the spiritual side of Zionism that insistently connected the Jewish present and revived future both to the land of Israel and to its pre-diasporic past.

In contrast to the Palestinocentrism that was endemic to spiritual and cultural Zionism, Herzl as a political pragmatist was prepared, in 1903, to accept an offer made by the British to reserve Uganda as a haven for the Jewish people, so desperate was he to find a place of refuge (though the offer was quickly withdrawn due to protests by the British public). For that very year was also marked by the most horrifying of the pogroms in Russian Jewish history, those at Kishinev. What marked these as particularly painful was that the pre-pogrom environment had been one of dénouement between the Jewish and non-Jewish communities, based in part on the higher level of secular education and therefore capacity for intellectual interchange in Kishinev than had been possible elsewhere. The pogroms in Kishinev cemented the sense Herzl and others had that anti-Semitism was a disease with no hope of a cure anywhere in the Diaspora. But Ahad Ha'Am and others were horrified at the very idea of looking anywhere but to *Eretz Yisrael* for a Jewish homeland.

The sense of the Diaspora as both hopeless with regard to a future and eminently forgettable because of fifteen centuries of past experiences would have implications for the terminology of the Zionist movement—so that once again we have returned to the realm of defining terms. Thus the Jewish State in the end would not be called *Juda*, which in English would translate as something like "Jewland," but rather *Israel*. This was a distinctively ideological, and not a casual or accidental decision. It marked the desire to leapfrog backward past the diasporic centuries of exile toward that period when the peoplehood of Judaism was in its golden age under Kings David and Solomon as the unified Kingdom of Israel.

Similarly, as the Zionist movement developed between the era of Herzl and statehood—and in the first decades after statehood—it thought of and sought to shape a "new man." Building on the notion of "muscular Judaism" that was taking shape in late nineteenth and early twentieth century Central Europe and subsequently borrowing, ironically enough, imagery spawned by the new Soviet State, Weimar Germany, and Fascist Italy in the 1920s, right-wing Zionist leaders such as Ze'ev Jabotinsky spoke of "a new psychological race of Jew."[53] As a practical matter, the word "Jew" was eschewed by the

Jabotinsky-ites as much as possible in favor of the term "Hebrew." "Jew" was by their definition being re-understood as an inwardly focused, bent-over, easily bullied, pale, urbanized, long-suffering victim of the Diaspora; "Hebrew" was intended to refer to a proud, handsome, athletic, farm-comfortable, suntanned, rural throwback and step forward to pre- and post-diasporic life.

There were also Jewish leaders who not only ignored the Zionist idea but who actively opposed it. It is fair to say that the biggest enemies of Zionism in its infancy were Jews. There were the Socialists and the Marxists who saw a Jewish nationalist movement as by definition antithetical to the universalist principles nuanced with regard to socioeconomics espoused by the Socialist and Marxist movements in which so many Jews had become active. These Jews believed that the eradication of socioeconomic divisions in the world was the key to ending anti-Semitism; that the liberation of all peoples would encompass the final Emancipation of the Jews. *Social* Zionism offered a response to that concern, which didn't mean all those voicing this particular concern were satisfied with such a response.

Ultra-Orthodox rabbis saw the movement as a heresy—also perhaps fearing that it would undercut their authority as community leaders. Many regarded it as offering a secularizing affront to the truths of religious Judaism. More profoundly they argued that it contravened the messianic idea as it had been spelled out by God for Judaism; to attempt to lead the Jews out of the Exile and back to the Holy Land before the advent of a divinely ordained Messiah was construed as sacrilege. But there also emerged Orthodox rabbis, like Abraham Isaac Kook, who shaped *religious* Zionism. He argued that since the messianic idea in Judaism is notoriously vague, there was no reason not to embrace Zionism, for it could be God's plan that we be the instruments of our own redemption; that the messianic idea was being fulfilled and not contradicted by Zionism.

On the other hand were those Reform Jewish leaders who feared that Zionism would compromise the societal gains that Emancipation had provided for Jews. One can certainly see this in the German Jewish community that had given birth to Reform Judaism back in 1810–11, but one sees it elsewhere as well. In England, for example, one of the most interesting instances of the Jewish Zionist versus anti-Zionist dynamic is the debate between two Jewish ministers in the government, Herbert Samuel (a Zionist) and his cousin Edwin Montagu (an anti-Zionist).

The first, who became the first British High Commissioner in Palestine, would be instrumental in furthering the sentiment that would lead to the "Balfour Declaration" in 1917;[54] the second, as minister of munitions and subsequently secretary of state for India, would fight against that sentiment.

Montagu's words on the subject, from a letter to Prime Minister David Lloyd-George, are instructive of the concerns of many secular and Liberal (Reform) Jews of that era:

> The country for which I have worked ever since I left the University—England—the country for which my family have fought tells me that my national home, if I desire to go there, therefore my natural home, is Palestine.

His concern as one who saw himself as a British Jew rather than a Jew residing in Britain was that the Zionist movement would encourage anti-Semites both to see Jews as not really British after all and to push for their emigration—in effect, their expulsion from Britain.

The hostility to Zionism on various Jewish fronts is nowhere more concretely apparent than in this: Herzl had intended for the First Zionist Congress to take place in Munich in August 1897, but at the eleventh hour he needed to switch the location to Basel, Switzerland, due to the intractable opposition of Germany's rabbis to the Zionist movement. There is particular irony, given subsequent history, both in Herzl's intention to center the nascent Zionist movement in Germany and in the steadfastness with which the German rabbinate articulated its opposition to that intention as something inconsistent with the sensibility that Jews ought "to serve the fatherland to which they belong with utmost devotion and to further its national interests with all their hearts and strength."[55]

7

ASPIRATIONS, INTERFERENCES, AND CONFLICTS INTO THE TWENTIETH CENTURY

Considering the same issue that exercised Montagu, Herzl arrived at the opposite sort of conclusion. He had reasoned that anti-Semites would ally themselves with the Zionist idea and help impel its success for the very reason that Montagu feared it. Herzl saw getting Jews out of Europe both as undercutting the negative consequences of economic competition between Jews and their Christian neighbors and as assuring the latter that the Jews who remained behind were unequivocally French or German or British or whatever European national. Herzl was also willing to compromise with his plan of Palestine as the Zionist goal, as I have noted above. His turn toward Uganda was also in part fueled by his sense of how impossible it would be to reclaim part of Palestine for the Jews.

Ottoman history had moved miles from the era of Joseph HaNassi and Suleiman the Magnificent. Although there had been a continuous Jewish presence in Palestine since antiquity, it had been a small one.[56] Herzl's audience with Sultan Abdul Hamid II to seek permission to establish a semiautonomous Jewish polity within the still far-flung Ottoman Empire had yielded little by way of a clear or concrete result. This was the same Abdul Hamid II who had issued a new constitution to his constituents in 1876, offering his Arab citizens a degree of cultural and linguistic identity, but who failed in most ways to live up to that promise. This was the same Abdul Hamid II who had tried to use religion as a rallying point to convince his Arab subjects to embrace rather than reject him as the Caliph of Islam (rather than seeing him as the Ottoman Sultan); who substantiated his claim to the Caliphate by repairing and embellishing mosques in Makka, Madina, and Jerusalem—and who even appointed a Syrian Arab, Izzat Pasha al-Abid, as his Second Secretary.

This was the same Abdul Hamid II who established a good relationship with the Prussians and their Kaiser Wilhelm II, who among other things helped reform the Sultan's military academies. The new officers being trained in modern methods of warfare and strategy included a handful of Arabs along with a majority of Turks. But when that new officers' corps rose up and, in 1908, succeeded in deposing Abdul Hamid II—this was the "Young Turks" rebellion—the Turkish officers who dominated it quickly turned their backs on their Arab brethren.

Thus once again the aspiration for Arab political fulfillment or even significant participation was thwarted. The consequence of this was the meeting that took place five years later—in July 1913, in Paris—of the First Arab National Congress. In other words, the Arab cultural, military, and political leadership finally acted on its own to push the movement of Arab Political Nationalism forward. So, too, the culmination of this movement may be seen to have paralleled the Jewish National Movement in approximate time and in organizing itself *away* from the Middle East where it was nonetheless rooted.

Even more so than in the Jewish Nationalist movement, the Arab Nationalist movement was fraught with questions of self-definition in three different ways. First because of the delicate balance between the sense of the convening Arabs as Muslims and as Arabs; second because of long-standing ethnic issues dividing communities within communities, such as the long-standing hostility between the Qais and Yamani groups dating from the eighth century in the faraway 'arav that continued into the twentieth century in Palestine where both migrated; and third because of political antagonisms that were already surfacing at that time, many of which survive to this day.

The interrelationship of Arabic with Islamic issues may be seen once again in the rebirth of the Wahhabi purist movement around this time in the context of religious support rendered to 'Abd al-'Aziz Ibn Sa'ud in his efforts to expand his base of power by annexing Hasa in 1913. In the aftermath of World War I, he would go on to annex Jabal Shammar in 1921 and the *hijaz* in 1924–25, which reshaped the majority of the peninsula into a new polity, the Kingdom of Saudi Arabia, by 1932. The family of Sharif Hussain, dispossessed of its power in that region, sought a new seat of power elsewhere. The British provided that seat in the central portion of the zone that came under their control after World War I.[57]

One of the significant definitional distinctions that ought to be offered here is the following: Jewish nationalism, as I have intimated, was modeled on various other forms of European nationalism in the sense of possessing a certain focus. Italian nationalism, German nationalism, French nationalism, Bulgarian nationalism, Serbian nationalism share the property of focusing on a particular piece of territory and its concomitants of identity for the Italian, German, French, Bulgarian, and Serbian peoples, in spite of any number of disagreements by their respective constituents as to how most efficiently to effect that identity. The ideology of Jewish nationalism was similar to these other European forms, as it evolved in Europe in the last third of the nineteenth century. By contrast, nationalism among the Arabs never coalesced in that sort of a focused manner. All Arabs might possess nationalist aspirations, but they were—at that time and to this day—rarely focused on a vision of identity for "the Arab people" or "the Arab nation." Recognizing this may help us understand how the history of Arab nationalism—or, better stated, *nationalism among Arabs*—has been consistently undercut by other religious, cultural, ethnic, and political aspirations.

On the other hand, although Jewish nationalism was inspired by and conceptualized by a European mind-set, it is significantly different in three obvious ways that are relevant to how it was and is perceived by Arabs. One, the nationalist sentiment that became Zionism and focused on *Eretz Yisrael/* Palestine came from no single place: the arrival of Jews from Europe cannot be simply compared to the arrival of the French or the British or Americans as missionaries or political colonialists. Those Jews who arrived, in arriving from diverse locations, were not seeking to *expand* the colonial *imperium* of their homeland as the French and British and other European nationalist expansionists were. They were seeking to *reconnect* to what they understood to be their historic homeland. Two, in an increasing number of cases, as time went on, there was no particular place—and often no place at all—to which such Jews could *go* if they left Palestine, unlike the Europeans who, if they left, simply went back to their own countries. There was no "their own country" elsewhere for the Jews, per se. And three, even before the turn from the nineteenth to the twentieth century, a large number of those Jews came not from Europe but from areas of the Middle East and North Africa.[58] Thus the discussion by Palestinian Arabs and others, at various times, of an *intifada* of the Jews from Palestine modeled on that against the Turks or the British, fails as a historical model, as I shall repeat later on.[59]

But I run ahead of myself. The Jewish nationalist hopes and the Arab nationalist hopes—the one shaped by a European consciousness and focused on an area of the Ottoman Empire between Syria and the *'arav*, between the Mediterranean and the eastern reaches of Palestine; and the other culminating its shape in Europe but framed by a Middle Eastern Arab consciousness and focused on an area more or less from Egypt to Persia and from Turkey to the *Yaman*, but without clarity as to how that vast region would or should be reconfigured—might either have met and achieved some sort of rapprochement or they might have simply collided, left alone by outsiders. But outside interference was unavoidable.

And since the various external actors had their own agendas, it was *inevitable* that the Arabs and Jews would collide *without* rapprochement. That collision interwove the collision of European interests that led up to and exploded into World War I. Put otherwise, a new round of the Crusades was beginning, albeit under a more overtly economic and political banner, with religion hidden beneath the surface.

Abdul Hamid II invited the Prussian presence into his realms to accomplish several tasks, including a reform of his military and construction of railroads between Istanbul and both the Persian Gulf and Makka. He wished to assert that he was not only the Sultan of a polity called the Ottoman Empire, but the Caliph and thus key leader of the Arabo-Islamic world. And it was important that he assert a more workable connection between his political capital and the spiritual capital of the Empire. As a practical matter, a railroad system would also allow more efficient troop movement across his domains. Abdul Hamid also hoped that the Prussians could help jump-start the failing Ottoman economy and replenish the dwindling contents of the imperial coffers.

We have seen that one of the most significant—if unintended—consequences of the Ottoman military reform program was the overthrow of the Sultan who put those reforms in motion. As for the railroad system, it was never completed, and it is probably fair to say that the project of replenishing the coffers moved forward but not as far as perhaps it might have had other issues not intervened. These issues were the British and the French—who, we recall, had been swallowing up bits and pieces of the Empire since 1830. By 1882, Britain had taken effective control of Egypt, although not in an "official" manner.[60]

More to the point, the British vision of a colonial empire that would stretch from India to South Africa—and perhaps of a triumphant return to the lands from which their Crusader ancestors had been ejected six centuries earlier—was obviously and significantly undercut by the Prussian presence now lodged in the very heart of that geographic vision. As if that were not enough, the matter of petroleum—oil—had by the late nineteenth century begun to assume enormous significance for any and all states expecting to be industrial, military, and political powers in the twentieth century. What is referred to in the history of science and technology as the "Third Industrial Revolution" was taking shape in the context of the discovery of oil and its uses. If Britain, home to the first coal-based Industrial Revolution of the late eighteenth and early nineteenth centuries, were to remain at the forefront of industrial capability and not fall behind Prussia, progenitor of the Second Industrial Revolution, then it could not stand idly by while the Prussians assumed control of a region rife with petroleum reserves. More specifically, Britain possessed a huge navy whose ships would be disadvantaged if they remained dependant on coal as oil was becoming available.

The gradual British encroachment into the heartland of the Ottoman Empire was thus in part a response to the significant presence of the Prussians as honored "guests" in that heartland. While it is true that World War I had among its causes disputes regarding Belgium and Hapsburg concerns, symbolized by the assassination of the Hapsburg archduke in Sarajevo, it seems clear that the most significant issue forcing the explosion of August 1914 was the question of the future of the Near (Middle) East.

Within the first year of the war, the British were already seeking Arab allies against the combined Prussian and Turkish enemy, using Arab nationalist aspirations and shaping the assertion that Arab assistance could remove the Turks from the scene and yield to the fulfillment of those aspirations as a wedge. In 1915–16, the British organized a revolt against the Ottomans in Syria. In exchange they promised an independent Arab state after the war. More precisely, "The Revolt in the Desert" was led by the Hashimite Sharif of Makka, Hussain Ibn'Ali and his sons, 'Ali, 'Abd'Allah, and Faisal.[61] The rebels conquered Makka and Aqaba, surrounded Madina and sabotaged the *Hijaz* Railway, the only portion of the Prussian-Ottoman railway project that had been completed.

By 1916, the British and their French allies were already meeting to consider in some detail how the Ottoman Empire might be carved up into their respective spheres of interest after the end of a war that they anticipated winning. The Sykes-Picot Agreement would leave the British in charge of the territory that extended from the northern edge of the Sinai to the southern border of Syria and from the Mediterranean shore to the Persian Gulf; the French would control the parallel territory north of the British region. They would retain their respective control or influence in the various areas in which they had already established themselves during the previous eighty-five years.

By 1917–18, the right wing of British General Allenby's armies—led by the Hashimites under Faisal—advanced into Palestine and Syria, and entered Damascus. The British permitted the raising of the Arab flag there.[62] Meanwhile, the British also made a gesture to the Jews in 1917 with regard to Zionist aspirations. The letter from Lord Arthur James Balfour to Baron Nathan de Rothschild on November 2, 1917, included the text of a statement that had "been submitted to, and approved by, the Cabinet" of His Majesty's Government, asserting that "His Majesty's government looks with favor upon the establishment in Palestine of a national home for the Jewish people . . . ." The letter with its statement came quickly to be referred to as "The Balfour Declaration" and interpreted by Zionists and their supporters as an edict calling for a Jewish state.[63]

So the promises to the Muslim and Christian Arabs in 1916 and to the Jews in 1917, each understood in distinct ways by the groups receiving the promises and the groups offering the promises, might seem to offer a collision course. The geographic non-specificity of the promises to the Arabs could suggest that a collision was not inevitable, assuming that they were to interpret those promises to refer to areas other than Palestine in its entirety. Nonetheless, the notion of a collision would not necessarily have worried the British: their colonial method was often to introduce conflict between groups—to divide and conquer or, as the case may be, divide and maintain control. This was a method that they continued to use in India virtually up to its independence, as when antagonisms between Muslims and Hindus were exacerbated by colonial governors. It may also be of interest to note that, meanwhile, the United States did not wish to get involved in all of this and only, in fact, became involved in World War I, on the side of the British and French, because of the 1917 sinking of the Lusitania, a distinctly nonmilitary ocean liner, by the Prussians. Part of the reason that—up to that point—President Wilson desisted from declaring war on Ottoman Turkey, who would have been the United States' natural enemy if Britain and France were considered allies, is the concern that American Christian missionaries and the small Middle Eastern outposts that they had established would be at risk if he were to do so. Thus, religion played a role in a political decision, not for the first or last time in this long history.[64] Wilson waited, preferring to remain neutral, until his hand was forced, and he then declared war on Prussia, but not on Ottoman Turkey. And of course the United States immediately withdrew from the scene after the Great War was over, barely a year later.

Within two years of the end of World War I, the British and French were in a strong position to divide the region into spheres of interest, influence, and control. The French Mandate—established in 1920—encompassed the area that would eventually yield the states of Syria and Lebanon in 1943 and 1944 respectively. The British Mandate of the following year encompassed the realm of greater Palestine and the area between Palestine and the Gulf. The latter region, comprising three *vilayets*—provinces—of the now-defunct Ottoman Empire would be cobbled together as the new geo-polity, Iraq, by 1932—just as a chunk of one of those *vilayets* would later be reconfigured as an independent polity, Kuwait, by 1962—by which time Iraq (in 1958) had already gained its independence.

Thus, in its desire to control the oil production from two different areas that, by the 1920s and 1930s were yielding more petroleum than any other sites in the Middle East, by putting them under one British-governed roof, the British colonial government created Iraq. In so doing, they brought together by administrative fiat three regions with little in common, historically, politically, ethnically, or even religiously: provinces made up of Muslim Kurds on the one hand and Arabs on the other; in the latter case, one group was Sunni Muslim Arab and the other Shi'i Muslim Arab. They also disconnected from what had been a continuum for several centuries under the Ottomans, that piece that came to be called Kuwait, for the same oil-driven reasons. The repercussions of this double decision would be felt all the way into the end of the 1980s and the beginning of the 1990s when Iraq invaded Kuwait and the Americans took the lead in restoring the British-made status quo from sixty years earlier.[65] They continue to be felt.

Similar things might be said of the other part of the British Mandate. Eastern Palestine would ultimately be reconfigured ethno-politically with the creation of a new state, Transjordan—named for the river that served as its western border—christened as a kingdom ruled not by a Palestinian leader but by the Hashimite family of Sharif Hussain. This was the family that had been so essential to the British against the Ottomans in 1917–18 and which held sway in the Kingdom of the *Hijaz* until 'Abd al-'Aziz ibn Sa'ud, with Wahhabi spiritual support, gradually increased his influence from the original annexation of Hasa in 1913 to Jamal Shammar in 1921 to the entire *hijaz* region in 1924–25. Sharif Hussain, having declared himself king in 1916, declared himself Caliph in 1924 but was shortly thereafter forced to abdicate and died in exile. His oldest son, 'Ali, sat on the throne for less than a year before Ibn Sa'ud drove him out; 'Ali died in exile in Baghdad.

By 1932, Ibn Sa'ud had created the new Kingdom of Saudi Arabia—and it was other members of the dispossessed Hashimite clan whom the British placed in power in eastern Palestine.[66] Decades later, September 1970 would become known in the Palestinian Arab world as "Black September"—for during that month and the period conintinuig thourgh early summer 1971, the King of Jordan killed more Palestinians than have been killed at least until 2010 in the many years of struggling with Israel. We may understand that part of the reason was King Hussein's fear of a Palestinian *intifada* against his non-Palestinian rule.

As for Britain's rule of western Palestine, given the promises and counter-promises made to Jews and Arabs—ignoring for the moment the definitional issue of Jewish Arabs—it is no surprise that it would offer a more imposing challenge than placing the entirety of eastern Palestine in Hashimite hands or even the shaping of a new Iraqi state. The complicated 1916 Allies' plan for Palestine actually placed the Lebanon area, reaching as far south as Safed, under French control and created an independent Arab state east of the coastal area. The plan also created an Arab state, but under British protection, south of Hebron on the West Bank, encompassing all of the area from the southern Gaza region across to the Dead Sea and down to Aqaba; and leaving the area between that east-west line just south of Hebron north toward Safed as a "new area" to be under joint British, French, and Russian protection, with the exception of the area around Haifa and Acre, both of which areas were to be under British rule.

In February 1919, the Zionists offered a counterproposal at the Paris Peace Conference, with their vision for a Jewish polity. They sought to have set aside for Jewish settlement the entire coastal area from Sidon in the Lebanon and down the Mediterranean seaboard as far as Rafa just south of the "Gaza Strip" and inland south by southeast to Aqaba; and with an eastern border that led from Aqaba north by northeast on what, at Ma'an, becomes a parallel line to the *hijaz* railway line, about twenty-five miles *east* of the Dead Sea and Jordan River, just west of Amman and coming to within twenty miles or so of Damascus. This proposal was rejected by the allies. In April 1936, the British appointed a royal commission to inquire into the effective working of the Mandate after a repeated series of Arab attacks against Jewish life and property. The result was the Peel Commission Partition Plan that in July 1937 suggested dividing western Palestine into a pair of Jewish and Arab states with a British controlled corridor from Jaffa to Jerusalem.[67]

According to this plan, the Jews would have been allotted the area along the coast from about thirty miles south of Tel Aviv to about fifteen miles north of Acre; east by northeast to Metulah and down along the eastern coast of the Sea of Galilee, continuing about fifteen miles south, toward, but just short of Beit Sh'an and then turning west toward Afula; the western border of the Jewish polity from that point and south would have more or less paralleled the coast, about ten miles from the Mediterranean. The remainder of the area as far as Aqaba, following the Jordan River to the Dead Sea and following a line southwest from the southern tip of the Dead Sea down to Aqaba would have been an Arab state. At that juncture, the Jews reluctantly accepted the plan and the Arabs rejected it outright. In the aftermath of the Peel Commission Report and partition proposal, the Jewish Agency once again put forth its own proposal. This one called for dividing the area west of the Jordan into six sections. Both Jewish sections were somewhat larger than what the British had proposed. Where the latter had seen a substantial Arab state and a small area to remain under British control, the Jewish Agency proposed three smaller areas as an Arab state with a much larger area to remain under a British Mandate. Jerusalem, rather than being encompassed by the British, would be on the border between and divided between the British and Jewish areas of governance.

In turn the British undertook another study of the situation by a group headed by Sir John Woodhead—the Woodhead Commission—later in 1938, which offered a proposal that reduced the two Jewish State sections to less than the Peel Commission had, but validated areas of Jewish-owned land within the proposed Arab State. The latter was similar to what the Peel Commission proposed in overall scale, but also granted to the Arabs an enclave around Jaffa and on the other hand officially acknowledged the Jewish-held areas within the Arab State and also expanded the continued British Mandate beyond where the Peel commission had taken it—it would encompass Ramallah to the north of Jerusalem and include territory to the south beyond Bethlehem.

Reflected in these assessments and reassessments, negotiations and compromises, are the overlapping and conflicting needs that made defining and allocating the territories of western Palestine (Palestine-Israel) such an astonishing challenge. How much more tangled the picture when one considers the entire region over the sweep of its incredibly long history.

PART THREE
TWENTIETH-CENTURY CONFLICT AND THE REMAKING OF THE MIDDLE EAST

8

WORLD WAR II, THE HOLOCAUST, AND THE TRANSFORMATIONS OF ISRAEL-PALESTINE

By 1938, Adolf Hitler had been in power in Germany for five years and his regime had begun both to deprive a range of groups—most emphatically, the Jews—of all their legal rights and to begin swallowing up pieces of nearby central European territories. World War II would break out "officially" the following year and the Holocaust of six million European Jews, together with the destruction of more than that number of other European civilians would define the period that ended in mid-1945.

For the Jews as the group toward which Nazi animosity most fully, consistently, and systematically directed itself, a question arose by the end of the 1930s with some urgency. Where might they go in order to survive? The Johnson-Reed Act of 1924, which finalized the quota system for immigration into the United States, and similar systems in Canada and elsewhere, definitively capped the numbers who might escape across the northern Atlantic. Some countries in South America offered refuge up to a point. So did some European countries, but if and when they were overrun by the Nazis the safety net became a death trap. Given the developments of the previous four decades, the obvious question was: what about Palestine?[68] Since Hitler had arrived into power, Arabs had begun working with his regime—specifically with Adolf Eichmann and the Waffen SS—toward military recruitment, sabotage, and propaganda; funded by the Nazis, Palestinian Arabs staged riots and attacks on Jewish communities within Palestine that helped encourage the British to minimize Jewish immigration to the area over the next several years.[69] The British preferred not to exacerbate their relationship with a Muslim and Christian Arab population that was not eager to absorb a large influx of Jews. The most famous pro-Nazi Palestinian Arab was the Grand Mufti of Jerusalem,

Haj Amin al-Husseini, who met Hitler in Germany in 1941. Without grounds for his claim, the Grand Mufti would assert in a Radio Berlin broadcast two years later that the Jews planned to destroy the al-Aqsa mosque.[70]

Winston Churchill would comment on this state of affairs in angry terms before the British House of Commons during this period:

> So far from being persecuted, the Arabs have crowded into the country and multiplied until their population has increased more than even all world Jewry could lift up the Jewish population . . . . We are now asked to submit, and this is what rankles most with me, to an agitation which is fed with foreign money and ceaselessly inflamed by Nazi and by Fascist propaganda.[71]

My intention is not to espouse or endorse Churchill's perspective, since I believe that he was quite capable of strong biases and overgeneralizations ("the only good German is a dead German" is ascribed to him as a sentiment). It is to supplement the other issues that I shall raise when I arrive at the discussion of selective and absolute memory and the implications of memory for moving forward toward solutions to the problems of the Middle East.

By the time of the outbreak of the war, no solution had yet been reached regarding a partition plan of Palestine into Arab and Jewish areas of political autonomy or semiautonomy, much less statehood. And as the situation of European Jews grew more desperate, the British, in part due to Arab pressure and in part due to their own convictions that the Jewish problem could find no solution in Palestine,[72] tightened restrictions both with respect to where Jews might continue to settle—the three main areas of Jewish settlement by that time, around Jerusalem and Beersheba and north of Acre became inaccessible to expansion—and with regard to how many Jews might enter Palestine anew: fifteen thousand per year between 1939 and 1944 was the maximum number of Jewish refugees allowed.

From the Jewish point of view, a large number of Hitler's *potential* victims were being forced into *actualized* victimhood, and those permitted to escape were being confined "to a small Pale of settlement similar to that which existed in Czarist Russia before the last war, and such as now exists only under Nazi rule."[73] From the Arab point of view, with the development of the Holocaust, permitting Jews to seek refuge in Palestine in whatever numbers was to import a European problem into the Middle East. Put otherwise, from the Arab Muslim perspective, the establishment of European Christian Crusader kingdoms was being echoed, albeit obliquely, by the establishment of small but growing European Jewish communities.[74]

From the Jewish point of view, the Arab stance loses whatever legitimacy it might otherwise have when placed against the Arab complicity in the destruction of European Jews and in the Nazi effort to defeat the British. In 1941, before either the Soviets or the United States had entered the war, and when it appeared that the British might lose the war, Arabs in general and Palestinian Arabs in particular, led by the Grand Mufti, were instrumental in fomenting a revolt in Iraq, the success of which would have been decisive in crushing the British. The Empire would have been sliced down the middle and cut off from its primary source of oil. After the war, in 1947, the American Christian Palestine Committee would offer a report commenting on how "it was indeed a critical moment that the Iraqi [Syrian and Palestinian] rebels, prodded and aided by the ex-Mufti of Jerusalem, chose for their uprising. . . At the call of Haj Amin . . . subversive elements throughout the Middle East were touched off into activity."

The report would further observe that:

> . . . now in 1947 we seem to be returning to the policy of appeasement in dealing with precisely those Arab leaders who did their utmost to aid the Axis powers. . . . It is not claimed that the facts stated in this document constitute a revelation. They do not appear to be in dispute in any reasonable quarter. There seems, however, to be a tendency to ignore them as no longer politically relevant. This (is) unfortunate, for the data herewith presented point to conclusions that are still valid with regard to the political reasoning prevalent among the Arab peoples.[75]

Whether the actions of a half a century ago should then—or can now—be used by non-Arabs as a guide to "the political reasoning prevalent among the Arab peoples" may be debated by many, but it is beside the point to the extent that non-Arabs perceive an "Arab mentality"—or a "Muslim mentality"—that is different from and cannot be bridged to a "Western Mentality." In other words, there are those who assert that two worlds are engaged in as fiercely an implacable struggle as were the United States and the Soviet Union during the darkest years of the Cold War.[76]

In a related complication that ties the Holocaust era to the decade that preceded it and has implications for how Israeli leaders are today measured with regard to their dealings with the Arab world: Haj Amin al-Husseini had been banned by the British from the territory of the mandate in the 1920s for fomenting pogroms and assassinating Arab moderates. Sir Herbert Samuel, the British Jew,[77] when he became High Commissioner, as an act of appeasement toward Arab extremists, pardoned al-Husseini, passed over the *three* winning candidates of a Muslim election, and granted to al-Husseini the post of Mufti—and with it the power to lead his followers into the active Nazi collaboration just described that followed not long thereafter. The memory of Samuel's act and its consequences has haunted every discussion of the past half century among Israeli leaders regarding negotiations with the Arabs in general and the Palestinians in particular.[78]

It should be noted, apropos of the question of Arab or Palestinian sympathies or assistance to the Nazi cause, that the *Yishuv* did not offer much help to European Jews seeking refuge during the Holocaust—perhaps because the *Yishuv* was itself too small and weak and struggling with both the Arabs and the British during that period, but afterwards there would even be some accusations of complicity between *Yishuv* members and the Nazis for personal or ideological reasons.[79] Those who argued that there had been Jewish traitors against the Jews asserted generally that the motivation *was* ideological: to give a final stamp to the notion that the only viable place for Jews to live real and secure lives was *Eretz Yisrael*.[80] Certainly many, including David Ben-Gurion, seem to have been less than overly sympathetic to the plight of European Jews, for either ideological or psychological reasons.[81] Others have seen significant evidence of feelings of guilt in *Yishuv* members in the aftermath of the Catastrophe precisely because they had been too helpless.[82]

A number of writers have taken up the question of how to evaluate the impact of the Holocaust on the founding of the State of Israel. The discussion and the efforts to actualize the discussion toward a Jewish state were in process from the end of the First World War to the end of the Second. But perhaps that discussion would have continued for a much longer period of time had the Holocaust not intervened to help impel something more active. Yet no further progress toward activation was made during or even in the immediate aftermath of the Holocaust; rather, a process continued to be fairly slow until 1947 and 1948. As Emil Fackenheim observes:

> Historians see a causal connection between the Holocaust and the foundation of the State of Israel. The reasoning is as follows. Had it not been for the European Jewish catastrophe, all the centuries of religious longing for Zion, all the decades of secularist Zionist activity, together with all such external encouragement as was given by the Balfour Declaration, would have produced no more than a Palestinian ghetto . . . Only the Holocaust produced a desperate determination in the survivors and those identified with them, outside and especially within the *Yishuv*; ended vacillation in the Zionist leadership as to the wisdom of seeking political self-determination; and produced a moment of respite

from political cynicism in the international community, long enough to give legal sanction to a Jewish State. Even so, "the UN resolution of 1947 came at the last possible moment."[83]

But Fackenheim continues: "This reasoning is plausible; no more so, however, than its exact opposite. Why were the survivors not desperate to stay away from Palestine rather than reach it—the one place on earth which would tie them inescapably to a Jewish destiny? (After what that destiny had been to them, the desire to hide or flee from their Jewishness would have been 'natural.') Why did the Zionist leadership rise from vacillation to resoluteness rather than simply disintegrate? . . . As for the world's respite from political cynicism, this was neither of long duration nor unambiguous while it lasted."[84] In any case, as the State of Israel was taking shape, and in the first two decades of its existence—until the eve of the June War of 1967—the Holocaust was a largely ignored—almost taboo—subject. This derived from a combination of the culminating sense of the need to separate Israel from diasporic Jewish history and of thinking of that history as one of passive victimization in contrast to the strong and actively self-sustaining present symbolized by the State of Israel.[85]

Fackenheim's discussion is offered by him in the context of the theological question of whether or not God allowed the Holocaust to take place, and if so why, and whether as a God-allowed event it was permitted in order for the State of Israel to come into existence. It does not seek to address the question of whether the Arab perspective is valid.

For that question one would need to approach it from a different angle of consideration from that of Fackenheim, who is looking at a piece of history with a theological issue in mind and with a largely Jewish audience in mind for his thinking about that issue. Rather than wondering about God's plans for the Jews, we need to consider the plans of humans, who both perpetrated the Holocaust and built the State of Israel. From the Arab perspective, the European Christians dumped the European Christian-Jewish question into the non-European, predominantly non-Christian Middle East. One may well be able to argue this simply from a "statistical" perspective: if the fact of Jewish refugees and the problem of where to settle them due to immigration quotas in countries such as the United States meant that that problem needed solution elsewhere, then the already-in-process matter of relocating Jews to the Middle East either as a politically independent entity, or not, surely offered itself. And one could argue that pushing from "either or not" to "definitively," a politically independent entity grew out of guilt for what was done to Jews and not done to *save* Jews during the Holocaust.

But that there was already such a process in place, that the discussion of a Jewish homeland and/or an independent Jewish state was taking place for half a century or more before the beginning of the Holocaust militates against limiting the answer to the question to such a perspective as often viewed by the Arabs. That discussion from within the Jewish world was accelerating, as we have seen, well before World War I and long before World War II. With regard not to the numbers of European and American immigration quotas, but of who was present in the Middle East prior to 1948, we have also recognized two things with regard to the Jews: first, that there were never *not* Jews in the region and second, that the number of Jews continued to escalate during the entire course of the modern era. Between the thirteenth and the nineteenth century, indeed, the Jews constituted the primary population in some parts of Palestine, specifically the area from Safed to Tiberias where Joseph HaNasi attempted to establish a semiautonomous state under Ottoman patronage in the sixteenth century.[86]

In the aftermath of World War II and the Holocaust—within and outside the Jewish community—there was a reinvigorated discussion regarding whether there might be a Jewish State and how it might be configured. While by April 1946, an Anglo-American Committee of Inquiry had arrived at a plan for a single binational state under British control, with an immediate grant of one hundred thousand immigration certificates to Jews and an end to the land purchase restrictions of 1940, once again the Jewish Agency put forth a proposal for two separate states west of the Jordan. The agency's plan would have created a Jewish state slightly larger than what was eventually obtained three years later after the Israeli War for Independence but would have created an independent Arab state on the West Bank and an independent Arab enclave around Jaffa; Jerusalem would have been put under international control.

The following year the United Nations—itself an offspring of the two World Wars and the failure to organize a concerted League of Nations between them—offered its own proposal. On November 29, the General Assembly voted to establish a Jewish State and an Arab State. This time the proposal called for three segments that touched each other but were barely contiguous to compose the Jewish State. The Arab counterpart consisted of three sections and the Jaffa enclave, similarly touching but barely contiguous, and Jerusalem and its environs were to remain an international zone. The plan also called for an Arab-Jewish Economic Union. As with the Peel Commission proposal of ten years earlier, the Jews reluctantly accepted it as a final validation of their statehood aspirations, and the Arabs rejected it. Over the following six months there was a virtually daily stream of small-scale attacks against Jews by Arabs and counterattacks by Jews against Arabs, or less frequently attacks by Jews against Arabs and counterattacks against Jews by Arabs.

The culmination of this process, which included the departure from Jewish-held areas of Palestine of nearly 120,000 Arabs by May 5, mostly encouraged to flee by their own leaders, was the Declaration of Independence of the State of Israel on May 14, 1948, and the invasion of the nascent state by six Arab armies—those of Egypt, Syria, Transjordan, Lebanon, Saudi Arabia, and Iraq—on the following day.

Although a truce was signed on June 11, it did not last long. Fighting ultimately continued until 1949. The final point of the war, brought to an end by way of a truce negotiated on the Island of Rhodes, had a threefold impact in its development. First, the Israeli forces enjoyed considerable success, so that, the longer the war raged, the more land was conquered, leading ultimately to a State of Israel after January 1949 remarkably close in size and disposition to what the Jewish Agency had proposed in 1946 and much larger than what the United Nations had proposed in 1947.

Second, a massive movement of populations ensued. Some 591,000 Jews from across the Arab world immigrated to the State of Israel, either out of fear of hostile activity against them by their host countries or because such activity was already taking place, or because the Zionist leadership encouraged them to come and to believe that such activity was imminent. Conversely, some 663,000 Arabs left the Jewish-held areas of Palestine, now parts of the State of Israel. Of these, some 256,000 were absorbed into Lebanon, Syria, Iraq, Transjordan, or Egypt. About 190,000 went only as far as Gaza and another 280,000 as far as the non-Jewishly held area of the West Bank—which, it was expected, would form the basis of an Arab State as the UN Partition Proposal had set forth. Additionally, over 160,000 Arabs remained in Israel or returned to their homes there during 1949.

Third, for those Arabs who neither remained nor returned to Israel nor settled in other already-established Arab polities—who anticipated shaping an Arab Palestinian State—disappointment rather than political fulfillment marked this period. Egypt occupied the Gaza Strip, which remained a kind of no-man's-land for the two decades that followed, its inhabitants limited as to their movement and as far as their ability to become part of the Egyptian world that was not only practically distant—its centers of life beyond the Sinai Peninsula—but culturally and politically very different: even Arabic dialects distinguished the Egyptians from the Gaza Palestinians. On the other hand, those Palestinians residing in the West Bank found their territory not merely occupied by Transjordan in 1948 but annexed to the Hashimite Kingdom in 1950. The annexation was opposed by the Arab League and recognized by only two members of the United Nations, Britain and Pakistan. It led to the formal renaming of the entire kingdom on both sides of the Jordan River as Jordan.

The condition of West Bank Palestinian refugees was economically somewhat better than that of their Gazan brothers and sisters—from which they
were now separated by Israel's territory—but still horrendous. One of the pre-
vailing debates regarding the shaping of both these populations pertains to
the matter of why they left Israel in 1948 and 1949 and did not return while a
window of opportunity presumably still existed—the peace treaties that Israel
signed with her neighbors were variously negotiated between January 24, and
July 20, 1948.

It seems certain that, initially, Arab leaders themselves encouraged emigration, promising a triumphant return that became increasingly unfeasible as the
Israeli army continued to expand its realm of conquest. But it seems equally
certain that, initially or after a certain point, the Israelis both encouraged such
emigration with words or in some cases physical violence—terrorism—that
pushed whole villages to flee in fear.

9

GOVERNANCE ISSUES IN THE MIDDLE EAST— BEFORE AND AFTER 1948

During the period between the Second World War and 1948, while geopolitical boundaries and populations began to shift, governance structures in the Middle East continued to experience a period of great transformation as well. This refers not only to the obvious reconfiguration of Israel-Palestine but also to many states and non-states within the region that one can observe going through major upheavals of leadership and political direction. If we point our lens back once again to the aftermath of World War I and then again to the era around 1948, there are at least three places where we might immediately examine things more closely to find the roots of this change.

The defeat of the Ottoman Empire and its allies in World War I marks a crucial fulcrum for our overall discussion. Having succeeded for the most part in ridding itself of its non-Arab, albeit Sunni Muslim, Ottoman rulers, the majority of the Arab world, both Muslim and Christian, found itself enthralled to new rulers. However, while the Christian British and French made any number of promises, as we have earlier observed, regarding a more independent future for the Arab world, the fulfillment of such promises was both slow in coming and/or complicated by counter-promises to others, including the Jews with respect to western Palestine. The ambition of the British and the French was not limited to the areas over which they assumed mandatory control. It included the entirety of the area north of their mandates—what was left of the former Ottoman Empire. But in that region, Mustafa Kemal, who would later be known simply as Atatürk, had taken control and managed to hold his own well enough against the British and the French that in the end they withdrew into more limited areas of domination and influence and thus, by 1923, the independent post-Ottoman state of Turkey was born.

But among the inhabitants of that state would be a substantial population of non-Turkish inhabitants, Kurds, who, concentrated in what became Eastern Turkey, northern Syria, and northeastern Iraq, were also promised some form of an independent polity by the allies during World War I but received nothing. Separated by redrawn geopolitical lines and divided among themselves along various tribal lines, the Kurds add yet another ethnic and political complication to the tangle of the Middle East and to all three post–World War I states that they inhabit. Nowhere is this more obvious than in Turkey, even now more than ninety years after Atatürk founded the new state.[87]

In founding the new state of Turkey, Atatürk created a secular republic in 1923. That is, he abandoned the notion that a predominantly Muslim state must be an *Islamic State* in the modern world in which he wished to see Turkey assume a role. Thus, for example, the Hagia Sophia, that, in its transformation from Church to Mosque after 1453 had become such a symbol of victorious Islam, was transformed into a secular State Museum. Its architecture and its internal artworks, both Muslim and Christian—its long-hidden twelfth-century Christian mosaics uncovered for all to see—now became part of the *cultural* heritage of Turkey, rather than the *spiritual* heritage of Sunni Islam and its caliphate. So, too, Atatürk dramatically disconnected the modern state from its predecessor by rejecting the Arabic writing system, which with its consonantal emphases was never particularly conducive to the vowel-emphasizing Turkish language, and adopting the modified Latin-letter system in 1928 with which Turkish has been written ever since.

These acts of secularization had repercussions that shaped the state during and after the time of Atatürk and would have peculiar consequences as recently as 2000. Speaking before the video cameras in the aftermath of the 9/11 attacks on the Twin Towers and Pentagon, Usama Bin Ladin asserted, among other things, that he was avenging the insult to Islam, and thus to God, meted out in 1923. That rather peculiar—and to most, obscure—reference was to the sacrilege of Atatürk. The validation of an act of violence and brutality by reference to an event nearly eighty years in the past, which most would not likely construe in any case as an attack on Islam recalls the thinking of the first Crusaders, who claimed that they were righting the wrong committed by al-Hakim in 1009 when he burned down the Church of the Holy Sepulchre in Jerusalem. Both assertions are symptomatic of a form of long-memoried religious extremism that has obvious implications not only for the region, but for the world.

A second instance of dramatic political reconfiguration occurred in the aftermath of the first Arab-Israeli war. After the signal failure to prevail against the nascent Jewish state, Colonel Husni al-Za'im seized control of Syria on March 20, 1949, one of the consequences of which was the setting up of a secular judicial system. Al-Za'im replaced the Qur'anic legal system with one based on the Napoleonic code. This would mean, among other things, that Syria would now follow Turkey in possessing a dual secular and Muslim identity, which was and is consequential for its relations both with other Arab—Muslim—states and with Israel.

In turn, since the primary clients for Syria's tobacco and grain were Jordan and Iraq—royalist friends of the West—al-Za'im was pushed into putting Syria into an economic relationship with the United States, in spite of the predominantly negative view of America as Israel's primary sponsor.[88] Syria would sway back and forth over the next six or seven years in its relations with Western powers and the Arab states. By the mid-1950s, a new party was on the rise, the Ba'ath Party, which saw itself as the party of Arab renaissance. It had been created by a Christian Arab, Michael Aflaq, and his Muslim friend Salah al-Bitar, and in 1954 it won 16 of 142 seats in the Syrian House of Deputies. As an entity, however, it was not confined to Syria, for as a champion of Arab unity it was able to sprout branches in Jordan, Iraq, and to a lesser extent, Lebanon.[89]

In the context of the 1956 Suez crisis, the USSR provided Syria with $140 million in technical aid, and relations with the United States soured. And in late 1957, the government sought political union with Egypt so that a new United Arab Republic (UAR) came into being on February 1, 1958, with Egypt's Abdul Gamal Nassir as its president. But on September 16, 1961, a new high command had taken charge within Syria and the UAR collapsed. In February 1962, a Ba'athist coup toppled the government of Iraq and the Syrian premier, Khalid al-Azm, sought a political merger; the new Iraqi government refused even to meet with the envoys from Damascus. On March 6, the army occupied Damascus, al-Azm was deposed and, with Michael Aflaq working behind the scenes, Salah al-Bitar established a new Ba'ath government. Two years later, al-Bitar was deposed by the army and Dr. Yussuf Zayin was put in place as premier—the fifteenth Syrian government in nineteen years.

Zayin's rapid reforms were essentially Marxist in nature and, as a result, he eventually sufficiently displeased General Amin al-Hafiz—who had installed him in power—that by December 1965, al-Hafiz deposed Zayin and reinstalled al-Bitar. However, this time al-Bitar lasted only two months before being taken into custody by another general, Salah Jadid, whom al-Bitar had sought to remove as chief of staff due to his excessively leftist leanings and who returned Zayin to the position of premier. Against this background, the disastrous June 1967 war with Israel took place.[90] Three years later, a second military disaster unfolded during the Jordanian Civil War[91] when the Syrian regime sent tanks to support Palestinian forces near the border but without air cover. The Jordanian air force easily demolished the Syrian tank column. The consequence was another coup, led this time by Chief of Staff General Hafiz Assad, who established a new government devoid of Marxist content and laying claim to the championing of Arab nationhood. Assad was elected president unopposed by 99 percent of the vote in a referendum held in March 1971. He remained in power until his death in June 2000, when he was succeeded by his son, Bashar.

This brief excursion into Syrian history offers yet another instance of what should give one pause as one considers the possibilities for unraveling the tangled web of the region. As this discussion has arrived by different paths toward the middle third of the twentieth century, by which time there was a number of new polities within the Middle East, we inevitably think toward the unresolved problem of the Israeli-Palestinian relationship as it moves through the second half of the century. But we ought not to be lured into the false assumption that the tangled web of the region is limited in its confusions and complications to the problem of the Israelis and the Palestinians or even the Israelis and the Arabs, as complicated as those issues are—a brief look at Syria makes that emphatically clear. As the second half of the century rolls itself out, there arises a range of issues involving both new polities artificially created by outside forces and old groups whose negative inter-involvements have never been cleared up.

Thus, in considering some of the array of complications that grow out of the reconfiguration of the Middle East between the end of World War I and the 1950s, one might also briefly examine the case of Lebanon. Lebanon offers a microcosm of the tangle of complexities facing the region as a whole and in some senses offers a parallel to part of the problematic of Israel, in its identity as a non-Islamic state within a mostly Islamic region. For Lebanon was, as an independent state, a polity with a largely Christian leadership. Created by the French as an enclave carved out of their mandate, it was designed to offer to a largely Christian Arab community what Syria proper, newly reconfigured, offered to a predominantly Muslim Arab community. The irony is that the configuration devised by the French, in extending the province to the sea, actually brought in many Muslims, diluting the Christian identity that had prevailed under the Ottomans for this *sanjak* (sub-province).[92]

Indeed, Lebanon is actually, over its brief independent history, surprisingly complicated. It stands out among Arab states in having established political stability with the help of the clergy, rather than by dismantling clerical power. The complexity of its religious configuration is echoed in the manner in which that power has been delicately balanced through most of its modern history.

Lebanon offers a Christian majority, of which about 70 percent are Maronites and the rest a mix of mainly Greek Orthodox, Syrian Orthodox, Syrian Catholic, Roman Catholic, Assyrian, and Chaldaean denominations. There are also substantial Sunni Muslim and Druze populations. In the initial phase of its independent, post-French condition, these three factions fashioned a fairly comfortable political arrangement that consisted of power-sharing signified by having a Christian president and a Sunni Muslim prime minister with a Druze foreign minister. The parliament was organized so that no sect could dominate and thus a union of Church and State would be impossible.

Lebanon's situation provokes several observations. The condition of the country as compared with that of Syria in the realm of terrorism vis-à-vis with Israel underscores how fragile the arrangement of power-sharing has been and how ultimately unstable and impotent that state has been. In contrast to Syria, which, for all its vocal animosity and aggression toward Israel, produced no terrorist incursions to speak of over the decades, Lebanon, without such animosity, was the source of frequent attacks that were not fully solved even by the Israeli invasion of Lebanon in 1982.

Further, with the French gone from the scene after 1946, the Syrian desire to exert control over Lebanon expanded dramatically. Although some Middle East specialists have observed that Lebanon does fine as long as there is no outside interference,[93] the withdrawal of the French created instability that only ended when, in the aftermath of the first Persian Gulf War, Syria was rewarded for its role as an ally against Iraq by being permitted, for all intents and purposes, to swallow Lebanon up with no interference from the West. Thus, while the country was stabilized, it came to be controlled by Syria and all but lost its independence.

In other words, Lebanon's stability derives from what most Lebanese would probably call outside interference, even as Syrians would assert that, by definition, their involvement is from within, since Lebanon was historically—pre-French Mandate—not a separate entity, but part of Syria. This is the same logic that Sadam Hussein employed to justify his occupation of Kuwait, which led to the war that yielded control of Lebanon to the Syrians. The issue of interference, particularly with respect to distinguishing "inside" from "outside," is one of the key drivers of conflict and dispute not only in Lebanon but in the Middle East as a whole.[94] Put another way, since the aftermath of the first Gulf War, Lebanon has ceased to be an independent *dhimmi*, or quasi-*dhimmi* state. The implications of that fact for the further discussion of Israel-Arab and Israel-Palestine tensions are profound. It raises the religion-based question of the ability and willingness of the Muslim Arab world to accept the presence of an independent *dhimmi* state—as Israel is—within the heart of the *Dar al-Is-lam*, i.e., the Muslim heartland (literally: "realm of Submission [to God]").

To answer that question, we must first return our thoughts briefly to the word *dhimmi* in the early and subsequent history of Islam.[95] If one believes that the earliest text of the *dhimma* as we have it derives from Muhammad's original agreement with the Jews of Khaybar, and if one believes that Muhammad's agreement was divinely dictated, then how can one possibly countenance an independent *dhimmi* state within the *dar al'Islam*? But nowhere is the *dhimma* specifically referred to, much less described in the Qur'an. Indeed, if one reviews what the Qur'an says about Jews—and other non-Muslim groups—one arrives at an ambiguous conclusion regarding the Prophet's view of them. In *Sura* 9:29 to "Fight against those to whom the Scriptures were given, who believe not in God nor in the last day . . . " But this by no means refers to the *dhimmi* in general, but rather to those *dhimmi* "who do not believe in God nor in the Last Day"—and by the way, this assumes that some form of the *dhimmi* concept is what the text intends, although the term itself only comes into actual usage after the creation of the Qur'an. More clearly and negatively, we read in *Sura* 5:51 "Take not the Jews and the Christians as friends." But we also read in *Sura* 2:256 that "there is no compulsion in religion" and in the same *Sura* (2:67) we read: "Believers, Jews, Christians, and Sabaeans—whoever believes in God and the Last Day and do what is right—shall be rewarded by their Lord; they have nothing to fear or to regret."

So the answer to the question regarding the acceptability of a *dhimmi* state will depend upon how one reads the Qur'an and which passages one selects as a guide for one's viewpoint. Whatever might further assist us that comes from the *Hadith*, is by definition not the word of God, but the word of the prophet or words about the prophet and, depending upon the nature of its transmission, of heavier or lighter weight in guiding our thinking.[96] If, finally, we examine the historical sweep from the seventh century to the twentieth century, we will encounter a range of conditions from Spain to the Holy Land to Persia, and to points yet further east with respect to the treatment of *dhimmi*.

This is not surprising, given the far-flung world of Islam, the range of schools of interpretation and of interpreters within those schools, and the manner in which politics and religion interweave across human history. That range includes conditions where *dhimmi*, primarily Jews, have been viziers to caliphs and sultans, and on the other hand, serious oppression was experienced by the *dhimmi*, with a variety of conditions falling between these two extremes. So history is no guide—and in any case, in no historical case do we see a fully independent *dhimmi* state within the *dar al'Islam* that could offer us a model situation. The closest we come, perhaps, is the brief and somewhat abortive attempt by Joseph HaNassi to create a semiautonomous Jewish polity in the vicinity of Safed and Tiberias under Ottoman patronage in the mid-sixteenth century.

Nonetheless, Islam's record of tolerance of non-Muslims when it is in control is far better than that of Christianity's tolerance of non-Christians, at least until the nineteenth century. But when not in control, as has been the case to varying degrees since the late seventeenth century, the story is often different. For many observant, devout Muslims who believe in the inviolability of a Muhammad-ordained *dhimma*, it may never be acceptable for a member of the *dhimmi* to be on a footing equal to, much less superior to, that of a Muslim. If Islamic fundamentalists comes to dominate the *dar al'Islam*—and fundamentalism has in recent decades surged in varying degrees in Jordan, Algeria, Tunisia, Egypt, even Turkey; and has been terribly feared by the Saudi leadership ever since the overthrow of the Shah of Iran—there is virtually no chance for permanent peace with Israel, since that would mean legitimizing a *dhimmi* state within the heart of the *dar al'Islam*.

On the other hand, interestingly enough, when the newly minted Hashimite Emir Faisal arrived at an agreement in 1919 with Haim Weizmann—the Zionist leader who would become the first president of Israel thirty years later—he did so based on supporting the idea embraced by him and other Muslims like him, that the Jews have rights to Israel. This derived from an interpretation of Q. 9:21—referring to "those who believe and have fled" to whom the "Lord gives . . . gardens . . . to dwell in"—and Q 17:4: "And we decreed to the children of Israel in the Book . . . ye shall rise to a great height . . . " Needless to say, not every Muslim agreed with Emir Faisal, who was probably assassinated by arsenic poisoning in 1933.[97]

The Muslim opposition to Israel is not a simple case of anti-Semitism—to think of it in those terms is to import a Christian European vocabulary into a Middle Eastern situation dominated by Islam. It's not that the Jews must be exterminated or even driven out, but that an *independent Jewish state* is unacceptable. The idea that an independent *dhimmi* state will not be accepted in the Muslim world is affirmed from the viewpoint of many Israelis not only because of the fate of Lebanon but by their own history. Israeli historiography records the attack on the nascent state by the armies of six Arab states. It does not—or did not until the beginning of the 1980s—remember the request from Syrian president Husni al-Za'im to meet with Ben-Gurion in 1949. Al-Za'im had apparently intended to offer a peace agreement under which Syria would have absorbed between 300,000 and 350,000 Palestinian refugees as permanent residents in exchange, according to Ben-Gurion's diary, for "half of the Sea of Galilee."[98]

Israel remembers the Suez crisis precipitated by Egypt's Nassir as the source for the Sinai war of 1956, in the aftermath of which the Israelis and their French and British allies withdrew under pressure from the United States, demanding in exchange negotiations that might lead to peace—a demand that was never met. It recalls the terrifying crisis leading up to the extraordinary victory of 1967 and extending the hand of peace in the aftermath of that war and once again finding the hand slapped back.[99] It mourns the high number of Israeli dead occasioned by the attack on Israel on Yom Kippur, 1973, in which, instead of preemptively defending itself, the Jewish State waited for diplomacy to do the work that it never did. Israelis cannot forget the incursions into the northern part of the state from terrorists lodged in Lebanon in the later 1970s and early 1980s.[100]

Connected to the question of whether Muslim Arabs can accept a *dhimmi* state is how one might understand the meaning of *jihad*.[101] Thus, with respect to struggling or striving with forces beyond one's internal self and outside the Muslim community, the Qur'an offers specific conditions under which one is obligated, or at least permitted, to fight. Among these the most relevant passage is that of *Sura* 22:39–40: "Permission [to fight] is given to those . . . who are driven out of their homes without a just cause." If the Palestinian view is that Muslim Palestinians have been driven from their land by Israelis or by Israel's existence, it is difficult to conceive how they would respond as Muslims other than by continuous warfare until that land is reclaimed.

Once again, we are confronted with questions of selective memory and historiography: how many Palestinian Arabs left, and for which reasons? How many were allowed to return after 1949, and how many did so? What was left behind and as such, how religiously valid would be an ongoing struggle to claim some or all of it?[102] The interpretive answer to these questions will affect any answer to the *jihad* question within the context of *Sura* 22.

There is also a more complicated twist to this last issue of *dhimma* and *jihad*. If Israel is an expression of secular Jewish *nationalism*, then what relevance does the matter of Jewish *religion* have to this entire issue? The PLO charter of 1968 denies legitimacy to the Jewish claim to any part of Palestine in part because "Judaism, being a religion, is not an independent nationality. Nor do Jews constitute a single nation with an identity of its own; they are citizens of the states to which they belong." This is the very issue with which Jews began to wrestle in the late eighteenth century and it is precisely the claim of Jewish nationalism that this sort of formulation is wrong. This is further complicated by the fact that the PLO—as it moved toward peace negotiations and the new identity of its dominant *Fatah* wing—began to renounce anti-Israel violence as a methodology by the end of the 1980s, and even to recognize Israel's existence as legitimate.[103] In contrast, the *Muslim Brotherhood* in Palestine, part of an Islamic revival movement founded in Egypt in 1928, reemerged along radical lines to fill in the "gap" left by the PLO's turn from violence to diplomacy. Thus *Hamas* and *Islamic Jihad* were born. Aside from the uncomfortable physical fact that they absorbed suicide-bomber methodology from *Hizb'Allah* is the spiritual fact of how they identify themselves.

Whereas the PLO in general and *Fatah* in particular were and are in effect secular organizations, so that the grounds for their relations with Israel are political-national, *Hamas* and *Islamic Jihad* shaped themselves as religious organizations. Thus where, for example, the PLO charter has asserted that Palestine is "an indivisible part of the Arab homeland," the *Hamas* charter refers to "the land of Palestine [as] an Islamic trust [*waqf*] upon all Muslim generations until the day of Resurrection." The PLO charter refers to the enemy as Zionist imperialists; the *Hamas* charter refers to "the unbelievers." The latter refers to a *Hadith,* which speaks of the Day of Judgment as arriving only when "the Muslims fight against the Jews and the Muslims kill them . . ." This returns the question of religious definition to the interior of Islam: if I accept this *Hadith* as valid, there is not much hope for reconciliation, but I can denounce a *Hadith* as not legitimate, or at least as not binding, since at *most* it is the word of Muhammad, and not the word of God.[104]

Conversely, of course, Israelis argued for years that Palestinian nationalism is not legitimate. Thus Prime Minister Golda Meir commented in 1969: "There was no such thing as Palestinians. When was there an independent Palestinian people with a Palestinian state?" Such a conviction continued through the 1978 Peace Accords with Egypt and as far as the Peace Conference in Madrid of 1991. It was not until 1993 in Oslo that Israel began the shift toward recognizing Palestinians as a distinct entity—and that the Palestinian charter slipped sufficiently into dormancy to allow for recognition of a Jewish state. But both sides of this equation remain fragile and clearly require reinforcement.

PART FOUR
THE PARADOXES OF ISRAEL/PALESTINE

10

ISRAEL AND THE PALESTINIANS

The *dhimma-jihad* sensibility militates against an easy willingness on the part of Israelis to believe that the Arabs will ever accept an independent Jewish State. This essential distrust of Arabs—Muslim *or* Christian—is reinforced each time some anti-Israel statement is made or action takes place. Thus not only the declared wars of army against army but the *intifadas* of civilians against civilians corroborates this distrust. Each such instance validates a sense of discomfort cultivated by the memory of the post–World War I through post–World War II era, of which Haj Amin al-Husseini is the foremost symbol.[105] Moreover, from the assassination of King Abd'Allah in 1951, by one of Haj Amin's followers in large part due to Abd'Allah's willingness to talk peace with the Israelis, until 1977 with Anwar Sadat's visit to Jerusalem, no Arab leader had been willing to talk with Israelis, as talking meant recognizing Israel's right to exist. After Sadat's historic visit, that situation began to change and the challenge became more narrowly focused on the Palestinians. And the question became: with *whom* should Israel negotiate?

There were Israelis who refused to recognize the Palestinians as a legitimate group with legitimate group aspirations, but the larger impediment was among those who were more open-minded but wondered: should we negotiate with the PLO? And then: *al-Fatah* or the PFLP or the DFLP or the PFLP-GC or with *Saiqa* or with the ALF?[106] And if with one or more of these groups, what of those that are left out of the negotiations? Will some continue to attack us while we are speaking peace with others? This situation would be made more complicated by Israel's own actions, specifically the 1982 Invasion of Lebanon that ended up producing *Hizb'Allah*. By the time of the 1991 Madrid talks, and certainly by the time of the 1993 Oslo Accords, this question had been swept aside, at least for enough Israelis, and the PLO and its leader, Yassir Arafat. Arafat had long since succeeded Ahmad Shukayri as PLO Chairman, as *al-Fatah* had long since become the dominant presence in the PLO. And Israel acknowledged the PLO as the legitimate opposite party with which to negotiate, even with the more limited but very noteworthy interventions by *Hizb'Allah* and *Hamas* during the period that followed.[107] But with the breakdown in the peace process seven years later, the level of distrust of those across the negotiating terrain escalated again.

At the inception of the period between Oslo and the Second *Intifada*, Israel also wrestled with whether and how to negotiate with Hafiz al-Assad-led Syria. Many Israelis worried that whatever concessions were made, including the return of the entire Golan Heights, Assad could not be trusted. There may be an irony here, since, historically, whatever else may be said of Assad, he could be relied upon to stick to the letter of his agreements, in contrast with more mercurial figures like Saddam Hussein. Nonetheless, the perception of him by many Israelis was an intensified microcosmic encapsulation of their broader distrust and fears. Nevertheless, negotiations proceeded, until the assassination of Yitzhak Rabin in 1995. They hovered again on the edge of possibility under Ehud Barak but fell apart definitively when the Israeli-Palestinian peace process collapsed in 2000.

But if we look to Israel's distrust of its Arab neighbors near and far as a significant issue militating against a simple solution to the Israeli-Palestinian and Israeli-Arab dynamic, we cannot limit the discussion to that issue. From the Israeli perspective—the Jewish Israeli perspective—there is also the larger picture of a Christian Euro-American world that cannot be trusted not to abandon Israel to destruction when push comes to shove. This second issue of fear and distrust is rarely articulated. But it is largely why Israel so consistently rejects the idea of international monitors to help supervise agreements, as for example when Secretary of State Colin Powell endorsed such an idea in June 2001.

Several interlocking elements feed into this gut-level response to the world and the siege mentality that, even now—perhaps especially now—more than six decades after Israel's independence and the development of one of the most powerful armies in the world, nags at the Israeli heart and soul. There is, to be sure, the powerful history of fifteen centuries of Jew-hatred taught—"the Teaching of Contempt"—and practiced at political, economic, social, and theological levels. And Jew-hatred did not disappear or even, apparently, dissipate with the secularizing tendencies in Western Christendom of the past two to three centuries.[108]

The culmination of such hatred arrived in the middle of the twentieth century in the form of the Holocaust. The significant thing about the Holocaust for this part of the discussion is not Nazism or its acolytes, per se. It is not simply all those whose ideology included an active interest in annihilating the Jews and Judaism and whose ideology perceived Jews insistently as racialized. It is rather those who aided and abetted the Nazi dream by refusing to act contrary to it—the Lutheran and Catholic Churches in Germany and their concomitants across Europe that embraced Hitler. The British who closed the gates to Palestine and the Americans who refused to bomb the train tracks to Auschwitz. We may read stories of this priest or that who risked his life to save Jews or of how the Danish king wore a yellow star in solidarity with his Jewish subjects. But as stunning as such stories are, they shrink in the selective memory to which all humans are subject against stories like that of the Slovakian Archbishop Kametko, approached by a former colleague and friend, a respected Slovakian rabbi, regarding the impending expulsion of the Jews.

> The archbishop . . . decided to enlighten him regarding the true fate that was awaiting the Jews in Poland. These were his words: "This is no mere expulsion. There—you will not die of hunger and pestilence; there—they will slaughter you all, old and young, women and children, in one day. This is your punishment for the death of our Redeemer."

There is also the comment of the Papal Nuncio regarding the same situation: "There is no innocent blood of Jewish children in the world. All Jewish blood is guilty. You have to die. This is the punishment that has been awaiting you because of that sin [the death of Jesus]."[109] One might argue rationally that the era of the Holocaust is long enough past that it should not cast a shadow over Israel's willingness to trust the Christian world monitoring and/or engaging the progress of its relations with the Arabs. But even were it possible for pure reason to eclipse emotion, many Israelis might find the record of Christian-Israel "relations" since the Holocaust troubling.

It is interesting to recall that until 1967, a substantial percentage of American Jews were not particularly interested in or supportive of Israel. They feared that to do so would find them the object of an accusation of dual loyalty, and indeed such accusations were common up through the 1970s. Others worried that, given the extraordinary and unprecedented opportunities that the United States offered to Jews, it would be foolish to focus on an enterprise ten thousand miles away with little relevance to the reshaped Jewish reality *cum* American Dream. In the case of the Ultra-Orthodox, the conviction that Israel as an enterprise that had not been created by a Divine act was a contravention of Divine Will and thus a sacrilege was still in place. These objections to Israel's existence echoed the layers of Jewish opposition to the Zionist idea at the turn between the nineteenth and twentieth centuries to which I earlier referred.[110]

The months leading up to the June War began to change that objectionist viewpoint in many quarters. As it appeared that Israel would be annihilated, and Western powers shrugged their political and diplomatic shoulders, acting as if there was nothing they could do about the situation, more and more Jews, particularly American Jews, sensed something all too familiar. With the Holocaust barely a generation behind them—and its memory fresh in mind due to the capture and trial of Adolf Eichmann only six years before—there emerged a sense that once again push was coming to shove and the Christian world, calling itself secular in the West and substantial parts of the Soviet East, would turn its back on a substantial Jewish population that was about to be destroyed. If massive Jewish support for Israel was one consequence of this sequence, the other, in spite of the stunning Israeli victory, was the affirmation of distrust for the Christian world, which might otherwise have dissipated within a generation or two after the Holocaust.

This is a fear that retains a grip on the Jewish-Israeli soul: if we don't take care of ourselves, nobody will. It is a fear rooted in a post-Holocaust history that has not been tempered in the decades *since* June 1967. The sense of imminent destruction on the eve of the 1967 war and the sense that the Christian world would do little to avert it was and is echoed in the inability of the Western powers to push for a cease-fire in the first two weeks of the 1973 Yom Kippur War. That no cease-fire could be arranged when the Arab armies were advancing successfully and Israelis were dying in much larger numbers than had been true in the previous two wars—although this quickly changed once the Israelis had counterattacked and encircled the Third Egyptian Army—is interpreted by Jewish Israelis as another symptom of how the (Christian) West cannot be relied upon.

Israeli Jews—and many of their coreligionists in the Diaspora—find sources of ongoing distrust in what they perceive as a double standard of expectation for their behavior from a Western Christian world—including the United States—that exhibits none of the morality on the political and military fronts that it demands of Israel. They find it in specific issues, such as the long-standing refusal of the Vatican to recognize the State of Israel, which only changed in the 1990s in the aftermath of Oslo and the Vatican's recognition of the Palestinian Authority in an equivalent manner. Every time the media shows a Palestinian being injured by an Israeli soldier without showing the attack on the Israeli soldiers that precipitated a violent response or the United Nations excoriates Israel for destroying an Iraqi nuclear reactor or airplanes on the ground at Beirut Airport with no loss of human life but ignores the bombing of a bus filled with Israeli schoolchildren, it confirms the conviction that the West is still dominated by Jew-hatred merely reconfigured as anti-Israel sentiments.[111] When the French Ambassador to Britain refers to Israel as "that shitty little country" and accuses it of being responsible for the world's problems and he receives not even a scintilla of a rebuke from his government, much less being recalled, it furthers that conviction.[112]

There has also emerged in the last thirty-five years another component to the reluctance of Israel to commit itself wholeheartedly to peace discussions with the Palestinians: religious conviction. One of the clear changes in Israeli demographics after 1967 was an upsurge in immigrants from the West—particularly the United States—with powerful religious sensibilities. These assert the divinely mandated legitimacy not only of an independent Jewish state, but one that extends from the Mediterranean Sea to the Jordan River or, in the minds of some, even to Mesopotamia. This is a classic case of interpreting God's word so that the revelation accords not only with one's spiritual beliefs but with one's political position. There is obviously a double irony here: much of the Orthodox and certainly the ultra-Orthodox Jewish community by and large disavowed the legitimacy of an autonomous Jewish State between 1896 and 1967; and American Jews in general were remarkably unconcerned and unsupportive of the Zionist idea during that same period.[113]

This religion-based demographic is complicated further by the fact that so many of the "settlers" *are* American. If establishing themselves in the heart of Hebron or the outskirts of Bethlehem—the Israeli frontier—is justified by their convictions regarding what God intended for this piece of real estate, deep in their guts is the sort of simple certainty famously expressed by the American actor John Wayne during the Vietnam era, when he observed that the United States should "just go in there and clean the enemy out" the way he so often did in his movies: walking into a bar and gunning down three or four bad guys at a pop. That cowboy imagery is wedded to the vision of settlers successfully protecting themselves from Native Americans (*Injuns!*) as they establish a growing number of beachheads for Euro-Americans across the continent. The very word "frontier" resonates with most Americans toward Wild West images.

It was the mid-nineteenth-century concept of "manifest destiny" that justified in the minds of thousands of Euro-Americans—well before there were movies to further romanticize their efforts—their God-given right and responsibility to push their presence all the way to the Pacific Ocean.[114] How many thousands upon thousands of Native Americans were dispossessed of their lands, livelihoods, and even their lives as Europeans settled the America that became the United States?[115]

This suggests that, psychologically, a majority of Israeli settlers—numbering close to 390,000 as of early 2015 on the West Bank and continuing to grow—have established themselves in the Palestinian Territories not only out of conscious Jewish religious-national convictions but out of an unconscious American frontier-heroic-cowboy-John Wayne sensibility. Note the terms "settlers" and "frontier" and their resonance with American history. Given this complicated psycho-spiritual condition, the possibility of simply removing them is nil, which means a different solution, if there is one, must be sought and that whatever role the United States might play in working toward an Israeli-Palestinian peace is more layered than one might otherwise suppose.

From a less religious and more historico-political perspective is the assertion that, just as the shape that the State of Israel took in 1949 was a consequence of a war fought because a more truncated version proposed at the United Nations in 1947 was rejected by the Arabs, so the expanded shape after 1967 reflected the rejection by the Arabs of the more limited version of Israel that had prevailed between 1949 and 1967. Therefore, just as the one became accepted by the international community, so ought the second—and besides, the times and places in world history where the changes in borders due to war have been reversed by concessions from the victor are few and far between. But the answer to that is simply that after 1967, part of the nonacceptance picture changed: a post-1949 Israel has been acknowledged as legitimate by Egypt since 1979 and by Jordan since 1994. Thus, if territorial concessions to the Palestinians will complete a new picture, of *acceptance*, then it is worth breaking with historical precedent.

Supposing an Israel that returns to its pre-1967 borders, and an Arab population within that Israel similar in size and disposition to that which existed prior to 1967, how can that population function with a sense of its own identity and yet as Israeli—as opposed to experiencing a sense of alienation from either Israel or itself or both? *How*, given both the very different Palestinian Arab consciousness that has evolved for that population not only since 1967, but since 1982 and especially since the Madrid-Oslo period of the early 1990s and the Second *Intifada* that began in the aftermath of the 1999–2000 collapse of Israeli-Palestinian negotiations? Put otherwise: how can even a geopolitically smaller, rather than greater, Israel remain both a Jewish state and a democracy?

The Israeli Declaration of Independence explicitly pledges that the new state will "foster the development of the country for the benefit of all its inhabitants; it will be based on freedom, justice and peace as envisaged by the prophets of Israel; it will ensure complete equality of social and political rights to all of its inhabitants irrespective of religion, race or gender; it will guarantee freedom of religion, conscience, language, education and culture. . ." This sort of declaration is reminiscent of the principles underlying the American Declaration of Independence and the US Constitution. And like the United States, Israel has not managed to live entirely up to the ideals its founding fathers posed for it.

It is true, for example, that Arabs serve in the Knesset, and that an Arab judge served for a year—but only a year—on the Israeli Supreme Court. It is true that the first Muslim Arab member of the Knesset, Abdulmalik Dahamsha, gave his inaugural speech in 1996 in Arabic, and succeeded in having a mosque established in the Knesset building, and that the Christian Arab Azmi Bishara—also elected to the Knesset in 1996—even mounted a campaign for election as prime minister in 1998. It is also true that Israeli Arabs are freer and economically better off than their counterparts *anywhere in the Arab world*, and that some of the limitations they endure derive from not doing army service, which has been a key to success in Israel both because of the respect accorded to those who serve and due to the connections one makes, practically speaking, while in the army—and their not serving in the army has, for most of Israel's history, been a mutually agreed-upon situation that recognizes potential conflicts of interest for Israeli Arabs.

The Arab representation in the Knesset, however, is still significantly lower than the percentage of the Arab population of Israel, and Bishara was stripped of his parliamentary immunity in 2001 to face charges of supporting terrorist organizations after he gave two controversial speeches. In August 2000, he had hailed the Israeli withdrawal from Lebanon as a victory for *Hizb'Allah* and the following year, in Syria, called upon Arabs to "enlarge the sphere of resistance."[116] I am not passing judgment on his treatment under the circumstances.[117] But by comparison, the 1983 Israeli commission headed by its Supreme Court president, Yitzhak Kahan, found Ariel Sharon guilty of "indirect, but personal responsibility for having disregarded the danger of acts of vengeance and bloodshed by the Phalangists" in the 1982 massacres in the Sabra and Shatila refugee camps in Lebanon, and as a consequence, he was forced to resign as defense minister; he was permitted to remain in the government as a minister without portfolio. More to the point, it may have taken nearly two decades, but ultimately he could—and did—mount a successful campaign to become prime minister.[118] In spite of such a—murderous—history.

What one might glean from this handful of data is that if Israel has not managed to fulfill the letter or spirit of its own Declaration of Independence, part of the blame for that failure falls on the complicated conditions in which Israel has existed from its inception: the fears and distrust of Muslims and Christians for long-term historical reasons in general, and more to the point, of its own Arab population in particular, given shorter-term history. This does not mean that more strenuous efforts ought not to be made to bring reality and the ideal of full democracy closer together; it merely reminds us that that effort will require multilateral and not unilateral attention. And if, for the sake of argument, a comparison is made with the American historical relationship with First Americans and with African Americans, Israel does not fare so badly both with regard to failure to fulfill its own ideals and with regard to the conditions that militate for or against successful fulfillment.

Numerous different thinkers in Israel have addressed this issue from their respective perspectives. Thus for example, Ilan Pappe wrote in a response to an article in *Ha'aretz* from 1994[119] in which he was quoted, that "I will continue to argue that we must resolve the serious contradiction between a Zionist and Jewish statehood and civil rights and democracy, not just as a way of repairing the injustices of the past, but mostly to make normal life in the future possible. A democratic and pluralistic Israel as part of the Mediterranean basin is also an Israel of varied historical narratives, of more than one truth. Such an Israel bears hope for a common future."[120]

When Minister of Education Yossi Sarid, leader of the left-wing Meretz Party, announced at the end of February 2000 that some poems by Mahmud Darwish—generally considered to be one of the greatest of the modern Arabic language poets, but an Israeli Arab who in political exile became a PLO leader— would be placed in the Israeli school literature curriculum, Uzi Landau, of the right-wing Likud Party responded with horror: "When they say more Darwish there's less Bialek.[121] There is less Zionism and more post-Zionism and less Jewish history and more fabricated Palestinian history and fabricated Zionist and Jewish history." Ron Milo of the Center Party commented: "My fear is that they're not studying enough Israeli history, that they are not studying enough about the land of Israel, that they're not studying enough history of the Jewish people. That's my fear. If they have that, I'm not scared of Darwish." Re'uven Rivlin of Likud said, "I understand that we are a nation that has to a large extent lost its need for symbols, for an ethos, for a tradition that has led us and brought us to this point, but still it is a matter of honor. . . There's no censorship. You can buy Darwish in every store. . . But to put him onto the school agenda—that makes a statement: that says there's no honor, you can do whatever you want with us, because we aren't worth anything."[122]

Ruth Gavison, a professor of law and an expert on civil rights has "likened the status of Israel's Arab citizens to the status of Jews in the United States . . . she does not believe that their [the Israeli Arabs'] sense of alienation justifies the assertion that Israel is not a democratic state" since they enjoy significant and equal political rights together with personal freedom and security. Should the Arab Israelis' *sense* of limitation or *actual* limitations "take precedence over the right of the Jewish people to a state in which it governs and in which it is the majority?"[123] Sami Smooha, an Arab professor of sociology at the University of Haifa, has called for cultural autonomy for Israeli Arabs: governed by The Basic Law of Human Dignity and Liberty, Israeli Arabs would be guaranteed democratic rights. They would function officially as they mostly currently do unofficially: as a non-territorially separate entity—the equivalent of the condition of the Ultra-Orthodox Jewish community in Israel, and in some parts of the United States—in which a supreme Arab council, empowered by the Knesset following a referendum of all Israeli Arabs, and centered around an executive committee, would represent the Arabs to the authorities in all areas of public life. Israel would remain functionally Jewish but more effectively democratic with respect to its primary non-Jewish minority.[124]

And more recently, Daniel Gavron argued in a January 12, 2009, article in *Newsweek* that "Israel could break the stalemate [regarding Israeli voters' views of how to achieve peace with the Palestinians] by fully enfranchising its Arabs, who make up about 14 percent of voters."[125] Largely excluded from proximity "to the center of power," an invigorated Israeli Arab voting population might have given Tzipi Livni's more leftist, two-state-advocating party the prime minister's office over Binyamin Netanyahu's more rightist, two-state-questioning, -doubting, (or even -opposing) party.

Writing prior to that election, Gavron observed that "[f]or that to happen, the Israeli peace camp must declare in advance its willingness to ally with Arab parties. Such an Arab-Jewish coalition would also have a galvanizing effect on Israel's population and help address years of discrimination. Israeli Arabs are feeling bitter about the Gaza attacks, but one of their own was the second victim of *Hamas* rocket fire in the first days of fighting, which should make it easier to emphasize that they are an integral part of Israeli society." Gavron's discussion seems almost too simple to me, as far as the bold title of the article is concerned, and more fundamentally, as far as turning the identity complications *felt by* Israeli Arabs into the political solution *derived from* Israeli Arabs. But even so, his articulation of the specifics of how the playing field might be made somewhat more level and the positive consequences of that leveling both for Jews and for Muslim and Christian Arabs within Israel—and perhaps also for Palestinians—deserves serious consideration.

The discussion within Israel is almost endless on this issue. Israel is, in this respect, at the opposite end of where its founders were over a century ago—and perhaps even sixty years ago—when the question of where the non-Jewish indigenous Arab population might fit into the Zionist vision seems not to have crossed anybody's mind. It seems to me that then the founders were being no better and no worse than humans everywhere, be they European, African, or

Asian, be they Western or Middle Eastern; and now the Israelis engaged in this discussion are living up to the positive side of a double standard typically applied by the outside world that demands of them that they operate from a Jewish perspective that is based on the best, most ideal of Jewish senses of justice, carved out during centuries of diasporic political, social, economic, and cultural disenfranchisement. The vociferousness of the debate is to Israel's credit as a democracy.

If in the end, Israel remains a state that follows a Jewish calendar and is attached to all sorts of Jewish cultural and even religious ideas, then it could be legitimately viewed as no more than the single Jewish mirror of the myriad of secular Christian and the very few secular Muslim states in which Jewish minorities live in relative psychological comfort and yet with what must be, at times, an intense sense of alienation. Whether we look at the United States—with a National Cathedral in Washington, DC, that is nominally both non-denominational and omni-denominational but actually Episcopalian (when was the last time anyone suggested that the stewardship of the Cathedral be passed over a multiple-year cycle, among leaders from various *Christian* denominations, much less Christian and *non*-Christian denominations?) and where Christmas breathes through every pore of the nation between Thanksgiving and New Year's Day—or we look at Catholic France or Italy or Muslim Turkey; we are looking at states that are theoretically secular but that actually, in varying degrees, pursue cultural and/or spiritual courses in which those who are not part of the majority can play only an uncomfortable or unreal part.

Can't Israel simply be—or can Israel simply *not* be—the mirror of such a condition, only with Judaism as the majority? In what way is this issue legitimate, and in what way might the very raising of it suggest a different standard to which Israel is being held than is held, say, by Americans for America?

All of the groups that served as primary elements in this narrative are joined not only in confusion and conflict but also fear, perturbation, and selective memory. This is in spite of several advances in Arab-Israel relations that emerged during the 1970s. The most obvious was the unexpected decision of Egyptian Prime Minister Anwar Sadat to come to Jerusalem to address the Israeli Parliament and ultimately to sign a peace accord with Israel in 1979.[126]

That stunning moment has at least two aspects that are important for this discussion. One is the context in which Sadat justified his offering of the olive branch to Israel. He distanced himself from the Arabs, rhetorically questioning why Egypt, a "non-Arab state" had spent the previous three decades fighting wars with Israel "on behalf of the Arabs." In this rhetorical question, we find the matter of definition with respect to the word "Arab" once more before us.

The other aspect is contained within the assassination of Sadat that followed several years after the peace with Israel. Muslim extremists—associated with the group calling itself *Islamic Jihad*—gunned him down on October 6, 1981, as he presided over an anniversary celebration of Egypt's success against Israel in the Yom Kippur War and conversely, the Egyptian-Israeli peace treaty.[127] In their court trial they argued that Sadat had betrayed Islamic principles, and thus the Islamic world, by an entire series of actions. Of these, the peace with Israel was only one and not the first on the list that they read before the court. Modernization and improper attire and behavior permitted to women such as Sadat's own wife were considered equally significant, as was the use of force during the previous month to suppress political dissidents. But Sadat's assassination might—and did—raise doubts among many Israelis regarding whether a larger peace with their neighbors would be possible, just as it would raise the bar of fear another notch for Arab leaders considering peace with Israel.

On the other hand, not only has the peace with Egypt held through the decades since Sadat's death, none of the conditions has been abrogated in the nearly forty years since Sadat and Begin signed the treaty—even if it has not been a warm peace. Moreover, one of the leaders of the group that assassinated Sadat—Karam Zuhdi—stated in a July 2003 interview that if he could go back in time, "I would interfere to prevent it [the assassination]." He suggested that *Islamic Jihad* misinterpreted the *shari'a* in perceiving religious grounds to justify Sadat's assassination. The point of this assertion is that even apparently intractable religious perspectives can shift if there is a desire to think and rethink spiritual matters and not to remain embedded in a given viewpoint.

However, Israeli fear can be stoked when, for example, a leading Palestinian like Salah Ta'mari, an important associate and supporter of Yassir Arafat, said that "I have not abandoned my dream of a democratic state in all of Palestine where Palestinians—Jews and non-Jews—will live together." For they interpret such a comment, for good historical reasons, as encoded: there will be no Israel, the Muslim Arabs will be in charge, and Jews may live here under a Palestinian umbrella as elsewhere across Arab Muslim-Jewish history and geography. Israelis hear *dhimma* in that comment and given the absence of a single democracy in the Arab world in the past or the present, fear the reality behind its generous-sounding words as an uncomfortable one. When they hear Ta'mari further comment, regarding Arafat, that "the minute he loses faith in this agreement [the Oslo-Wye Accords], Arafat does not lack the courage to say 'the agreement is finished, and we are no longer abiding by it.' He has great courage, both in war and in peace"—they hear duplicity, not courage, and a reinforcement of their conviction that they could not trust Arafat or the Palestinians.[128]

In the years since Arafat's death, a good deal more water has flowed under the bridge. Arafat's "successor" Mahmud Abbas, has shown little capacity to deliver on initiatives with the Israelis. More to the point, he and the *Fatah*-based Palestinian Authority found themselves unable to sustain a position of leadership, much less unity, within the Palestinian world at large. They were removed from power by the electorate of Gaza in 2006–7, leaving that side of the playing field entirely in the hands of *Hamas*, which has fairly consistently denounced the Oslo Accords and any arrangement that provides for the ongoing existence of the State of Israel.[129]

In a related irony, the Israeli decision—under the leadership of Ariel Sharon, of all people—to unilaterally pull out of Gaza in 2004,[130] as a presumably preliminary act of a negotiation, has led only to disaster. It caused internal Israeli political and religious debate: a coalition of right-wing rabbis pronounced a curse on Sharon;[131] and his key intraparty competitor, Binyamin Netanyahu, mounted an internal offensive against Sharon's continued leadership. There have also been many outside Israel who questioned Sharon's motives, based in part on an October 8, 2004, interview in the Israeli newspaper, *Haaretz*. There he asserted both that peace could only come when the Palestinians renounce terrorism against Israel but also that the withdrawal from Gaza would freeze the peace process.

So it is not clear exactly as to where Sharon thought to go next, peace-wise. But in the aftermath of the withdrawal, if there *had* been such a renunciation of terrorism from the Palestinian side, then the net effect would not have been to freeze the process, presumably, but to further it.[132] However, in the aftermath of the Israeli withdrawal, it is not clear that there was an effort on the part of the Gazan leadership—at least after *Hamas* took charge—to shape anything resembling an effective, forward-looking infrastructure, along cultural, social, economic, or political lines. Dependng upon whose account one reads or hears, there was some effort or on the contrary, everything seems to have moved in a retrograde direction.

While the Israelis had been present in Gaza, they had invested in a good deal of construction besides houses and several synagogues, including, for example, an extensive array of greenhouses, using hydroponics to produce food and other flora in the fairly unforgiving natural environment. Rather than continuing these projects, the Gazan leadership—or so it seemed to many Israelis—simply destroyed them, exhibiting little but pointless rage, the endpoint of which was to deprive themselves of resources that were theirs for the taking. That, at least, is one version of what happened.[133] Other accounts suggest that since the departing Israelis actually destroyed about half of what they had constructed—withdrawing without destruction from the other half, after an American Jewish fund-raising effort compensated the settlers with $14 million for the investment that they were abandoning—there was insufficient material left with which to work.[134]

A third account suggests that once the settlers left, massive looting began, which the Gazan leadership lacked suffficent manpower resources to prevent.[135] A fourth account details the productivity that nonetheless proceeded and the hopes for expanding agricultural production. This last account also points out a further complication: the only passage through which the fruits and vegetables being produced can find a viable market is Israel, so potential delays created by the checkpoint system can spell disaster, since such products require a quick arrival into the marketplace.[136]

A related but separate issue pertains to the assumption of power in Gaza by Hamas. The rage and frustration with the *Fatah*-led Palestinian National Authority leadership's corruption and inability to provide leadership, services, or hope—abetted by the Bush administration's forcing the issue of free elections and openly expressing its support of *Fatah*—led to an overwhelming victory by *Hamas* in the elections of 2006 and a change in Gaza's leadership, after a civil war between *Hamas* and the *Fatah* by 2007. Aside from how one might abhor the intense violence enacted by members of *Hamas* against their defeated political opponents, one might also feel dismay that they in the end seem to have offered relatively little improvement in the lives of Gazans.[137] The *Hamas* track record of providing social services and their concomitants has been very little in evidence, particularly if one accepts the assertion that they used human shields when engaging the Israelis militarily—although there are those who assert otherwise. [138]

What *Hamas* did do was to expand and extend a program of military activity against Israel, raining hundreds of rockets from Gaza into southern Israel. Those attacks waxed and waned over the course of the next few years—there was even a brief cease-fire, which, depending upon whose perspective one assumes, either means that *Hamas can* renounce violence under the right circumstances and come to the peace conference table; or that *Hamas'* renunciations are smoke screens behind which they consistently prepare greater violence. In any case, after two years of this, the Israelis finally responded with a merciless and blistering attack on Gaza in December 2008 and January 2009, in which not only members of *Hamas* but hundreds of Gazan innocents lost their lives.[139]

Thus, from the increasingly majority Israeli perspective, pulling out of Gaza led only to endless harassment until the ugly day of reckoning finally arrived, for which most Israelis felt there was no choice. Moreover, in a pattern reminiscent of the circumstances in 2000 of failed Israeli-Palestinian negotiations that helped bring Ariel Sharon into the prime minister's office, certainly the catastrophic relationship with Gaza culminating with "Operation Cast Lead" helped return Bibi (Binyamin) Netanyahu to that office—and Netanyahu has not—to date—expressed enthusiasm for any sort of Palestinian state.

On the contrary, he has presented the impression of someone willing and even eager to establish further Israeli settlements in the West Bank. Israelis on the political left are struggling to provide an answer to the question of who on the Palestinian side should be their counterpart—and whether the government of Mahmud Abbas, still in power in the West Bank and still nominally engaged in dialogue with the Israelis, can deliver a true peace treaty with or without the cooperation of the Hamas-led Gazans.

11

THE PALESTINIANS AND ISRAEL

After the June 1967 war, the areas where Palestinians had been resident outside Israel but not assimilated into Arab countries—Gaza and the West Bank—fell under Israeli rule. In military terms, Israel became the occupying authority, echoing the British and Ottoman Turks that came before them as an outsider presence.

So from the perspective of the Palestinians, the nearly fifty years since have mostly been years of humiliation and frustration. Particularly in the last few years this has become intensified by the post-peace-talks collapse and with it the *Second Intifada* on the one hand and the Sharonist and post-Sharonist mood of Israel on the other. It is certainly true that suicide bombing targeting children on school buses and teenagers in discos or celebrants of Passover Seders fall outside the lines of behavior that might fill Israelis with trust in the humanity of the Palestinians. But so are the events precipitated by an occupying authority that people fear that every flower contains an explosive within its pistil, thus undermining Israeli humanity as it *affects* Palestinians.[140] From crowded border checkpoints, to the construction of a security fence and sometimes wall that slices and dices the West Bank, to the overwhelming attack on Gaza, many—perhaps most—Palestinians despair of the willingness of the Israelis to really live side by side in peace with them.

What choice do the occupied have in this state? Most Israeli Jews think that because the Palestinians refused to accept the "generous offer" they wished to impose on them, they should have waited patiently and continued talking indefinitely. But since February 2001, if not earlier, the Palestinians have not had anyone to talk to or anything to talk about, apart from cosmetic changes in the way they are being dominated or an agreement to turn the occupation state back from temporary to permanent. . . And the occupation continues, the violence continues, the dispossession continues. What choice do the Palestinians have?[141]

I can imagine what it was like in Ram'Allah when an F-16 bombed the police station there. I am not talking about civilians who were killed there—cooks from Gaza, not troops. I am talking about bombing a densely populated city. I am talking about liquidating people on the main street, from a helicopter, with three passersby also killed. It's impossible today to say that this was "collateral damage," that we didn't intend to kill civilians, because when a plane bombs a populated city, you take into account that civilians could get killed. . . I read this week what the head of the Civil Administration, Brigadier General Dov Tzadka, said about the authorizations he gives to demolish houses and groves, and how the army then goes hyperactive and levels the area he authorized twice . . . I am constantly dumb-founded at how these people get up every morning and go to work. . .[142]

The PA [Palestinian Authority, empowered with responsibility for civic affairs in the Territories after the Oslo Accords] was given responsibility for civic affairs, like sewage, education, and road-building, for three million Palestinians. . .

But. . . it was administrative control over people without authority over most of the area in which they lived, and without any room for development, a requirement for every government... Nearly every administrative function by the PA required approval by the Israeli authorities. . . Israel controlled—and continues to control—all external borders, the passages inside the West Bank and from it to Gaza and back, the water sources, the economy, the movement of population into the Territories, and the registration of the Palestinian population.[143]

The authors of the three passages quoted above are neither Palestinian nor Arab, neither European nor American. They are Israelis who are part of the small but significant voice that persistently speaks out regarding how impossible conditions have been for nearly fifty years and have become increasingly so for at least fifteen years for the Palestinians under the Israeli occupation, as well as the deleterious effect of occupation on the Israeli soul. The point is: if patriotic Israelis feel this way, how must the Palestinians themselves feel? How can they be expected to trust Israel when, with the shift from one regime to another, the mood of reconciliation seems to alter so dramatically? How can they overcome their distrust and distaste honed through decades of this experience and come back to the table of negotiation?

And if we step back beyond 1967 to 1948, we may see this condition as exponentially multiplied: the Palestinian view is that of having largely been pushed from lands that then became Israel in that year, into land much of which was occupied by Israel in 1967. Rashid Khalidi puts it simply that "most of the population of the Strip is not originally from there, but rather from a swath of villages in the southern regions of Israel, whose inhabitants were driven or fled there during the fighting of 1948–49, and were never allowed to return from there to their homes."[144] Put otherwise, the rocket attacks into southern Israel from a Gaza Strip are viewed—at least by some Palestinians— as attacks into territory from which they had been forcibly ejected in 1948 and therefore *still* as attacks against occupiers, not legitimate inhabitants.

The question then becomes: is there a solution to a problem in which fundamentally the two antagonists both feel legitimately entitled to the same piece of property? This is particularly vexed when we have no way of gauging in an objective manner who was precisely where sixty years ago, who did or did not try to return to where when it was possible, and how possible it was at that time. We might then further ask to what extent violence is justified if the one committing the violence feels fundamentally dispossessed and that there is no other way to reverse the dispossession? And we might ask how to weigh the levels of violence from the two sides of the conflict: is there a different weight to be given to the two sides, Israeli and Palestinian, given who dwells where and who possesses the more substantial military power?

Moreover, if we are to grasp the layers of this issue within the larger context of the Middle East, it is important to keep in mind that during the nearly fifty years since 1967, the complications of functioning as a people have not been limited to those imposed on the Palestinians by Israeli governance. The most obvious example is the massacre achieved by the Jordanians under King Hussein between September 1970 and July 1971—known in Palestinian historiography as Black September—in which more Palestinians died than in all of the combined confrontations with Israel between 1948 and 2000.[145] And when the Israelis invaded Lebanon in 1982, because that is where militant factions of Palestinians had established themselves in the aftermath of the Black September debacle, they were initially hailed as liberators by the local population, which had been brutalized and oppressed by the Palestinian militants among them for several years. Nonetheless, just as Israel both overstayed its welcome in Lebanon and facilitated actions against Muslim Palestinians by Christian Lebanese allies of the Israelis in the 1980s, so the mainstream population of Palestinians found themselves in increasingly straitened conditions as the Israeli occupation plowed on through the 1970s and 1980s and into the early 1990s.[146]

More fundamentally, Palestinians became increasingly aware that their future would not be guaranteed by external forces: the various Arab states that made noises or even supplied guns or money for their cause would, in the end, not be able to pressure Israel sufficiently to provoke consideration of a Palestinian State. With that in mind, the willingness to escalate antagonistic efforts toward an *intifada* of the Israelis grew. There is a further ironic twist in this. The Israeli incursion into and continued presence in Lebanon after 1982 had, as one of its unanticipated consequences, the creation of a new Palestinian organization. In the aftermath of the hornets' nest of interrelationships that had been stirred up, there emerged *Hizb'Allah*—the "Party of God"—a radical Shi'i movement that had, in part, drawn its inspiration from the religious revolution in Iran that had replaced the Shah with the Ayatollah Khomeini in 1979. The tactic that they adopted—of suicide car bombings—which first manifested itself in the attack that left 241 US Marines and 30 Israeli soldiers in Tyre dead in late 1983, would eventually redirect itself, after the Israelis finally pulled out of Lebanon, into Israel itself.[147]

By then, a complication and a breakthrough for Palestinian life arrived at the center of the historical stage. This was the eight-year-long war between Iraq and Iran in 1980–88 and in the aftermath of that war, the invasion of Kuwait by Iraq and the attack on Iraqi forces by an American-led coalition that shaped the period 1990–92. What this complication meant for the Palestinians was twofold. First, hundreds of thousands of Palestinians making very good salaries in Kuwait, whose labors supported the economic infrastructure back home, were suddenly out of jobs and forced out of Kuwait and back to Palestine. Second, Yassir Arafat's ill-fated attempt to act as a go-between in the period leading up to the Iraqi invasion of Kuwait and from the invasion to the time of the American-led coalition's arrival on the scene, ironically, worsened the Palestinian leader's image and the Palestinian position in the West, as well as among the Arab leadership that joined the coalition. It was difficult to distinguish Arafat as a go-between from Arafat as a supporter of Saddam—coupled with the cheering by some Palestinians for the Scud missiles that Iraq sent toward Israel, the image was created of Palestinians as supporters of Saddam Hussein. All of this undercut the Palestinian cause by creating a perception throughout much of the world that they were not interested in peace.

Nonetheless, a breakthrough came shortly after the complication of these events with the Madrid negotiations of late 1991 and Oslo Accords of 1993 that suddenly seemed to open new possibilities in Israel-Palestine relations. The Israeli Lebanon venture had something to do with this breakthrough, as well. Increasing numbers of Israelis were beginning to doubt the inviolable sanctity of their army as a consequence of that debacle, and from that doubt they questioned where occupation was leading them. The internal debate had many extraordinary side moments, as when Yael Dayan, a new member of Parliament and daughter of Moshe Dayan, icon of the 1967 June War, met with Arafat in Tunis (to which he moved his headquarters after the dual removals by the Jordanians from Jordan in the early 1970s and by the Israelis from Lebanon in the early 1980s) and referred to him as a "symbol of peace and compromise," rather than with the virulent descriptive language typically aimed at him by Israelis.

After the handshake on the White House lawn in September 1993 between Yitzhak Rabin and Yassir Arafat, there was a period of heady hopes on both sides of the Israel-Palestine fence. Those hopes were nurtured by several factors. The first of these was Rabin's capacity to think outside the box of historical fear, to focus less on history and more on future possibility, and to convince a majority of Israelis to follow his lead. There was also the willingness on the other side for Arafat to believe in and convince Palestinians that the path on which they were now moving would ultimately lead, *finally*, to the end of their frustrations and humiliations and to the realization of their dream of an independent state. These hopes were further stoked by the skillful diplomacy of Bill Clinton, commanding the trust of both sides, and mediating between them to facilitate their coming closer together as negotiations moved forward.

In the aftermath of that moment on the White House lawn, a flurry of events pushed the peace process forward . . . and then backward. King Hussein of Jordan signed a peace agreement with Israel in 1994, at the same time renouncing any further interest in the West Bank territory that had been under his control between 1948 and 1967. This arrangement, together with Egypt's abandonment of Gaza, accomplished several ends simultaneously. The peace between Israel and two of its most significant Arab neighbors, which had evolved between the end of the 1970s and the early 1990s, paired with the peace negotiations with the Palestinians, seemed to presage a broader and fuller peace in that corner of the region.

Hope evolved in spite of the unresolved relationship between Israel and Syria and in spite of the question of Lebanon, vis-à-vis Syria, the Palestinians, Israel, and itself. At the same time, the precise answer to the question of how to shape a Palestinian future, placed simply into Israeli or Israeli and Palestinian hands, now presented itself as a potential time bomb should certain things go awry. The question had arrived after more than twenty-five years not only of Israeli military occupation of Gaza and the West Bank, but of expanding settlements of Jews in both those territories.

Things did go awry but in the unexpected form of the assassination of Rabin by a Jewish Israeli right-wing extremist. Encouraged by his rabbi both to believe that Rabin's movement toward denouement was leading to the giving up of lands divinely designated for the Jews and to imagine that murdering the prime minister would be justified, indeed praised by God, a man named Yigal Amir shot Rabin down at an enormous peace rally in Tel Aviv on the evening of November 4, 1995.[148] In retrospect, what the madman murdered was the hope for peace for both Israel and the Palestinians—at least until such time as another leader capable of thinking outside the box of fear would arise. However, initially this may not have seemed to be the consequence of Rabin's death; negotiations between Israelis and Palestinians continued, some progress continued to be made with regard to Israel's relinquishing authority to the Palestinians over some areas within the Territories, limitations with regard to new settlements remained, and a moratorium continued on terrorist attacks against Israelis by Palestinians.

As the Clinton administration slid deeper into its second term, discussions moved to the lush setting of the Wye Plantation outside Washington, DC, and complicated arrangements shifted forward. The Wye River Memorandum signed by Prime Minister Binyamin (Benjamin) Netanyahu and Palestinian Authority Chairman Yassir Arafat, witnessed by President Clinton on October 23, 1998, provided an interim agreement in which "The Israeli side's implementation of the first and second Further Re-Deployment will consist of the transfer to the Palestinian side of 13% from Area C as follows: 1% to Area A and 12% to Area B. The Palestinian side has informed that it will allocate an area/areas amounting to 3% from Area B to be designated as Green Areas and/or Nature Reserves. The Israeli side will retain in these Green Areas/Nature Reserves the overriding security responsibility for the purpose of protecting Israelis and confronting the threat of terrorism. . . ."

The memorandum put into place both more detailed redispositions of territory than had been articulated in the Oslo Accords and further delineations of cooperation not only between the Israelis and Palestinians but, under prescribed conditions, trilateral activity that involved the United States as well. It encompassed security issues and matters such as the opening of an International Airport in the Gaza Strip and broader cooperative economic issues. It laid out an intricate and precise timeline for events and meetings, to culminate with a meeting scheduled for May 4, 1999, by which time the matters encompassed were to have been dealt with and plans for the next phase of negotiations would take place.

Those familiar with Israel's political scene and hopeful of progress toward a final peace with the Palestinians, that would ultimately include a viable independent Palestinian state and an agreeable handling of Jerusalem from both Israeli and Palestinian perspectives, breathed a collective sigh of relief when Ehud Barak became prime minister in 1999. Whereas Netanyahu had been a reluctant partner, pushed hard by Clinton toward the negotiation table, Barak seemed very much to be cut in the Rabin image: a soldier with leftist sympathies who was eager to make peace.

With optimism, the last round of Clinton-mediated talks moved forward, reconvening at Camp David, the historic site where Jimmy Carter had successfully brokered a peace agreement between Israel and Egypt that marked the first crack in the wall of hopelessness of Arab-Israeli relations two decades earlier. There Prime Minister Barak offered to withdraw from between 86 and 91 percent of the West Bank—but then suddenly everything collapsed. Ostensibly, the reason for the collapse is that, although Chairman Arafat was presented with terms that eventually offered 97 percent of what he sought and, rather than either accepting or suggesting that he would need to consider and counterpropose, he argued that what he had been offered was not enough, that it would be suicidal for him to accept it—and he stormed out of the negotiations. There is little question in most analysts' minds that Arafat was an important part of the problem; that he was ultimately much more comfortable as an embattled revolutionary than as a paper-pushing diplomat seeking to engender a stable state in peaceful coexistence with the erstwhile object of his revolution.[149] As Salah Ta'mari, one of Arafat's strong supporters, observed in 1998, "When it comes down to it, it's not so romantic dealing with sewage, taxation, salaries, and unemployment."[150]

But a closer look at what he was offered helps explain his response, although responding with a counterproposal would unquestionably have been more fruitful than merely storming out of the negotiations. The precise structuring of territories—in which barrier settlements and roads that divide the territory were to stay in place—would have deprived a newly independent Palestine of most of what it needed to function. This includes, to give one salient example, control of water supplies through access to the aquifer below *the surface* of the area under discussion.[151] It may well have also made it very difficult for the Palestinians to believe that Israel would ever accept a genuine Palestinian state without Israeli barriers imbedded within it.

What the world saw was Arafat's tantrum, but what it failed to perceive was the precise nature of what he rejected. What it also heard little about was the continuation, in spite of the tantrum, of discussions between Israeli and Palestinian negotiators determined to arrive at a solution to their joint problem. After Camp David, these discussions took place back in the Middle East, in Taba, Egypt. It was there and then, in January, 2001—during the very last days of the Clinton administration—that the next impediment to peace emerged. The Israeli elections approached and Barak's apparent failure to assure a stable and solid peace had pushed the Israeli electorate toward the unabashedly hawk-like stance espoused by Ariel Sharon, who had led the brutal incursion into Lebanon in 1982 and made a personal fortune as the housing minister. Amidst this, Barak suddenly pulled his negotiating team out of the discussions that had been inching forward.[152]

Barak presumably imagined that in so doing, and thus in presenting himself as more hard-line than his earlier stance had suggested, he might not lose the election. But more fundamentally—perhaps when push came to shove— he could not step outside the box of distrust and fear that would have moved the discussions forward, instead of abandoning them to the violence that has ensued in the seventeen years since. It is certainly true that Arafat did nothing to help assuage this distrust and fear, but Barak's fear cannot be discounted when trying to understand what ultimately drove the situation toward failure.[153] Sharon was elected, the "Second *Intifada*" was duly begun, the brutal attempts to suppress it blossomed, and the circle of fear, mistrust, and violence spiraled upward.

If Barak and Arafat, each in his own way, contributed to the collapse, Sharon was doubly at its heart. Not only did he cast his corpulent shadow across Barak's consciousness but he also personally blew on the very sort of embers that could and did become the flames of the *intifada*. I refer to his notorious visit to the Temple Mount/Haram al'Sharif area on September 28, 2000. It was certainly his right as a Jew, as an Israeli, as a human being—as a private individual—to make that visit. But to do so accompanied by a retinue of one thousand policemen, as the head of the Likud party, both gave to the visit an official air and offered an obvious provocation to the Palestinians. In the context of still-delicate questions regarding the ultimate status of Jerusalem in a future two-state reality, it smelled of a political statement, an assertion that Jerusalem would remain non-negotiable, all-Jewish property. Confrontation with Palestinian demonstrators followed; these led to the deaths of four Palestinians, the injuring of some two hundred, and the wounding of fourteen Israeli policemen.

While it is true that a subsequent investigation by an American-led commission concluded that the visit by Sharon ultimately seemed to be "no more than an internal political act; neither were we provided with persuasive evidence that the Palestinian Authority planned the uprising," nonetheless the Palestinians would continue to see the event as provoked by Sharon and the Israelis would continue to see the demonstrations and subsequent rioting as part of an Arafat-initiated *intifada* designed to help scuttle the peace talks. Thus the beginning of the "Second *Intifada*"—also known as the *al'Aqsa*

Intifada—actually preceded the collapse of the final-attempt talks at Taba, and no doubt added fuel to Barak's inability to think outside the box of fear and distrust.

Before moving forward to pick up the thread of what has transpired between the disaster of 2000–2001 and the present, it is important to step back for a moment and to readdress the matter of selective memory and the recurrent theme of fear and distrust. It has become too common in the last few years to assert two things that confound all efforts to resolve tensions in the Middle East. The first is to speak or write as if the sole complication for the region is the Israeli-Palestinian issue; that to solve *that* problem would be to lead us out of the overall regional morass—although, arguably, ISIS/ISIL has recently helped mold an awareness on the part of a growing number of people that there are, indeed, other issues within the region's morass that have little to do with the Israeli-Palestinian issue. The second is to speak or write as if the Israel-Palestine problem emerged in 1967 with the Israeli conquest of the West Bank, Sinai, and the Golan Heights, and therefore that the root of the problem is Israel's intransigence regarding matters such as Palestinian statehood and the status of Jerusalem.

It is certainly true that Israel has gradually come to hold most of the cards in this matter. It is also true that a key to the failure to resolve this particular problem is the inability of a majority of Israelis and their leaders—particularly now that we have arrived full circle from Sharon back to Netanyahu—to think outside of fear and distrust. That has led to unilateral actions such as the highly charged decision to build a barrier to separate Israel and protect it from Palestinians, every one of whom seems to be assumed by Israel's leadership to be a potential or even likely suicide bomber. It must be noted that, on the one hand, this "security fence" has cut down the number of suicide bombings within Israel by more than 90 percent. However, on the other hand, the decision of precisely where the barrier goes and what it encloses and excludes was not only arrived at unilaterally, but seems to maximize both the discomfort level of the Palestinians and the comfort level of particular Israelis, namely those inhabiting the "settlements."

More fundamentally, as occupiers, the Israelis have grown into the ugly role they too often now play, unfamiliar to the principles that undergird Judaism but all too familiar to history at large. In other words, they have not been able to escape normalizing—a desideratum when it was articulated by Herzl over a century ago, and perhaps a desideratum where hamburgers and shiny cars are concerned, but not where oppressing and humiliating another people is concerned. This development can be seen in scores of incidents, small and large, involving Palestinians at checkpoints and elsewhere. It is also true that the consequences of nearly fifty years of Israeli occupation, culminating with a post-failed-peace-effort-era of unprecedented cruelty, has imbued the Palestinians with profound distaste for Israelis and, more important, profound distrust of them. They are as certain that the Israelis will never yield to peaceful coexistence as the Israelis are that the Palestinians never will.

And just as every frustrated radical who becomes a suicide bomber is construed by Israel to be a component of a monolithic Palestinian bloodlust, every God-clinging Jewish radical who pitches a tent in the Territories and every Israeli soldier who is abusive in his interrogation of a Palestinian youth—or old man or pregnant woman—is construed by Palestinians as a component of a monolithic arrogant Israel, lusting for more territory. As every Jewish settler in Hebron thinks of every Arab in the city as a blood relative of those Arabs who massacred sixty Jews in the riots of 1929 and don't even acknowledge that there were Arabs who hid whole Jewish families to protect them at that time, every Arab in Hebron believes that every settler is another Baruch Goldstein, who gunned down twenty-nine worshippers in the Ibrahimi Mosque in February 25, 1994.[154] Fear and frustration feed frustration and fear from both ends of an endless line.[155]

To untangle the tangled web of issues defining the Israel-Palestine conflict, we must not only step out of received patterns of explanation but take into account the threads that began their interweave before 1967. We might step back as far as the period between World War I and 1948, during which no proposal, however modest as far as allotting territory to the Jews, was acceptable either to the Palestinians or to their Arab brethren. If we have seen that the British and the French certainly helped sow discord between the Jewish and Arab communities, nonetheless during those decades it appears at least that the Palestinians and their brethren were the intransigent ones.

We might jump from that era to the next, between 1948 and 1967, in which many Palestinians neither stayed nor returned to Israel after its independence; it was an admittedly small window of opportunity to return, and it is fair to say that Israel was not encouraging it, but then neither were Arab leaders at that time. Nonetheless, the result was that these individuals found themselves in territories controlled by Jordan and Egypt. It was the Jordanians and the Egyptians who created the refugee camps in which for two decades enormous frustration built up; that frustration was already firmly in place when the camps and the territories where they were located fell into Israeli hands after the Six-Day War. I might add that at that time, Israel seems from most accounts not to have intended to maintain control over those territories, but hoped to use them as bargaining chips in the peace negotiations for which the

Jewish State was at that time so desperate, and in which the Arab states, for their part, seem to have had no interest.[156]

Nor, it must be further added, did the Arabs as a whole exhibit much concern for their Palestinian brothers and sisters after 1967 either. It was only in the aftermath of the 1973 Yom Kippur War, when the military option regarding Israel's survival or destruction seemed clearly to have failed, that the larger Arab world began to use the Palestinians and concern for their welfare as a chip with which to generate anti-Israel sentiment on a world scale. If we continue forward toward the Oslo Accords and their aftermath in the mid-1990s—recalling that the darkest moment for Palestinians between 1967 and 1992 was Black September—we find the following situation. That apart from the Israeli failure to be more aggressive with regard to dismantling recent Jewish settlements in the Territories, and in thinking seriously toward the shaping of a Palestinian state with a capital, possibly in Jerusalem, there were other issues militating against success, including that neither the Arab nor the Western powers, who promised funds to help develop a Palestinian infrastructure, came forth with the volume of support that had been promised. Moreover, of the funds that *were* poured into Palestine, there is good evidence that a disproportionate amount ended up in Yassir Arafat's Swiss bank accounts. There seem, then, to have been failures on all sides, the repercussions of which were furthered exponentially by the assassination of Rabin.

All of which must be kept in mind, if meaningful efforts to end the conflict are to be pursued. Since 1973, to repeat, Israel has been largely in charge of the situation. Arafat was placed by Israel under house arrest;[157] settlements continued to be built in the Territories; suicide bombings were rising and falling in number without a rational reason; both the Israelis and the Palestinians were in the grips of terror regarding each other; and the United States, under the Bush administration, rather than assuming a role of leadership and intermediation, had reduced itself to a blind backer of Israeli policy and a source of both Palestinian and Arab distrust, not only because of its unqualified support of Israel but because the president refused even to speak with Arafat who, regardless of what one might think of him, was the duly appointed and elected leader and spokesperson of the Palestinians.[158]

At the same time, interestingly enough, President Bush pushed for a conclusive plan—"a detailed blueprint for an Israeli-Palestinian permanent status peace agreement . . . based on the Clinton parameters of December 2000," and building "on former permanent status negotiations, including those held in Camp David and Taba." The two sides continued to hammer out details for two years, until October 2003, at which time the Swiss government stepped in to offer Geneva as a site in which to finalize the remaining details—for example, regarding water. The "Geneva Accord offer[ed] a real and mutually agreed upon possibility for ending the conflict between the two sides . . . " Alas, despite the efforts of fifty-two Israeli and Palestinian discussants and sig- natories—from politicians to poets—the positive energy that held sway during the discussions never translated to a new reality outside them.[159]

In recent years, two important changes have come about, which require further comment. The first is the change in the American presidency from Bush to Obama, and with that change, new possibilities that seemed to be taking shape with respect to the overall discussion of the Middle East morass and the specifics of the Israel-Palestine issue. The second matter within the matrix is that in the aftermath of the 2005 Israeli pullout from Gaza and the arrival to political hegemony there by *Hamas*, there followed a fairly continu- ous rain of small-scale rockets onto Israeli towns and villages within striking distance of the Gaza border. The eventual Israeli response was, as has been noted, a massive assault on Gaza, which some have seen as justified and others as excessive.[160]

There are several angles from which to view the Israeli counterassault. The Israeli perspective—that there was no choice—I considered toward the end of the previous chapter. The regional and international perspective I shall con- sider in the chapter that follows. For the issues being addressed in this chapter, we must pay further attention to the Palestinian perspective, which sees the strike as confirmation that Israel cannot be trusted not to resort to extreme violence when conditions become uncomfortable: they see themselves as always looking at the Israelis from the receiving end of a gun barrel and never being quite sure when it will go off.

More than that, there is what Rashid Khalidi refers to as:

the obstinate refusal of both the Bush administration and the Israeli government to accept the results of the 2006 Palestinian Legislative Council elections, and their international campaign to try to force the Palestinians to go back on their democratic choice, [which] is also crucially important in understanding why Palestinians were fight- ing over the ruins of their refugee camps in 2007. This campaign has included Israel's withholding of Palestinian taxes, and an American- led international financial and diplomatic boycott of the [*Hamas*-led] PA. . . . [I]t involves the Israeli refusal to ease its choking restrictions on movement and goods . . . and most ominously, the Palestinian slide into the abyss involves United States government arming, training, funding and encouragement of *Fatah* in order to bring it to attack its rivals.[161]

A reader of the above passage should recognize that Khalidi writes without attempting to minimize the responsibility of the Palestinian leadership in general or *Hamas* in particular in shaping the conditions to which the Gazans were relegated by 2007. He was writing before the major escalation toward the incessant rocket attacks into Israel orchestrated by *Hamas,* which in turn culminated with the 2009 Israeli attack into the Gaza Strip. But that time-blip matter underscores the issue of perspective: the Israelis felt provoked by the rockets; the Palestinians felt provoked to support *Hamas* whether or not most of them supported the rockets. The desperation leading to that support is a function of conditions since 1967, but also since 1948—and perhaps ultimately even a good deal further than that: even beyond 1920 and beyond 1517 to what starting point?

This brings us to a final issue with regard to the paradoxes of Israel-Palestine history, memory, and perspective. For Jews in the second half of the twentieth century there are, as we have seen, two major events that have defined that century, the Holocaust and the establishment of the State of Israel. Jewish Israelis have come to commemorate the one event and celebrate the other in back-to-back proximity among the annual cycle of celebrations and commemorations that mark their calendar. Both of those types of events coincide as one, as it were, on the Palestinian calendar. The process of establishing the Jewish state was a process that included among its details the destruction of more than four hundred Arab villages during the exodus of their inhabitants. The moment is referred to in the historiography of those refugees as *al-Nakba*—"The Catastrophe."[162]

My intention here is not to weigh the comparative responsibility of Arab and Israeli leadership in provoking that exodus and its attendant destruction or in creating the refugee community, because each side will argue its case until it is blue in the face without convincing the other, and I have yet to read an outsider's account that failed to exhibit strong prejudice in one direction or the other. The issue is also not to argue the objective legitimacy of comparing the Palestinian *Nakba* of exile and destruction to the mass murder of Jews accomplished by the Nazis. If this were a matter of sheer numbers, that would be absurd. As Anton La Guardia observes, "the extermination of the *Shoah* belongs to a different universe of evil to the dispossession of Palestinians in the *Nakba.*"[163]

Nonetheless, as Israel has remained the governing authority in the Territories for nearly five decades now—particularly during the last sixteen years, in the context of the Second *Intifada*—the security methodology of occupation has increasingly morphed in ways that to *some* historians echoes the method enacted toward Jews in Nazi Germany in 1933–39. But that does not justify the injudicious and angry labeling of the Israelis as Nazis. The Final

Solution evolved by the Nazis for their Jewish victims has no counterpart at all in the Israeli treatment of the Palestinians.[164]

One of the starting points on both sides of the Israeli-Palestinian conflict must be to acknowledge and respect both the suffering and the *sense* of suffering that each side has endured. Jews, some of whom still retain the house keys taken by their ancestors from Spain after the expulsion of 1492 must recognize at least equal legitimacy of emotion pertaining to Palestinians who retain the house keys taken by their grandparents or great-grandparents after fleeing the nascent state of Israel in 1948. Palestinians need to recognize the differences between the Jews who arrived into Palestine and have shaped a state and the Turks, British, and French who arrived into the region with very different goals in generations and centuries past. Such rethinking can be the crux of reconciliation in its deepest sense.

12

THE UNITED STATES, THE INTERNATIONAL COMMUNITY, AND ISRAEL-PALESTINE

One might ask what it is that the three principal current forces—Israel, the Palestinians, and the United States—might consider as a way out of this conundrum.[165] What follows in my discussion assumes a greater level of both reason and courage than is apparent in the current leadership, so I recognize that we are not likely to find my "proposals" executed in the immediate future.[166] But I would hope that they would at least provoke thinking as serious as that necessary to grasp the complexities that I have been seeking to unravel.

The first shift is one that I would make were I the prime minster of Israel to combat the cycle of violence. It would be not to dismantle Jewish settlements in the Territories, but to unilaterally withdraw Israeli military forces from the Territories—or at a minimum, to withdraw them to encompass the three areas conceded by the Palestinians at Camp David in exchange for comparable territory from behind the "Green Line." Or to withdraw them into a series of security outposts.

There is an interesting aspect to what at first may strike some readers as overly simplistic. Among the institutions within Israel that were either born or received a new lease on life in the aftermath of the Six-Day War of 1967 as part of the upsurge in Jewish religious fervor that the six-day "miracle" yielded was *Merkaz ha-Rav* Yeshiva in Jerusalem. It was founded by the first Ashkenazi Chief Rabbi of Palestine, Avraham ha-Cohen Kook—to whom I earlier referred as the Orthodox rabbi who had embraced Zionism in the first part of the twentieth century and argued to his followers that Zionism's secular shapers might well be instruments in God's hands for bringing about messianic redemption.[167]

When Rabbi Kook died in 1935, leadership of the yeshiva passed to his son, Rabbi Tzvi Yehudah ha-Cohen Kook, and in the course of the 1950s the ideological rapprochement between Orthodox Judaism and the secular Zionist community—now the State of Israel—tightened to the point that the *Merkaz* became a center of nationalist religious thought, asserting the state and its strong right arm—the army—as holy elements in God's plan.

It was the *Merkaz* and its leader, the younger Rabbi Kook, who in turn became the center of religious rightist assertions after the 1967 war regarding the God-given intention for a Greater Israel. If at first glance all we might note is the irony that so many ultra-Orthodox who opposed the Zionist idea now oppose anything less than its broadest geopolitical interpretation—and thus offer a solid stumbling block on the road to peace—a second glance offers hope.

Religious passion impelled Rabbi Kook, on Israel Independence Day, 1967, to deliver a sermon in his yeshiva in which he rent his spiritual garments rather than celebrated—because parts of the land intended by God for the Jews had been given into Arab hands after the 1948 war.[168] The same passion caused him to expound upon the events of a few weeks later as divinely accomplished, and to teach thereafter that to give up any of the land of Greater Israel was a sin as serious as idolatry and murder.

Rabbi Kook viewed the State as part of the Divine Plan for Redemption and its leaders therefore as individuals who "should be honored as 'the judge that shall be in those days' (Deut. 17:9). What to do when the state failed to follow God's will to settle the land? The conundrum was resolved by according to the state a conditional holiness. *The state was the means of settling the land, as opposed to the traditional Zionist view of settling the land as a means of creating the state.*"[169] But in that case, my proposal should accord perfectly well with the needs of Orthodox settlers in the Territories: if the state pulls back to the Green Line, that does not eliminate their divinely appointed work of settling the land. This would also be consistent, in fact, with Spiritual Zionism as it was espoused from the beginning by thinkers such as Ahad Ha'Am, for whom statehood was the wrong goal of a Zionist movement whose purpose was the spiritual rejuvenation of Judaism, not a physical refuge for Jews.[170] I am not being "cute" with this argument; I am addressing the religious right in its own terms.

If, in turn, a fence need be built to assure security, then build it, but along the Green Line, rather than in and out of gerrymandered potential Palestinian areas of governance. I would certainly negotiate with the Palestinians to allow the Jewish settlers to stay—but settlers should know that they would now be citizens of the new state that I would be the first to recognize: the independent

State of Palestine. And in withdrawing to the Green Line, I would also be leaving behind not only sufficient landmass, but sufficient landmass of quality with respect to water and other resources to make a Palestinian state viable. More than that, I would be leading Israelis to a perspectival change in attitude: leaving behind not only Palestinian territory but, more significantly, surrendering control of Palestinian life.[171]

Were I the leader of the Palestinians, I would reiterate to the Israelis and to the Palestinians how emphatic my intention is to arrive at a final peace with Israel. This would include doing what Arafat never did, discrediting and delegitimizing terror—not merely *renouncing* its use, as Arafat did do in September 1993, but emphatically *condemning* its use. I would make every effort to root out extremists and express with warmth my hope and expectation that Jewish settlers who choose to live within our borders would be accepted, safe, and indeed welcome. I would make it clear that I do recognize how limited is the paradigm that inspired *al-Fatah* in the early 1960s: that, as the French could be evicted from Algeria through armed struggle, the Jews could be evicted from Israel by similar means. The Jews are not France and the Palestinians are not the Algerians.

The counterpart of the change in Israeli attitude toward Palestinian Arabs would be the change in Palestinian attitude that I would promote: that we are not merely and always *victims*. That sensibility, shaped into a strategy and not merely a condition by Arafat, has led to a sense of not being accountable and of not being required to compromise. As Shibley Telhami puts it, "This tendency to avoid accountability has become an aspect of the political culture of the Middle East. In part, it is explained by a pervasive narrative of victimization.... This sentiment is held by governments in the region as well as members of the public."[172] In abandoning that strategy, I would be leading the Palestinians forward toward an ability to negotiate successfully with the Israelis and offering the Israelis reasons to believe that negotiations could succeed.[173]

These measures on both sides might help push all parties beyond the confines of fear and distrust, given time. They would also make feasible the negotiation of another matter: Jerusalem. And I would, were I leader of the one side or leader of the other, express my willingness to share the city as a dual capital. To a certain extent it has functioned that way since 1967, in that the Muslim Holy Places have been administered not by the Israelis but by Palestinian authorities. So to extend that principle to the point where one authority is not subsidiary to the other, but both stand on equal ground and join together to maintain the city, is far-fetched more for psychological than for logistical reasons. In fact, negotiators on both sides had arrived virtually to that point of agreement before the entire situation collapsed in 2000.

Part of the oddly interesting reason that they had come to agreement on this arrangement was that Bill Clinton posed to both sides a question designed to help them think about the earthbound Jerusalem, instead of being so intensely focused on its heavenly counterpart. The two groups of negotiators were enjoined to come up with—and did so with a remarkable degree of ease and consensus—a list of sixty municipal needs that the two sides could share. They laid out a tentative "plan" to deal with everyday details—from garbage disposal to water and electricity service to the delivery of mail. To coadminister the mundane aspects of the city and leave the sacred sites to the various religious authorities may not please everyone, but surely the majority of reasonable individuals on both sides who hope for peace rather than more violence could embrace such a notion.

There are, I believe, compelling arguments that could convince my fellow Israelis and my fellow Palestinians to follow my lead, which does not, of course, guarantee that they *would* listen. I would argue to both sides that the only hope for our children and our grandchildren to grow up in an environment that might be construed as normal is one in which "basic training" refers to sports and not war; that if we wish for long, prosperous lives for our descendants then we can only wish for a framework of peace in order to accomplish that. I would argue to my Israeli constituents that no wall, however high, and no fence, however strong, will guarantee this as effectively as a determination to live side by side in peace. I would remind my Israeli constituents that if we remain in control of the Territories, we will be a minority within our own country by the year 2020—or 2025, or 2035, but sooner or later—and that accordingly, either the nature of Israel as a Jewish state or as a democracy will by definition be lost.

I would argue to my Palestinian constituents that no number of suicide bombers will drive the Israelis out or destroy the State of Israel—that the Israelis are not the Turks or the British, regardless of where the Zionist ideology and its initial primary population derived from geographically or ethnically, and I would remind my Palestinian constituents that an enormous percentage of the Israeli population derives from the Middle East and Africa. Their parents, grandparents, and ancestors for many generations have suffered too much for too long for them to give up and go—and there is no other *home* for them to go back to.

I would remind my Israeli constituents that the Oslo Accords set in motion a series of significant forward movements with regard to Arab-Israeli relations even if it was less than most would have wished. Thus, not only did Jordan move rapidly to conclude a peace agreement with Israel, but Morocco, Tunisia, Qatar, and Oman began to develop economic relations with it as well. Moreover, acts of terror precipitously dropped year by year between 1993 and

2000, from Oslo to Camp David, one of the consequences of which was that Israel's economy boomed as it was able to focus on more than its military.

I would argue most strenuously that refusing to think toward a Palestinian shaping of what Jews had demanded be shaped for them a century earlier—an independent, autonomous state—cuts deeply into the very Jewishness that, in its most justice-obsessed sense, defines Israel at its best. It is indeed embodied in Israel's own Declaration of Independence; the difficulties of living up to the democratic ideals posited in that document are rendered exponentially more difficult by the Occupation.[174]

The moral Jewishness of the Jewish State is being sacrificed to—hijacked by—the inevitable inhumanity of being an oppressor.[175] Far from having merited the right to oppress others as long-term victims in history, the Jews—of all people—are obligated to learn from history and to seek to eradicate oppression wherever they can, nowhere more emphatically than in the heart of a Jewish state. This is contained in that most essential of rabbinic phrases, *tikkun olam*.[176] I would plead with my Israeli constituents not to forget the history of the Jews that led up to and culminated in the Holocaust; that to oppress another people is virulently antithetical both to Jewish teachings and to what, as humans in the best (as opposed to the worst) sense, Jews should have learned from our own experience.

Ultimately, I would argue to them that they have no choice. As long as the current status quo remains, with occupiers of a territory whose inhabitants are dispossessed and disenfranchised in their own lands, humiliated daily, and frustrated constantly in their attempt to live lives of dignity and hope, that as long as that situation obtains, violence will breed itself and Israel will have no choice but to humiliate, frustrate, and suppress the Palestinians. The cycle of viciousness will continue to circle around itself. The only solution to that problem is to change the status quo. The only means of changing the status quo, to change the conditions that are deleterious both to the Palestinians *and* to the Israelis, *both* physically *and* spiritually, is to pull back from "the Territories" as well as from an attitude of control, both recognizing a Palestinian State and leaving that state sufficient space and resources to shape itself.

Such changes in conditions and mind-set are easier said than done. It requires a capacity for pushing past inherited distrust and fear—for both Israelis and Palestinians. Barak ultimately lacked it, as did Arafat in the end as well. Did Sharon, ironically and in the end, develop it? The stroke that took him out of the picture as quickly as bullets took Sadat and Rabin out of the picture left us with only speculation regarding how far he might have gone along a peace-seeking road. What of Olmert and Netanyahu? What of Abbas—and those who lead *Hamas*? An important corrolary to this is the matter of past-future thinking. As ugly as the Israeli occupation became in the thirty years between 1967 and 1997, by the end of that time, as the Palestinian Authority (PA) took over control of those areas ceded to it by Rabin, Perez, and then even Netanyahu, the PA operated the prisons with more infamous gusto than the Israelis had: more Palestinians died in *Palestinian* prisons during the first four years of post-Oslo PA control of Gaza and West Bank cities than in *Israeli* prisons. The point is that from whichever side of the fence, the protagonists have to examine their own conduct and not only scrutinize what is happening across the barbed wire.

Here is where another paradox enters the picture. One might argue that if all other parties, near and far, removed themselves from the situation and left the Israelis and the Palestinians to themselves, the situation would have a better likelihood of yielding a successful outcome. But strangely, while that may have been true a century ago or even half a century ago, it certainly is not true now. First, because the Middle East, even where only the Israel-Palestine corner of it is concerned, is not actually limited to Israelis and Palestinians; and second, because of the overly large volume of fear and distrust that has been built up over the decades between Israelis and Palestinians.

With this in mind, the other Arab states must come forth and put their signatures where their mouths have been. Thus beyond Egypt and Jordan, Syria and Iraq, the Saudis and the Libyans must make it clear that they have abandoned their decades' long hostility toward the State of Israel. Obviously, Syria is particularly significant in this matter. It is arguable that Syrian unwillingness to follow Jordan and Egypt toward peace discussions with Israel, even when progress toward peace between Israel and the Palestinians was in place, helped maintain the necessary sparks of antagonism that with the failure of Camp David and Taba became a conflagration. But there is also strong evidence that Hafiz al-Assad was thinking toward peace as he lay dying of cancer. Would he have gone forward or backward had he lived?[177]

This brings back into focus the matter of the Golan Heights—the fear and distrust factor from the Israeli side at the thought of returning the Heights to Syria would require major psychological surgery. This, despite repeated analyses by *Israeli* military experts arguing that with Israel's current level of technology, the Golan is not what it was before 1967 as a potential security threat, and even as it must also be noted that virtually none of the terrorist activity against Israel has come from across the Syrian border in more than forty years. And it is highly unlikely that without a discussion of the Golan the Syrians will come to the table of negotiation. What this demands is a major gesture of peaceful aspiration on the part of the Syrians to convince the Israelis that giving up what, real or not, many view as a large strategic advantage is in Israel's long-term interest.[178]

With the current deterioration of Syria, after more than five years of civil war, many of these points are effectively moot. Nonetheless, the strategic shape of Israel's physical security in the immediate past, present, and future as compared to fifty years ago, and the question of non-Palestinian Arab groups' interest in peace with Israel remain salient, particularly as the Russians have become increasingly reengaged with Syria. And there remains, astonishingly, a real possibility that the situation in Syria could in the future, for better and for worse, revert to something like what it was back in 2009.

In pure Arabic terminology this means: *salaam*, not *sulh*. Both of these terms may be translated into English as "peace," but whereas the first implies a full peace, the other does not. *Sulh* implies something between a cease-fire and a full peace; it implies a temporary peace until such time as war becomes an option. *Salaam* derives from the same root as the word "Islam" and with the root meaning of "submission"; it is a powerful statement of a serious interest in peace. To the extent that *salaam* is understandable as cognate with the Hebrew word *shalom*, it implies "fullness" and not the mere absence of armed conflict.

It is obviously essential for Israel to feel that the arrangements arrived at with the Palestinians, the Syrians, and other Arab states fall into the category of *salaam*. Put in other terms, it is essential that these states, all of which are Muslim, declare themselves capable and willing to accept a *dhimmi* state within their midst. The Arab states need to do more than accept Israel's existence; they need to embrace Israel's legitimacy so that they denounce and not merely renounce terrorism. Arab leaders need to support the proposition that not only Israel, but also the Palestinians and the Syrians need to be willing to compromise if all sides are to walk away from the negotiation table with something substantial.

Moreover, the anti-Semitic bombast that continued to pour out of the Palestinian and larger Arab—particularly Egyptian—press between the time of the Wye Memorandum and the collapse of the Camp David and Taba talks must unequivocally stop. Particularly when we consider that the media in most of the places under discussion are state run, then altering public perceptions about Jews and about Israel, rather than reinforcing the negative imagery that has prevailed for so long, should be one of the foremost tasks of these outlets.[179] This is an issue parallel to and reminiscent of what forward-thinking Catholic and Protestant theologians refer to as the problem of the "teaching of contempt" for Jews and Judaism and the importance of ending such teaching.

More will also be required of the Arab states in terms of material investment. The wherewithal to create the infrastructure of Palestinian statehood will necessitate the sort of financial help that was promised and not fully delivered after Oslo, albeit not only from the Arabs. It will require a more proactive interest in the fate of everyday Palestinians. An obvious sort of gesture could and should be offered by the Kuwaitis, for example, who as a practical matter could reemploy at least some of those Palestinians who were expelled at the time of the first Gulf War, thereby slicing significantly into the economic shape of myriad Palestinian communities.

Interestingly enough, the beginnings of what I have just prescribed for the Arab states was actually put into play toward the end of 2001. The Saudi plan, put forth by Crown Prince Abd'Allah called for full normalization of relations between the Arab nations and Israel in return for full Israeli withdrawal from the occupied territories. The proposal even called for adjustments that would, in incorporating some settlements into Israel, thicken the country's narrow waist, for which comparable territory, perhaps bordering Gaza, would be transferred to Palestine. The Plan was unanimously adopted at the Arab League's summit in Beirut in March 2002. But by then, the Israelis were in the midst of the Sharon administration, obsessed with the explosion of the new *intifada* and also under no pressure from any allies to consider the plan, and it was rejected.

Indeed the one ally whose pressure might have pushed Israel to look at the Saudi proposal with serious eyes—the United States—was not willing to push. And strangely, given the history of the last 130 years or so, and the overall negative impact of Western involvements in the Israeli-Palestinian, Arab-Israeli and overall Middle Eastern picture, this proposal will necessitate the involvement of the West—particularly the United States—as well. As the frequently referred to "sole superpower" on the planet, the United States is in a unique position to do what it so successfully did during the Clinton years: act as a go-between to help the Israelis and the Palestinians think and talk together.

But there are prerequisites to our ability to function that way again. The first is changing an attitude and a policy that was reflected in President Bush's refusal to meet with Chairman Arafat.[180] We can hardly act as a go-between if we ourselves refuse to talk with one of the principals! We can hardly expect the Israelis to step beyond their own fears and distrusts regarding the Palestinians if we simply corroborate their most negative view of the Palestinians as enemies, rather than as partners.

We can hardly expect the Palestinians—or the rest of the Arab and Muslim world—to accept us as mediators if they perceive us as one-sided in our view of the situation. That we are perceived this way and that we in fact operate this way on an official governmental level is not only corroborated by our unwillingness during the Bush years even to speak with the Palestinian leadership; it is demonstrated by the absolute carte blanche we ceded to the Sharon government (and its Olmert-led and Netanyahu-led successors) to do as it will with regard to the Palestinians.[181] Happily, a shift in attitude was reflected when Barack Obama made it clear from the outset of his presidency that the United States under his administration would both function cooperatively and not dictatorially where our allies are concerned, and reach out with words and gestures to all protagonists on the global (and not just the Middle Eastern) stage. He sought to balance support for Israel with a serious recognition of Palestinian issues.[182]

We support Israel for a number of reasons. One is that Israel is the only democracy in the Middle East; it is our only natural ally and our only consistent ally. Stated from a larger perspective, it *is* the outpost its founders hoped it would be, of Europe and the West in the Middle East. Whatever its demographics, its governmental, economic, and societal infrastructures mirror our own and thus it offers a natural focus for our sympathies. Another, in the post-9/11 era, is that we have become capable of seeing ourselves mirrored in a different, more negative way, every time we read or hear of a suicide bomber blowing him/herself up at a Jerusalem bus stop. We perceive the Israelis to be fighting the same war against terrorism that we are. Since, in our unilateral arrogance during the Bush-Cheney-Rumsfeld years, we determined to fight that war our way and without cooperation from most of our European and other allies—including, critically, Muslim allies—Israel's role as parallel to our own is even more accentuated.

Many experts today will argue that the "real" reason behind American support for Israel, particularly as it largely became blind support, is the Jewish lobby on Capitol Hill. While that view is quite accurate as far as the present moment is concerned—the Jewish lobby is currently the most successful on the Hill—it does not explain the history of American support, except by retrofitting the present onto the past. American Jews were not overly supportive of Israel until 1967, as I have earlier noted.[183] They feared that Israel might upstage the Promised Land that they had found here, particularly by the 1950s and early 1960s, and they feared the accusation of double loyalty.[184]

When President Truman met with Haim Weizmann prior to the United States' recognition of Israel's statehood, he did so virtually in secret and without enthusiasm; recognition and subsequent support came other than through a lobby or love. Nor were American Jews organized yet as a lobbying force in any case. In the 1950s, they were beginning to become seriously involved in the process of candidate support and to develop the skill of translating such support into elected officials' support of their agenda. It would be some time before that involvement and that skill would emerge as significant and before that agenda would push support of Israel to the top tier of Jewish concerns. In the early 1960s, for example, the struggle against denominational prayers in nondenominational public schools came well before concerns for Israel.

Nonetheless, the beginnings of American support for Israel both predate the existence of the State and came in the larger context of the Cold War. During World War I, more than a generation before the State of Israel existed, the US government sent aid to the Jews of Palestine and conversely, one of the "Hebrew" battalions that helped in the defeat of the Ottoman Turks was organized in America. Mordecai Ben-Hillel HaCohen wrote in his diary at around this time: "The entire national enterprise in Palestine has fallen on America's shoulders."[185] In the aftermath of the War, in spite of the overt central position of the British and French in the region, America's significance was already being recognized: Ben-Gurion, who would emerge more than twenty years later as Israel's first prime minister, was already directing his efforts on behalf of the Zionist movement to the United States, rather than to Great Britain, in the 1920s.

Indeed, America's interest in the region was already piqued in the late eighteenth and early nineteenth centuries because of coffee—a growing beverage-taste fire that the Ottoman Turks had kindled in Europe as they extended their dominion westward in the sixteenth and seventeenth centuries, so that coffee shops began in Budapest and spread to Vienna and then to Paris. Barely was the United States a presence in the world and the taste of coffee was beginning its spread on this side of the Atlantic: and the Middle East seemed to be the source toward which to turn in order to fulfill the need for it. By the mid-nineteenth century, as we have seen, the American interest had also become religious.[186]

By the time the British and French were jockeying for final predominance in the region, in the 1930s, the United States was also finally beginning to awaken to the issue of oil. In the aftermath of World War II, American interest was driven by the strategic concerns of the Cold War. These included but were not limited to the growing question of how to prevent the Soviet Union from gaining access to the enormous oil reserves that were by then known to reside in the region, from Iraq to Saudi Arabia—the consequences of which concern are repercussive up to and through both the Gulf War under Bush the Elder and the second invasion of Iraq under Bush the Younger.

During the Cold War, the United States began to worry that Israel, whose birth and infancy had been strongly supported by the Soviet Union, might join the Soviet bloc. So it developed a special fund with which to disseminate American books, periodicals, films, and music to Israel. CARE packages were delivered to Israel, and shortly before the first Israeli parliamentary elections, the American Export-Import Bank agreed to extend a $100 million loan, an enormous sum at that time, to Israel to assist with immigrant absorption and development projects. As much as this pattern of American patronage soon became the norm, an Israeli might have initially worried that, with the collapse of the Soviet Union as a counterweight to its own power, the United States might rethink it alliances.

However, this hasn't proven itself to be the case. The fact is that the United States has, by now, established a long track record of supporting Israel, both in United Nations votes and other international fora and in dollars loaned or granted outright to the Jewish state. This condition puts it in a unique position, one notably ignored by Bush the Younger, to apply pressure on Israel's government in a way that a state such as France or Britain hardly could.[187]

But what kind of pressure? The kind that links American fiscal support with a shift in Israeli policy away from the construction of state-supported settlements in the Territories and toward renewed and serious discussions with the Palestinian leadership, toward expressing recognition of the validity of a Palestinian state and away from offering bits and pieces of semiautonomy that leave room for neither infrastructure nor self-esteem. Pressure not intended to be punitive in the absence of such a shift, but that speaks eloquently and forcefully about the future of Israel, both physical and psychological, with regard to both security and spiritual well-being.

Of course, the Israel-United States relationship has become considerably less simple in the past half-dozen years, since Mr. Netanyahu made it clear during the 2008 US presidential election that he would prefer a victory for Obama's opponent, John McCain; and that he even more emphatically supported Mitt Romney in 2012. Obama, to an extent, followed the sort of pressuring course to which I have just referred, while continuing to be cordial to Netanyahu; however, the pressure that he tried to exert was not close to maximal and whenever it was applied, it inevitably provided his Republican opposition with grounds for articulating doubts as to whether the president's support for Israel was unequivocal.

In other words, internal American politics have aided Netanyahu's efforts to reclaim the sort of *carte blanche* position that Israel had when George W. Bush was president. That said, the American Jewish community itself has become tremendously divided regarding Israel's policies and the American relationship to Israel. Nowhere was the question of how to consider and how to *shape* the next phase in the American-Israeli relationship more obviously problematic than in the moment when Netanyahu was invited to speak before the US Congress in 2015, without the usual diplomatic conditions that would have involved the President's Office, specifically to weigh in on the forthcoming American decision regarding the reshaping of relations with Iran.

So as much as a more evenhanded position has not been detrimental to Israel in the least—I would argue, in fact, that pushing Israel back to the negotiation table and away from actions that make negotiations impossible is useful to Israel—because Obama, as the purveyor of that greater evenhandedness, inspires such vehement opposition from members of the Republican party, his position did not carry the situation nearly as far forward as one might have hoped for. And perhaps, part of this is also a consequence of there being so much ground that needed to be made up in the aftermath of his predecessor's eight years in office.

There should be two objections to the idea of how the United States can use its resources to guide the Israelis and Palestinians toward the negotiation table, beyond the fear and distrust problem. First, that even a viable Palestinian state offers a logistical problem given that its two parts, the West Bank and Gaza, will be separated by Israel. I would argue that, under the sincere peace conditions that this plan envisions, untrammeled passage across that stretch of Israeli territory—across a double border that, at the outset will be a double point of nervousness and tension—can in the *long* run become as uncomplicated as the passageway that winds through the Pyrenees between Spain and France or that marks the transit between the Netherlands and Germany in the aftermath of the shaping of the EU.[188]

But I would not wait for that long run to arrive, and for several reasons would propose a slightly different solution. It is modeled on the experience of India and Pakistan, which were shaped as modern states at around the same time that Israel was being first fashioned. Muslim Pakistan was separated into Eastern and Western Pakistan by primarily Hindu India; this proved disastrous for decades until finally a decision was arrived at to disconnect the two Muslim states from each other, leaving one as Pakistan and renaming the other Bangladesh. Why not do the same with non-Jewish-dominated Palestine? Instead of a two-state solution, then, I am proposing a *three*-state solution.

This proposal would offer several advantages. It would eliminate the majority of the logistical complications pertaining to the communication between the two Palestinian parts of a two-state solution. The notion that has been floated by any number of individuals—for example, in the popular press, by way of Daniel Klaidman's January 12, 2009, *Newsweek* article, "A Plan of Attack for Peace"—of creating "a land corridor connecting Gaza to the West Bank and allowing for the free flow of people and commerce between the two" seems ill conceived as an on-the-ground practicality. That plan effectively cuts Israel in half: how do Israelis then flow from north to south of the corridor? There have been other proposals, for extensive tunnels or bridges connecting the two sides of a Palestinian state, but these, too, are a logistical challenge.

Certainly, one of the more creative and careful proposals presented in a bilingual (English and Arabic) 2005 study, "The Arc: A Formal Structure for a Palestinian State," and published by the Rand Corporation, calls for a high-speed train that would connect Gaza and its projected airport near Rafa to the West Bank and eight key cities between Hebron and Jenin.[189] There would be no ingress/egress stops between Rafa and Hebron; from Jenin it would continue, again without ingress/egress options, to its terminus in Haifa. The proposal suggests the possibility of an automobile toll road with very limited ingress/egress options following a path parallel to that of the train.[190]

But still, the only advantage of this idea is that it offers perhaps the most workable way in which to maintain a singular Palestine consisting of Gaza and the West Bank. This may appeal to a theoretical emotion that "we are all Palestinians," except that everything about the governance, socioeconomics, apparent attitude toward Israel and, ultimately, identity militates against such a sense of unity except in an automatic, knee-jerk response to the idea of separating the two areas that are in fact physically separated and have been for nearly seventy years. Two separate states for Palestinians would accord more realistically with the current facts on the ground: *Hamas* controls Gaza and *Fatah* currently controls the West Bank. Creating two separate states would allow each of these groups to develop according to its own strategies and plans.

As a practical matter from the perspective of Israeli security, one might assume that the vast majority of Palestinians and their PA leaders on the West Bank are willing and ready to think and act in favor of peace and to move toward normalized relations both with Jordan and with Israel—and with the world within and beyond the Middle East—but that *Hamas*, embedded in Gaza, remains more intransigent. The three-state solution would make it possible for Israel to focus in one way, toward normalized relations with the West Bank, *Fatah*-led Palestinians, and in another way with defense measures a more central issue, with the Gazans. *Hamas* and its intransigence has a greater chance of being isolated and its ugly intentions—if they remain ugly—thereby undercut if it is completely disconnected from the West Bank; the possibility of being voted out by the Gazan Palestinians themselves, it seems to me, would increase.

The notion of a three-state solution neither complicates nor simplifies the mundane issues of garbage collection and mail delivery. Nor does it further complicate or simplify the matter of Israel's security fence/wall—except that, should the West Bank relationship move toward greater normalcy while the Gazan relationship does not, it is much simpler to construct or maintain such a fence on the Gaza border than along the extremely irregularly configured Green Line. Nor does it simplify or complicate the issue of the settlements on the West Bank. I reiterate my suggestion for these, that they not be dismantled, but that their inhabitants become citizens of Palestine as there are Arab Palestinian citizens of Israel—even dual citizens of those two states.

Finally, the three-state solution does not affect the issue of Palestinian refugees seeking repatriation to what is Israel in any way differently from how a two-state solution would. If Israel were willing—as for the past decade and a half its leaders have claimed that they are[191]—to allow a limited "law of return" to apply to some Palestinians—an international court could seek to adjudicate the claims over the following years of those coming forth either to ask for return rights or compensation.[192] But as I have observed above,[193] the number of those claiming to have "always" been in Israel's part of Palestine is much smaller than a close look at the history of the region in the last 150 years suggests. Others would be resident in one of the two new Palestinian states, and still others would be finally accorded citizenship in Syria and the other states where they have resided as stateless persons for so many decades.[194]

Nor, it should be noted, does this proposal eliminate the possibility that in the future—if things were to change with regard to *Hamas* and its attitude both toward Israel and toward the PA, and if in general, peaceable relations on a substantial level evolve on both Israel-Palestine borders—the two Palestinian states could be united under one administrative or federated roof. I do not see that happening very quickly, but as we have repeatedly observed, the region is renowned for sudden changes in attitude and relationships.

The second objection to the proposal regarding a dominant American position in Israeli-Palestinian discussions is that the role of the United States may *sound* as patronizing as those of the British and the French a century ago. To this second objection I would respond that Israel—and Europe and half the world—has followed and swallowed the lead of the United States for three-quarters of a century; that the culture and socioeconomics of the United States has swallowed Israel and Europe and half the world on many levels, from McDonalds to Democratic values, for better and for worse. Certainly, Israel has embraced the United States in many ways other than as a client state and its patron. So to invoke the Americans as a force to push the Israelis out of their box of fear and distrust and to push the Palestinians and the Arabs out of theirs is perfectly appropriate. It merely requires the interest and the will on the part of an American leadership committed to long-term peace in the region and not to American hegemony.

There is, in fact, another irony in this. Israel learned democracy from the United States, and as of this writing, particularly but not only with regard to the issue about which I am writing, Israel often practices democracy much more efficiently than does the United States. In the United States, one heard virtually no public debate during the Bush years regarding Israel or regarding Israel and the Palestinians. Not only was speaking out in disagreement with the federal government on *any* issue treated by that administration and its champions as treasonous—as anti-American—but to speak out against the blind American support of Sharonist policies that ignored both the moral infrastructure and the future survival of Israel was to be perceived as anti-Semitic if the speaker was not Jewish, or percieived as treasonous if the speaker was Jewish.

To be sure, there have been and will be anti-Semites who attempt to cloak their animosity toward Jews behind anti-Zionism or, a few years ago, anti-Sharonism and more recently, unqualified horror at the Israeli attack on Gaza without any references either to what provoked the attack or to the effort exerted by Israel to make it less of a horror. But it is also true that there were strong *supporters* of Israel at the time of Sharon and since that time, who were also ultimately anti-Semitic; and Jews and non-Jews alike who remain loyal to and are in love with the State of Israel and are for these very reasons critical of its stance vis-à-vis the Palestinians. In the first case, for example, there are members of the Christian religious right, including many of those who were closest to and most supportive of President Bush. Their rhetoric would suggest that their strong support of Israel derives not from philo-Semitism, but rather from the conviction that the Second Coming must be preceded by the ingathering of the exiles. This means that the Rapture will follow the return to Zion of all the Jews. Its corollary is that the Jews will then participate in the Rapture, having recognized the Christhood of Jesus—or be swallowed up with everyone else whom the Apocalypse swallows up, in the event that they fail to see the Light of His Return for what it is. So their Zionism is in fact a function of their supercessionist perspective.

In the second case, it is not only Americans who do or would speak out were they given a forum in which they would not be excoriated. This category also includes a growing array of Israelis from different walks of life, including soldiers and scientists, former cabinet ministers and heads of the *Shin Bet* (Israel's internal security services), to say nothing of professors and doctors, lawyers, and journalists, who have spoken and/or written in no uncertain and often extremely angry terms against the policies of the Sharon administration and its successors with regard to the Palestinians.

So I am referring here to both the right and the obligation to speak out in calling on our own government to effect attitude change, and for that change on the part of our government as a complement to the words, actions, and thought-pattern changes that I am suggesting as necessary for Israelis, Palestinians, the Arab world at large—and, for that matter, the European and Middle Eastern Christian and Muslim worlds at large.

American Jews, while Bush was still president, were already becoming more vocal with regard to a new relationship to Israel that did not accord it carte blanche on any and all fronts. This is evidenced by the emergence shortly before the 2008 presidential election of a Jewish organization called *J Street*, made up primarily of—and intended to appeal to—American Jews concerned about Israel's survival, but who see that survival as underserved by unequivocal boosterism. This surging, grassroots effort to enact exactly the sort of attitude change that I am describing called, in late May, 2009, for American Jews to impress upon President Obama and Secretary of State Hillary Clinton that they must stand firm with the just-then visiting Israeli Prime Minister Netanyahu with regard to an absolute freeze in West Bank settlement construction.[195]

I might add a further note on this specific issue in the interests of reminding the reader of potentially significant details that rarely find their way into public view. In a public dialogue with Geoffrey Kemp called "Middle East Update" held on Monday afternoon, August 1, 2016, at Chautauqua Institution, Dennis Ross noted in passing that 80 percent of the settlements have been built on 4 percent of the West Bank.[196] The implications of this datum, if it is true, are as follows: it has been a continuous principle, going back to the post-Oslo discussions under Bill Clinton, that the final determination of the borders of the Palestinian state would include some areas previously within Israel's 1949–67 borders and exclude a precisely equal volume of area—that would become part of Israel—from the former West Bank.

The total volume of land to be exchanged would amount to 3 to 5 percent of the entire Palestinian/Israeli landmass. In that case, the settlement growth under the Israelis, and in particularly in recent years under Netanyahu, might not pose as large an obstruction to peace negotiations as would at first appear. This does not, however, exonerate the Netanyahu administration with regard both to the principle of unilaterally undertaking construction when the precise areas of exchange have not yet been determined and to the negative publicity and thus psychological obstruction that the ongoing construction offers to the peace process.

In any case, that the Obama-Biden-era atmosphere invited debate on this as on other issues was also evidenced in the March-April 2009 issue of *Moment* magazine, a left-of-center Jewish publication that covers politics, culture, and a range of diverse subjects. In that issue, two opinion pieces from opposed sides of the spectrum appeared—separately, not on facing pages, so that they were simply two different pieces with two different viewpoints.

Gershom Gorenberg's brief piece entitled "It's Time for American Jews to Speak Up!" asked whether "American Jews [will] dare to ask the same questions that are regularly asked by the Israelis themselves . . . will they listen to their own opinions? Will they dare to voice them publicly and without embar-rassment?. . . I'd like to believe that [party line-towing Jewish American lead-ers] . . . doubt the wisdom of expanding West Bank settlements, or question the attempt to ban two Arab parties from Israeli elections, or feel qualms about the firepower that Israeli forces directed at civilian areas during the war in Gaza. But if they have those doubts in private they don't agree with themselves in public."[197]

In the same issue, David Frum wrote in a piece titled "Force: An Inconvenient Truth," that "[d]uring the Gaza war, many American Jews were gripped by . . . self-destructive sympathy . . . They anguished as much (or more) over the suffering inflicted by Israel's defensive actions as by the danger and terror of *Hamas*' aggression." Frum turns to a quote—from his "friend and coauthor, Richard Perle . . . [who] likes to repeat a story of an encounter with a peace protester. 'War solves nothing,' the protester said. 'Well,' Richard answered, 'it has a better record than social work,'"—in order to underscore his point that force is the only solution to this problem. After the Gaza war, he noted, "*Hamas* has been relatively quiet." He argued that Israel, pushed to make peace at any price over the years, lest time run out on her, has continued to flourish while refusing to accede to such pressure, while "Israel's enemies, by contrast, fell farther and farther behind."[198]

I will not judge whether Frum's hawkish perspective is a valid existential one for Israel in either the physical survival sense, or the moral and psycholog-ical sense in which Israel might be measured by more than her technological achievements. I won't judge whether Gorenberg is stepping out on a dangerous or naïve limb by his commentary. The reader can probably deduce well enough by now what my opinion would be on this. My point, though, is that the juxta-position of these two radically different perspectives in a public forum of sorts bespeaks a willingness on the part of the publication's editor and publisher to promote such discourse, however controversial, out of recognition that Israel and everyone else is better served by discourse than by silence.

It is fair to express dismay at the crushing weight of the Israeli attack on Gaza, but only if one expresses dismay at the two years of continual rocket attacks into southern Israel that preceded that attack and also takes note of Israeli efforts to minimize the weight. One ought to note the times when Israeli soldiers exhibited the opposite of restraint, but only if one acknowledges the myriad times when Israeli soldiers exhibited restraint and/or expressed grief at the damages that they perpetrated—and only if one also expresses outrage at the fact that *Hamas* has forced scores of Gazan children into forced labor to dig smuggling tunnels between Gaza and Egypt—and at how many dozens of children have died doing such work.

It is interesting, in passing, to observe how the Arab world at large was remarkably subdued in its verbal response to the Israeli Gazan incursion. Did they hope that *Hamas* would be dismantled? If so, was it because of their concern for the spread of *Hamas*-like ideology to other parts of the Arab world where other regimes would be threatened? We may well recall that part of the reason that the Saudis permitted the encampment of American and other non-Muslim troops on their soil during the first Gulf War was the fear of the regime-toppling instability that Saddam's incursion into Kuwait might generate.

Given the pre-Black September trauma that the Kingdom of Jordan had experienced at the end of the 1960s, the Saudis can surely recognize the potential provided by *Hamas* for regime-threat.[199] Or was it because of their sense that *Hamas* was a fly in the ointment of furthering the Israeli-Palestinian peace process? Did they *get* the issue of the Israeli perception of all of those rocket attacks into southern Israel? That relative verbal restraint offered quite a contrast to the response from much of the world beyond the Middle East. The nature and future of the peace process for Israel/Palestine is as unpredictable as every other aspect of this narrative.

PART FIVE

CROSS-REGIONAL ISSUES AND THE FUTURE OF THE MIDDLE EAST

13

THE LARGER ARAB CONTEXTS OF PEACE AND WAR

Let us assume, for the sake of argument, that the Israel-Palestine problem *were* solved; that a pair—or better, a trio—of secure and viable states were to shift into place side by side, and even that their interface evolved in a positive and productive manner for all three of them. What then, of the region overall?

To repeat an important mantra: the situation in the Middle East is more complicated than Israel and Palestine, Israel and the Arabs, or the complexities of Islam, Christianity, and Judaism. It includes the ethnic struggle between Arab and non-Arab entities, as in Iraq versus Iran, Syria versus Turkey, even Egypt versus Jordan or Libya—to say nothing of the Kurds within Iraq, or the Kurds within Turkey, in which last case *neither* side is Arab—or the Arabs in the Sudan. It also involves intra-Arab conflict between Islamic and Christian populations, as in Syria and Lebanon, or intra-Islamic conflict between Sunni and Shi'i populations, as between Iran and Iraq.

These issues are also interwoven with socioeconomics, as in the objection on the part of some of Usama Bin Ladin's followers to the ongoing impoverishment of so many Saudis while an inner circle continues to swallow up billions in oil revenues. And the region is defined by complex governance politics. Even within the limited context of the Palestine Liberation Organization, we see this in its range of different suborganizations. Beyond the PLO are more than a dozen other Palestinian liberation organizations, and the PLO, while it has become virtually synonymous with *Fatah*, is dominated by but not limited to *Fatah*.

Some of these organizations are Muslim; some are Christian. Some seek a peaceful solution to their conflict with Israel; some simply and unequivocally want Israel destroyed. The identifying nomenclature of Palestinian organizations has shifted in the last decades and the last few years (the *Fatah*-dominated PLO became the dominant component of the Palestinian Authority in the wake of the 1993 Oslo Accords, but the PA is not merely a continuation of the PLO or of *Fatah*). This shifting nomenclature is particularly apparent where the more distinctly anti-Israel groups, such as *Hamas* and *Hizb'allah*, are concerned.

Jordan has in important ways removed itself from engagement with the Palestinian problem, first by the conflagration of Black September in the early 1970s and later by the peace treaty with Israel in the 1990s, in which the Hashimite Kingdom renounced all interest in the West Bank. In both cases, King Hussein was trying to lessen the sense of threat to his throne deriving from the ethnic matter of his non-Palestinian family ruling over a Palestinian population. Israel inherited the problem on both occasions. When the PLO and its entourage relocated to Lebanon after Hussein drove them out of Jordan, Lebanon became a locus of anti-Israel activity and ultimately the object of Israel's problematic 1982 invasion.[200] And the West Bank Palestinian problem remains both unsolved and one that is essentially an Israeli problem now that Jordan has extricated itself.

Similarly, if the Syrian-Lebanese border is quiet, it is because the United States and its allies allowed Syria to swallow Lebanon in all but name in the aftermath of the first Persian Gulf War, as a reward for Assad's support of the anti-Saddam coalition. But Syria's borders with Turkey and Iraq are rarely silent. Part of this derives from ethnic hostility, as the Turks are neither Semites nor Arabs. Part of it is religious, as the Iraqi community bordering Syria is Shi'i; the Syrians are primarily Sunni. Part of it is ethno-religious: substantial numbers of Kurds, who have never had their aspirations for political self-determination, addressed, promised since World War I, are located largely in the northern and eastern areas of Syria, which borders Iraq and Turkey, respectively, as well as inhabiting eastern Turkey and northwestern Iraq.[201] And the Kurds are themselves not a monolith; aside from their location in several different states. In Iraq, for example, there are at least two major, often mutually antagonistic, factions.[202]

In Iraq, the Kurdish region encompasses not only the Zagros Mountains within its territory, but more importantly, most of the Mosul oil fields in which the British and the Iraqis in turn have been so interested. Indeed, the British had considered creating a Kurdish state after World War I in order to protect the Mosul-Kirkuk oil fields—and promised this to the Kurds in that region— but the conflict that this would have brought about with the French as well as with Russia, and Iran caused them to later abandon the idea.[203]

By 1967, after the June Arab-Israeli War and under the regime of Colonel Abdul Salam Muhammad Arif, the Kurds and Iraqis seemed to arrive at a *modus vivendi* in which the former retained autonomy in the mountains and the latter were ceded control of the Mosul oil fields. This tacit agreement was made more formal in March 1970, and by then included oil revenue sharing between the Iraqi government and the Kurds. But already by January 1972, new fighting had broken out between the two sides. More recently, of course, the Kurds suffered genocidal attacks at the hands of Saddam Hussein; while in Turkey they have engaged in terrorist activity against the Turkish population and regime. On and across the borders of all three countries—Iraq, Syria, and Turkey—they have been a part of the complications, challenging the political order.

By the time that the Baghdad regime had worked out an arrangement with the Kurds in the late 1960s and early 1970s, "Iraq" had changed hands several times. Having deposed and assassinated King Faisal II in 1958, Brigadier Abdul Karim Kassim assumed control of the government. At that time, he sought to assert himself as the leader of the Arab nation. In this he opposed the claim of Arab leadership asserted by Abdul Gamal Nassir and Egypt—but the issue became moot when he was executed in his own apartment in 1963 by the court-martial instituted by the National Council of the Revolutionary command. He was then succeeded by Colonel Arif, whose support came from the Ba'ath Party. One might assume that this would have meant good relations with Syria, also by then controlled by the Ba'ath party—but the party of the same name in Syria at that time (the mid-to-late 1960s) preferred independent socialist development in each Ba'ath-led country; while in Iraq, Arif's notion was pan-Arab, including Egypt.

While Arif was in Damascus discussing a unity plan, the Syrians with whom he was meant to be negotiating—al-Bitar and Michael Aflaq—were discussing a plan with his Deputy Premier, Salah al-Sa'adi, behind his back that would create an economic Syrian-Iraqi merger that would exclude Egypt. Al-Sa'adi ended up expelled from Iraq. Aflaq and al-Bitar flew to Baghdad and attempted to seize control of the Iraqi government in the name of the international Ba'ath Party; the Iraqi army expelled them, restored Arif and his government to their positions, and the Ba'ath party was banned from Iraqi politics.[204] Thus, a significant part of the tension between Syria and Iraq in the past two generations has been based on the fact that each is led by a branch of the Ba'ath Party and each has asserted that it should be the true leader of that party. This issue was not improved with the assumption of power in Iraq by Saddam Hussein.

Iraq is better known to the world for other relationships than that with Syria, however. In 1980, Saddam's troops entered into a protracted war with

Iran that would last for eight years, at the end of which he could claim victory since it was the Iranians who actually sued for peace. But both peoples were exhausted, their resources decimated. Saddam's forces gained enormous experience and confidence in this war, during which he also experimented with chemical and biological weaponry—both against the Iranians and against the Kurds within Iraq. It is important to note here the role played by the United States in the eight-year war. Since barely two years earlier the Iranians under the Ayatollah Khomeini had taken American hostages and released them after an extended period of tension and difficult negotiation, and since the Ayatollah's regime had been consistently antagonistic toward America in its rhetoric, it is not surprising that the United States took the Iraqi side and provided much of the weaponry that brought Saddam his success—at least initially.

Actually, a more detailed look at the United States' position during the war reveals that, in its middle phase, when it appeared that Iraq was gaining a decisive advantage, and in spite of the strong public stance against Iran, the Reagan administration began secret negotiations to supply Iran with arms in exchange for assistance in negotiating the release of a second group of American hostages—in *Lebanon*. So, arms began to make their way to Iran from the United States in the form of antitank missiles in 1985.

Adding a further twist to this somewhat bizarre piece of information, the missiles that were sent to Iran were provided by Israel.[205] By the following year, when Iran seemed to be gaining the upper hand, particularly after Iranian forces conquered the Iraqi Faw Peninsula near Kuwait, the United States began to worry again, not as much about Iraq as about the threat to oil shipments coming from and through Kuwait. Thus, not only did American support swing back more clearly toward Iraq, but by 1987 Kuwaiti ships began to fly American flags and therefore boasted the protective support of the US Naval forces in the Gulf.

Another matter of particular relevance to our discussion is that Saddam, at the end of the war, represented himself as the champion of the Arab world against "the Persian menace." Having exhausted his funds and incurred enormous debts in the course of the war, and also aware of the power of his army, Saddam turned rapidly after the end of the war to the other Arab states, and to Kuwait and the Saudis in particular, with a demand for financial support and relief. In a long note to the Secretary General of the Arab League on July 15, 1990, Iraq's Minister of Foreign Affairs, Tariq Aziz, wrote in part:

Before the war Iraq was one of the main oil producers, with about 2.6 million barrels a day. . . [but] Iraq's losses during that period [1980–85] rose to $106 million.

In point of fact, this sum has gone into the coffers of the other oil-producing countries of the region. . . A simple calculation is enough to show that Iraq's "debts" to Kuwait and the Emirates are easily compensated for by the surplus profits they made, thanks to their increase in oil production during the war.

The question we must ask is: since Iraq took on all the responsibility for defending the security and dignity of the Arab nation and for protecting the wealth of the countries in the Gulf—which would have fallen into foreign hands if Iraq had lost—must it still, despite everything, consider the aid it was given as a "debt"?

. . . How then can we continue to consider the amounts given to Iraq by brother Arabs as debts, when it contributed many times those amounts from its own treasury, and its youth gave its blood in defense of Arab land, dignity, and wealth?

Aziz emphasized Arab unity many times in his note, asserting that "if only there existed a feeling of being part of Arabness and a desire for the security of the Arab nation," the situation would be a happier one for all concerned. These comments reflect the complicated world of Arab politics and of a long history of ethnic and political as well as religious and cultural strife militating against the desire for Arab unity. And they resonate from the failed intra-Arab negotiations that began in 1990, which were meant to prevent the Iraq-Kuwait war that began in early August.

Once Saddam began increasing his war-bound rhetoric, there are many places in which one can see this failure taking shape. When intra-Arab diplomacy was still hopeful and active toward preventing the Iraqi invasion of Kuwait and its consequences—and a summit meeting was still scheduled to take place in Jeddah—the Kuwaiti Emir wrote to his brother, Crown Prince Sheikh Sa'ad al-Sabah, in part: "It is noteworthy for us to keep in mind our national interests; therefore don't listen to whatever you may hear from the Saudis or Iraqis in regard to brotherhood and maintaining Arab solidarity. Each has his own interests to cater to."[206] That sensibility is reflected in nearly every phase of the negotiations undertaken in their various stages to prevent the war from taking place.

Part of Saddam's rhetoric with regard to Kuwait focused on an assertion that Kuwait was a natural and historical part of Iraq and, thus, were he to "liberate" it from the Sabah family and bring it back under Iraqi governance he would merely be restoring the integrity of his land. Two interesting historical data come to mind regarding this. First, that on the one hand Saddam was right, in that Kuwait was an artificial contrivance of the British; but that on the other hand he was wrong, since Iraq itself was similarly an artificial contrivance of the British from the same period, and "Iraq" had never in its history existed as a unified entity of common ethnicity with distinct borders.[207] Saddam was also not the first Iraqi ruler to assert this. Back in 1961, Abdul Karim Kassim had asserted sovereignty over Kuwait by means of the same sort of claim: that the oil-rich area had always been—and topographically still was—a natural part of Iraq. At that time, the British, Egyptians and Saudis allied together to prevent an Iraqi takeover.

On Augst 1–4, 1990, Iraqi troops swiftly invaded Kuwait, driven by Saddam's lust for conquest and its concomitants, and multiplied by his frustration regarding the nonresponse to his demands from other Arab states and also by the mixed signals from the United States regarding what its response to an attack on Kuwait would be. When the invasion of Kuwait arrived, the Egyptian Foreign ministry put out a statement condemning it, which provoked shock from Jordan's King Hussein: "This destroys everything. And it gives all chances of broadening the conflict."[208] If half the Arab world was shocked by the Iraqi invasion of Kuwait, the other half was concerned about the American response that would surely follow. The majority of the Arab League's twenty-one foreign ministers adopted a resolution condemning the invasion and demanding that Saddam withdraw his troops from Kuwait unconditionally. Seven—Djibouti, Jordan, Libya, the PLO, Sudan, Yemen, and of course, Iraq—did not vote for the resolution.

According to King Hussein of Jordan, Saddam had expressed willingness to discuss a withdrawal from Kuwait, if a mini-summit of certain key Arab leaders were to be convened and provided that the Arab League did not condemn his actions. Given the adoption of the resolution, the summit could never take place. Nonetheless, astoundingly, Saddam was apparently shocked that the summit that had been scheduled for August was canceled, even after his invasion and the publication of the resolution of condemnation. It is perhaps a symptom of his irrationality that he was so surprised.

The resolution also called for Western Powers not to deploy troops on Arab soil. It would take one week for the United States to turn that point of view around. An important element in the about-face was the achievement of Soviet support for intervention in the situation. The mere attempt to gain that support reflected several developments. First, with Gorbachev in charge, the Soviet Union was rapidly moving at this precise moment toward *perestroika*, and so the decades-long American goal of keeping the Soviet Union out of the Middle East had suddenly shifted: Secretary of State James Baker's strategy of *involving* the Soviets went against a dogma that had been in place since the Truman administration.

A second key element was getting the Saudis to agree to host American troops. American satellite images showing concentrations of Iraqi troops in Kuwait and near the Saudi border were ultimately sufficient to convince King Fahd to agree to permit the temporary stationing of American troops on Saudi soil—and a secret protocol was agreed upon: that when events permitted, the American troops would be removed, but permanent bases would be established for multinational troops in the nearby Emirate of Bahrain and in Kuwait itself, once it had been freed.[209]

A further element in rendering the deployment of Western troops on Arab soil feasible was the configuration of that multinational force: it included Arab and Muslim states, thereby eliminating the possibility for Saddam to present the impending conflict as one in which he represented the Arab and Muslim worlds against an infidel and/or foreign imperialist enemy. These developments reflect important lessons for current and future challenges in the Middle East. Notably, they signify the possibility that countries with counter-valent interests, if they find common interests stronger than those that are antagonistic, can work together. In theory, at least, not only the United States and this or that Arab or Muslim state, but even Israel and those states, or, as the case may be, the Palestinians who don't yet have a state, could work together if they found sufficiently compelling common interests.

We can connect this to an earlier chapter of the region's history. If we look to February 1957, we find that the most apparently implacable of Arab Muslim enemies, the Hashimite Crown Prince Abd'Allah of Iraq and King 'Abd al-'Aziz Ibn Sa'ud of Saudi Arabia—with a mutual enmity between their families going back centuries—were meeting in Washington, DC, under the patronage of President Eisenhower and secretary of State John Foster Dulles, agreeing to an alliance in order to fend off the Arab revolution that threatened both. This historical chapter speaks to the United States' ability to function as a go-between in facilitating cooperation even in the most delicate of conditions, if the will and the wiles are there.[210]

But even as these key elements needed to oppose Saddam Hussein shifted into place, negotiations with him continued. It is not clear, as they began to achieve success in shaping a far-flung alliance against Iraq, whether the American leaders of the coalition wanted a negotiated settlement or became increasingly eager for a military confrontation that would afford the opportunity of dismantling Saddam's now considerable military infrastructure. Certainly the adoption of an UN-sponsored resolution on November 29, 1990, calling for a precise date of Iraqi withdrawal from Kuwait has been interpreted by some as an indication that the window for negotiations was being rapidly closed.

On the other hand, President Bush (Senior) announced the following day that he would send Secretary of State Baker to meet with Iraqi Foreign Minister Tariq Aziz to facilitate negotiations. Remarkably, the meeting only took place by the skin of its diplomatic teeth—on January 9, 1991, six days before the UN Resolution demanding Iraqi troop withdrawal—since for the five weeks between that time and President Bush's call for a meeting the two sides could hardly agree on a proper time and place for negotiation! Pierre Salinger asserts that "a top Iraqi source told me that all that was needed to set up conversations involving Tariq Aziz, George Bush, James Baker, and Saddam Hussein was for Bush to pick up the phone and call Saddam Hussein to discuss it with him. This was part of Saddam Hussein's mentality."[211]

If the statement is true, then what of "Saddam's mentality"—is that *his* mentality or "*Arab*" mentality? In either case, how far should the President of the United States be willing to go in catering to that mentality in order to avert a military conflict? If the statement is true and President Bush chose not to pick up the phone, was that his *own* mentality of dislike or distrust of Saddam or his sense that if anyone should pick up the phone it should be Saddam, calling Bush, and not the other way around? Or did he not wish to avert the military confrontation—either for internal reasons, related to a reelection effort soon to come and waning popularity; or for external reasons, related to American hopes to dismantle Iraq's military capabilites and therefore alter the balance of power in the Middle East?

In any case, the January 9 meeting between Baker and Aziz that took place in Geneva lasted more than six hours, during which the world waited and, due to the unexpected length of the meeting, began to hope that perhaps a diplomatic solution was being worked out. It wasn't. Aziz had come to Geneva to assert that the January 15 deadline for Iraqi troop removal be lifted: "We can't negotiate with them unless they do."[212] Baker handed Aziz a letter to be given to Saddam, but reading it, Aziz refused to deliver it. Aziz later asserted at a press conference that "the language in this letter is not compatible with the language that should be used in correspondence between heads of state." Again, if this was so, was the issue a function of American insensitivity or Iraqi hypersensitivity?

By January 10, the United States had decided that unless Saddam actually withdrew his troops from Kuwait, the attack on those troops would begin on January 17, at 2 a.m. Baghdad time. The aftermath of that moment—and the provisional cease-fire that arrived at six weeks and four hours later—was that the military capability of Iraq had been crushed and its infrastructure more or less ruined. More than that, the Arab world that had placed itself on both sides of the coalition fence was more shaken and divided than it had been in a long time. A number of American and Western military bases came to populate the region. But Saddam remained both uncaptured and, when he resurfaced, unrepentant, and as time went on, whatever positive aura had accrued to the United States for its role in the war began to fade.

In the years that followed—after the Persian Gulf War, the events of September 11, 2001, and the invasions of Afghanistan and Iraq—Iran regained some of its military potency and found itself included on the second President Bush's short list of nefarious states. But in the aftermath of our second invasion of Iraq, in 2003, the capture of Saddam the following year, and the dismantling of any and all parts of a potential Iraqi infrastructure, Iraq's neighbors such as Saudi Arabia and Jordan grew concerned that the currently ambiguous shape of Iraq could adversely affect them. It is not merely the fact of instability that worried them, but specifically, that the Iraqi Shi'is might find common ground with the Shi'i Iranians, creating a block of power potentially destructive to the two kingdoms.

Before addressing the consequent regional issues, it is important to consider several matters that emerged from the situation of Iraq in 2003–4 and its aftermath. One pertains to American conduct and its implications for the future of the American role in the Middle East. In the first instance, there is the question of whether we should have engaged in that invasion at all, and the lies the Bush-Cheney government told Americans and the world to justify our intervention to remove Saddam from power: that he was an ally of the Bin Ladin Islamists who masterminded the attacks of September 11, 2001—he was not; he was as secular a Muslim as you could find—and that he was harboring hordes of weapons of mass destruction, for which we never had any evidence.

Beyond the troubled course that led to the war, the casualness with which we approached the conflict of our own making was nothing less than horrific. The phrase, "collateral damage," which Donald Rumsfeld was so fond of using, is cast into sharp relief as reflecting an attitude of moral emptiness when one considers a mere handful of specifics to which it might pertain. For instance, toward the beginning of the war, the Bush administration was under the impression that Saddam was eating at a particular Baghdad restaurant; US warplanes leveled it, killing more than a dozen civilians. These included children and one young woman whose headless body was recovered by her mother, as reported in the Associated Press. *The London Independent* cited this attack as a "clear breach" of the Geneva Conventions' ban on bombing civilian targets. There were many more of these acts, nonetheless.

The range of thoughtlessly administered civilian deaths and what they reflect of American values ought to give all Americans pause.[213] So should the extreme instability that followed our incursion into Iraq, the removal of Saddam and, most fundamentally, our failure to undertake the invasion with a clear sense of the country and the region around it, and the likely consequences, for both, of our intervention. Things became further complicated when the American government eventually determined that it could not put US troops in Iraq in the position of possibly being prosecuted by Iraqi courts for war crimes if they fought in the country without a Status of Forces Agreement (SOFA). The Iraqi parliament, however, which was essentially being asked to vote to keep American troops in its country, not surprisingly refused to pass a SOFA. After 2003, the parliament was dominated by the Ahrar party, whose members were followers of Shi'i cleric Muztada al-Sadr. Al-Sadr's followers centered their political ideology on anti-imperialism. So, even aside from being upset by the large volume of civilian casualties occasioned as "collateral damage" by the American invasion and ongoing occupation, they were not going to vote, essentially, to enable a continued US presence in their country. This meant that when Obama assumed the presidency, he could not maintain that presence without contravening international law.

A student of Iraqi history of the previous five centuries or so would not be surprised at the gradual disintegration of the country into areas dominated by Arab Sunnis, Arab Shi'is, and Kurds in the years following 2003. Nor, particularly given the history of the previous half century, should one be surprised by the bloodshed being spilt specifically between Shi'i and Sunni Arabs.

Through the war, we removed the Sunnis (Saddam's infrastructure) from power and replaced them with the Shi'a. We then blindly supported the new Shi'i Prime Minister Nuri al-Maliki—largely because he was presumed to be diametrically opposed to Saddam, and inadvertently empowered him to completely marginalize Sunni Iraqis as he shaped a Shi'i-dominated government. We also helped facilitate the removal of virtually all of the predominantly Sunni leadership within the army, including around three thousand officers—as noted by former General David Petraeus in a public lecture on Thursday, August 18, 2016, at Chautauqua Institution.[214] On that occasion, he commented that we sent them out into the wind, with nowhere to turn and no reason to support a state that we hoped would simply assume some stable shape.

It is also important to reiterate that Saddam wasn't a Bin Ladin Sunni with strong religious convictions; he was a Ba'athist, with, to repeat, a very secular ideology. When his regime fell, however, and the Shi'a were installed by American forces, this caused Sunni extremists to form groups connected to al-Qaeda, and, later, to shape what would become the so-called Islamic State (i.e., ISIS/ISIL), in an Iraq dominated by instability and in the process of being swallowed by a vacuum of power. There had been no al-Qaeda in Iraq before our 2003 intervention. But—in spite of distaste for Saddam as a virtual infidel and a demagogue—operatives poured in to fight American troops at that time, first gathering under the rubric of al-Tawhid ("Unity") and led by the militant Jordanian Abu Musab al-Zarqawi, who ran a military camp in Afghanistan. Al-Zarqawi had had a poor relationship with Usama Bin Ladin at first, but he made peace with his Saudi-born opponent in order to fight the American presence in Iraq, joining al-Qaeda and forming a Mesopotamian branch of the organization in 2004.

Al-Zarqawi may be credited with turning an insurgency against American troops in Iraq into an all-out Sunni-Shi'i civil war, sending out numerous suicide bombers into areas where either Americans or Shi'i Iraqis might be found—and possibly arranging the bombing of three hotels in Amman, Jordan, in 2005. After he was killed by American troops, the new Iraqi leadership declared itself the Islamic State of Iraq, further deepening its al-Qaeda association. However, it would eventually be pushed into Syria in 2011. Driven from local governments and effectively forced out of the New Iraq, Iraqi Sunnis regrouped in Syria, where they developed a far more religiously radical view than they had previously possessed, ultimately building on the al-Zarqawi-led version of al-Qaeda. They formed the Islamic State, with the expressed goal of creating a far-flung Sunni Muslim polity. And once the United States pulled out of Iraq, ISIS/ISIL/Daesh came back across the border from Syria and retook areas that had been under American control.

Simply put, under the Bush/Cheney administration, we broke Iraq and made no legitimate attempt to fix it, either by taking the initiative to recreate three autonomous stable states as had been the shape of that area under the Ottomans, or by pushing for more effective power-sharing among the Sunni and Shi'i Arabs and the Kurds. If our real motive was control of the oil, then arguably we did not consider this ethnic/religious issue for the same reason the English didn't nearly a century earlier. If our motive pertained mainly to avenging the alleged attempt by Saddam to assassinate the senior Bush, then such an emotion-driven project was being undertaken without thought or concern for its larger consequences. Whatever the motive, we did little to reconstruct what we destroyed.

Syria, Iran, and Iraq are all now dominated by Shi'a leadership. ISIS/ISIL would like to depose all of these regimes, while at the same time viewing the overly secular Saudi (Sunni) leaders as infidels, which is how they viewed Saddam. Syria's role as a player in establishing a stable region was compromised by the rebellion against Bashar al-Assad's leadership that began in 2011 and the ongoing civil war that has torn the country apart, effectively exterminated or exiled the Christian minority, and created an unprecedented wave of refugees, the sheer volume and volatility of which has also threatened the stability of Turkey as well as generated fear of spreading Muslim extremist terrorism across Europe and the United States. Syria's dire condition has from the outset been further undermined by ISIS, which revels in expanding instability, chaos, and violence in the region. Thus, when civil war broke out in Syria, the Sunni radicals who had evolved into ISIS in Syria and then Iraq once again returned to fight in Syria in order to create an "Islamic State in the Levant," which includes both Iraq and Syria.

It is also important to recognize that the combination of deconstructing Iraq and empowering its Shi'i Arab population at the expanse of the Sunnis opened wide the door for Iran to expand its position of power within the region. And an alliance between Iran and Shi'i Iraq could not only reinforce the tenuousness of the situation of Sunni Iraqis but enhance a sense of threat felt by the Sunni Gulf States, particularly Saudi Arabia.

The return of Iran to regional prominence also quickly raised the level of concern for Israelis, specifically regarding the possible development of Iranian nuclear power. The sense of uncertainty shared by the Saudis and the Israelis regarding the degree to which they could count on the United States to crush the threat of Iran has also yielded the unanticipated consequence that those two countries—behind the scenes—have been talking in friendlier tones than ever before. Thus, a positive, if ironic and unanticipated, consequence of the 2003 invasion of Iraq is that some seeds for peace may have been sown between perhaps the most important Sunni Arab Muslim country in the region and the Jewish State. Nonetheless, it remains to be seen how all the relevant actors will respond to this development.

Regional complications multiply further when we extend our view across North Africa. Within Morocco, the struggle between a secularizing Islamic monarchy and a rising fundamentalist faction are interwoven with the question of how to maintain a dynamic balance between the constitutional and monarchic elements that govern the state. This has increased the level of violence and chaos in that country over the past two decades. Morocco's next-door neighbor, Algeria, has further provided some of the fuel for that violence by breeding the fundamentalists who concern not only Moroccans but also Tunisians. And the Tunisians are equally wary about the intentions of their neighbor to the east, Libya, whose former leader, Mu'amar Qaddafi, had by 2008 begun to re-seek a place on the regional and global stage, but whose prior support of terrorism had yielded disputes with both Tunisia and Egypt, aside from complicating relations with Europe and the United States.

Qaddafi's death in 2011, in the context of the so-called Arab Spring, has not necessarily removed Libya as a source of regional agitation. On the contrary, with Qaddafi's demise, rebel groups turned against one another in a series of turf wars, culminating in full-scale civil war by summer 2014 when Islamist parties were sharply defeated in the June elections supervised by the UN. The Islamists and their allies rebelled against the newly elected parliament, forming the "Libya Dawn Coalition" and seizing Tripoli. The new government fled eastward to the city of Tobruk, near the Egyptian border. Thousands died and some four hundred thousand Libyans were rendered homeless. All of this is apart from the attack on the American Consulate in Benghazi on September 11–12, 2012, that left the American Ambassador Christopher Stevens dead, among others.

It is also apart from—though directly connected to—the beheading of twenty-one Egyptian Coptic Christians in early 2015 by a Libyan-based branch of ISIS/ISIL, which is the group that has most benefitted from the Libyan chaos of the past few years. The Copts were Egyptian migrant workers captured in December 2014 and January 2015; the video of their execution was broadcast on February 15, 2015. The next day, Egyptian planes struck extensively at ISIL facilities in Libya. Libya is a strong reminder of how far the areas that are relevant to "the Middle East" extend, and of the diverse ways in which politics and religion are essential parts of the complex web of the region.[215]

All of these complexities, in fact, derive from a combination of political and religious issues. They are also, as always, interwoven with ethnic and tribal matters. It is because of such complexities that I have questioned the label of "Arab Spring." I am skeptical of an image that suggests a growing promise toward a blossoming summer for events that, while they removed a handful of autocrats from power, have left a trail of problems and questions that evoke, if anything, the congealing of deep winter.

It is also notable that a key location for the efflorescence of the so-called Arab Spring was Egypt, the ethnicity of which raises questions about the simple use of the adjective "Arab," as we have noted previously. Egypt has at times seen itself as ethnically Arab and even as a leader of the Arab world—as in briefly under Nassir, after the revolution of 1952, particularly when forging a United Arab Republic together with Syria in 1958. At other times, however, as when Nassir's successor, Sadat, signed a peace agreement with Israel in 1979, Egypt has viewed itself as other than Arab.[216]

Regional complications extend beyond the Arab world, in any case, including into areas south of Morocco, Algeria, Tunisia, Libya, and Egypt. Thus to Egypt's south, the Sudan was, seven or eight years ago, the location of the worst racial and ethnic genocide anywhere on the planet, which was being meted out against the Christian and Animist blacks of the south, in and around Darfur, by the lighter-skinned Muslims of the North and their Arab allies. While the intensity of horror slowed somewhat eventually—and has virtually fallen off the media pages of a Western world with a very limited news-focus attention span—it has by no means subsided completely.

The regional complexity in its beyond-the-Arab-world aspect also, needless to say, certainly includes Iran, both before and after the dissolution of Iraq, as well as Turkey, Afghanistan—where the Taliban offers its own version of al-Qaeda, and where Usama Bin Ladin ultimately organized himself, among other things, toward the judgment day that he designed on September 11, 2001—and Pakistan. Unfortunately for direct stakeholders and outside analysts, the countries relevant to an understanding of the region seem to multiply continuously.

14

WIDER CONTEXTS OF PEACE AND WAR

The reemergence of Iran in the aftermath of the Second Gulf War makes necessary a more detailed review of that country, and the same must be said for Turkey, since these are the two key non-Arab Muslim states in the region. Both nations also have particularly extensive, distinguished histories, of which their populaces and leaders are cognizant and proud, to a fault.

Iran was historically known as Persia, although since the term "Iran" comes from the Indo-Iranian root "Ira-," meaning "best," the modern designation is by no means objectionable to most Iranians.[217] A long and august history reaches its first high-water mark more than 2,500 years ago when Cyrus II "the Great" and his Achaemenid successors held sway—an Indo-European dynasty, the main languages of which, Avestan and Old Persian, are closer to English than to Arabic—from the western Indian subcontinent to the edge of Libya.

It was Cyrus who, in the aftermath of the fusion of the Medes and Persians to create the Achaemenid power, swallowed up the Semitic Babylonian (Chaldaean) Empire—more or less today's Iraq and parts of Syria, Jordan, and Israel-Palestine—and permitted the Judaeans to return to Jerusalem to rebuild their Temple in 538 BCE. Part of the secret of the Persians' success, in fact, was their administrative innovation: they permitted a great deal of leeway to diverse ethnic and religious groups, provided that they toed the political line.

The Achaemenid Persian Empire, under Dareios III, was dismantled around 331–330 BCE by Alexander the Great, but about a century later its successor emerged in the form of the Parthian, or Arsacid, Empire, achieving independence from the Seleucid successors to Alexander and melding Persian and Greek cultural ideas. The Parthian Empire lasted for five centuries, offering the Roman Empire serious competition for domination of the Middle East during much of that time; the Parthians were particularly renowned for their skill as archers.

They were, in turn, displaced by a successor Persian conqueror, Ardeshir I, who in 224 CE defeated the last Parthian king, Arbanus V—in hand-to-hand combat. Ardeshir's successor, Shapur I, consolidated and expanded the Sassanian Empire after assuming power in 241 CE—and took the Roman Emperor, Valerian, prisoner at Edessa, in 260. It was also during Shapur's reign that a new faith, spun off from Zoroastrianism, Manichaeism, began to spread. It was thus a largely Zoroastrian and Manichaean imperium that, having controlled much of the region for four centuries, gradually dissolved between 638 and 651 through a succession of losses to the oncoming Muslim Arabs.

A succession of Shi'i Muslim dynasties held sway, beginning with the caliphate of Ali, the Prophet's son-in-law, in Kufa in 656. Ali was assassinated there five years later, but Ali's second son, Hussein, soon challenged the dominant Muslim dynasty, the Umayyads, whose capital was in Damascus. Perhaps the most remembered moment for Shi'i Muslims, particularly Iranians, was the battle of Karbala in 680, in which Hussein and his small force of seventy-two warriors were slaughtered by an Umayyad army, engendering a definitive schism between Sunni and Shi'i Muslims.

It should also be noted here that the emotional quotient of Persian culture is very high. The story of Hussein at Karbala has been told and enacted with great passion again and again, as if the events were happening at the time of the telling—in a manner reminiscent of medieval Christian Passion Plays—so much so that the audience would often become engaged with the actors on the stage as if there were no boundary between audience and actors.[218]

Culturally, the fusion of Persian and Arab cultures led to an extraordinary output of a wide range of visual, literary, and musical arts in the eighth through tenth centuries, during the political heyday of the Abbasid Dynasty in Baghdad, after the elimination of the Umayyads in 750. What is now Iran and parts of what are now Iraq, Azerbaijan, and Afghanistan were dominated by a succession of dynasties asserting themselves side by side with the Abbasids, and derived from diverse ethno-linguistic sources. The briefly lived Ghaznavid Dynasty, for instance (994–1030) was Turkic-speaking. The arrival of another Turkic group, the Seljuks, in the eleventh century—whose defeat of the Byzantines at the Battle of Manzikert in 1072 would start the process leading to the first Crusade—signaled the beginning of the slow swoon of the Abbasids and other, smaller dynastic groups.

Genghis Khan's Mongol army would help transform that swoon into a final demise—when he swallowed up the Khwarezmid Empire in 1221, every person in the key city of Nishapur who could not escape was beheaded, their heads stacked in pyramids. Similarly, Tamerlane (Timur the Lame) killed seventy thousand people when he sacked Isfahan in the 1380s; with him came the Timurid Dynasty. The most significant of Iranian dynasties, perhaps, was the Safavid, whose founding figure, Shah Ismail, declared Shi'i Islam the official state religion in 1501. The rule of Shah Abbas I, however, marked the dynasty's high point, beginning another "Golden Age" that extended from 1590 to 1722. The Shi'i Safavid Persian Empire often vied for hegemony in the region with the Sunni Muslim Ottoman Turkish Empire.

After the collapse of the Safavid Empire and nearly half a century of civil war, Persia was unified in 1796 under its last imperial dynasty, the Qajar, which, over the course of the nineteenth century, engaged in several losing wars with Tsarist Russia and Armenia, as well as Georgia and Northern Azerbaijan (1813). It also began selling tobacco and concessions for discovered oil to European companies (1890)—full oil rights were granted to Britain in 1901—but finally more or less collapsed under its own corruption in 1906 when a briefly lived constitutional democracy, looking to the United States as its model and inspiration, asserted itself, and a *majlis* (parliament) was formed to push the country into the modern era.

The *majlis* stuttered and was dissolved two years later, then restored and again dissolved in 1911, as Iran—still nominally governed by Qajar shahs—was under the thumb of the Russians in the north and the British in the south and east. With the arrival of World War I, during which as we have earlier noted, the entire region was used as needed by the key European protagonists, Iran gradually subsided into political, social, and economic chaos. This only resolved itself after the Great War, when Iran agreed to become a British Protectorate, in order to avoid full occupation by Russia—but the *majlis* reconvened in 1921 and rejected that condition.

As British troops withdrew, more chaos ensued, enabling Reza Khan, a not particularly well-known officer in the army, to stage a coup. His self-appointed succession of roles from minister of war to prime minister culminated in a decision, in 1925, to formally depose the last Qajar leader and to become Shah. He was, in part, persuaded to do this rather than to become president of a new republic by key religious leaders who feared that their own roles in a democratic republic would shrink.

He was thereafter known as Reza Shah. Ironically, under his new imperium, the clergy's role *did* diminish as he pushed heavily for a western-style modernization and secularization of the country. He even replaced traditional Islam-rooted religious holidays with those based on ancient Persian customs. And one of his first orders of business was to fortify his central authority by shaping a more disciplined standing army and undercutting the authority of tribal leaders. He also provided public education, opened Iran's first modern university, opened schools and the workplace to women, and abolished the wearing of the veil—all of which further undercut traditional religious authority. Furthermore, as part of an industrialization effort, he also built roads, bridges, state-owned factories, and a transnational railway. But alongside these modernizing efforts, Reza Shah dissolved the *majlis* definitively and crushed free speech—his troops massacred hundreds of protestors against his antireligious policies in 1935, the same year in which the name of the country officially switched from "Persia" to "Iran."

He elected to remain neutral as World War II broke out, but the Soviet Union needed the Trans-Iranian railway to supply it with wartime materiel and so the British and the Soviets invaded and occupied Iran in 1941, deposing Reza Shah and forcing him to abdicate his leadership. He died in exile in South Africa in 1944. His playboy son, Muhammad Reza Pahlavi, was installed in his stead as Shah. At the end of the war, the USSR established the Azerbaijan People's Government, in Iranian Azerbaijan and in the following year the Soviet–backed Kurdish Republic of Mahabad declared its independence from Iran—the first hint of an independent Kurdish polity in the course of decades of European promises. The following winter Iran would regain control of both Soviet-declared regions.

The events of the following decade are crucial for understanding much of the specific undertones of the relationship between Iran and the United States up to the present day. On the one hand, British troops withdrew from Iran in March 1946 and pressure from the US-led UN forced the Soviet forces to pull out of Iran's northwest province two months later, the only territory that had been occupied by the USSR during World War II that was vacated by Stalin. This reinforced the position of the United States in Iranian eyes, going back to the beginning of the century, as a pro-justice model to be admired. Iran formally became a constitutional monarchy in 1949.

On the other hand, emulating the American model, the Iranians once again pushed for a democratic republican government two years later: the second constitutional revolution led to the reaffirmation of the *majlis'* political position, the election of Muhammad Mossadeq as prime minister—the first true, democratically elected Iranian leader in its history. This also led to a law proposed by Mossadeq and passed by the *majlis* that would nationalize Iran's oil industry, wresting it from British control. The British froze Iran's sterling assets and took the case to the International Court of Justice—which ruled in Iran's favor. Defying the court decision, the British amped up the pressure on Iran by placing a complete trade embargo and enforced it with their navy, leading to a collapse of Iran's economy.

Perhaps even more significant in the long run was the decision made by the American CIA under the influence of British Intelligence—that asserted that Mossadeq was pushing Iran toward an overly warm relationship with the Soviet Union—to join the British in staging a coup, known as "Operation Ajax," under the command of Kermit Roosevelt, Jr. This ultimately brought down Mossadeq's government in 1953 and confined him to prison for three years and then house arrest until his death in 1967. One might recall that this was the time when the Cold War was reaching a high-water mark reflected in particular in the United States by the activities of Senator Joseph McCarthy and culminating in June of that same year (1953) with the execution of Julius and Ethel Rosenberg. In other words, it was an era marked, in the United States, by a profound paranoia of Communism and in particular the danger to Americans of an expansive Soviet Union.

The British pushed hard on this issue, to draw the Americans into the coup. One might also keep in mind that Mossadeq had followed the lead prescribed by the *majlis* in 1951 and nationalized the Iranian oil industry that—up to that point—had disadvantaged Iran while favoring the British—who, aside from drawing the United States into the plan for the coup orchestrated a worldwide boycott of Iranian oil and froze Iran's sterling assets. Anglo-Iranian oil became British Petroleum in 1954.

In the midst of these events, the Shah, believing that the coup had failed, fled to Rome, but was shortly thereafter brought back to Tehran and reinstalled. We can only imagine the enormous disappointment of the Iranian people at the role that the previously admired Americans—the light on the hill—played in the tumbling of the first real Iranian democracy. This disappointment intensified as the young Shah developed SAVAK—the eyes-everywhere secret service—with assistance from the CIA a few years later.

Like his father, Muhammad Reza Pahlavi pushed hard toward the West: his "White Revolution" of 1962–63 undertook major land reforms, championed workers' rights and women's suffrage, but was poorly executed and, reminiscent of Stalinist "five-year plans," did not succeed as intended. When the most notable religious leader in the country, the Ayatollah Khomeini, attacked the reforms in a series of public addresses, he was jailed; released a year later, Khomeini resumed his harsh criticism of the government and was then exiled to Najaf, in Iraq—from which position he continued to criticize the Shah through written pamphlets and sermons recorded and distributed on cassettes.

Over the next decade, Iran experienced rapid economic growth and relative stability—public health, educational institutions, highways, bridges, railroad tracks, water and sewage projects, factories, hospitals all expanded significantly, as did the country's military strength. The Shah's personal obsession with the latest military technology, and his expanding oil revenues, made him an ideal client for what President Dwight D. Eisenhower called the burgeoning American military-industrial complex.

Among the significant moments and developments during the twenty-year period following the 1953 coup one might note the grandiose, multimillion-dollar celebration effected by the Shah in 1971, at the ancient site of Persepolis, to mark what he called the 2500-year empire, referring to his regime as a continuation of the imperial Achaemenid Medo-Persian creation of Cyrus II "the Great." One might also note that the Arab oil embargo of 1973, following the Yom Kippur War, bloated Iran's own oil revenues to 20 billion dollars a year, enabling the Shah to accelerate his timetable of westernized modernization. This included an enormous pile of arms added to the Shah's arsenal by Nixon beginning in 1972 in order to counter Soviet influence; by 1976 Iran had spent 4 billion dollars on American military hardware.

SAVAK's spying, repression, torture, and killing of Iranian citizens also expanded significantly during the mid-1970s—together, on the other hand, with "Ugly American" incidents in which Americans were immune from prosecution, thanks to a "Status of Forces Agreement" (SOFA), which the Shah had agreed to in 1964, granting immunity to American citizens in Iran. The SOFA was one of the things against which the Ayatollah Khomeini most strongly spoke out both before his arrest and during his exile in Iraq. SAVAK's arrest and torture of key religious leaders, such as Rafsanjani and Khamenei, reached its peak in 1974. By the following year, oil revenues had begun to shrink and economic hardship and inflation set in. In 1975 Khomeini's forty-nine-year-old son suddenly died and SAVAK was largely suspected of having murdered him. The unrest of the following year—in which Khomeini shifted his exile to Paris, gaining access to the international press—due to the extremely uneven distribution of wealth, yielded the deaths of hundreds of protesters by the Shah's police in various cities. But the unrest continued to expand, so that the Shah once again fled on January 16, 1979; he died a year later in Egypt—after a brief interlude in a US hospital where President Carter had invited him for cancer treatments.

Two weeks after that flight, Ayatollah Khomeini, the figure around whom diverse Iranian factions had united in opposition to the Shah, arrived into Tehran on February 1, and then the Islamic revolution began. Thus the year in which the Egyptians and Israelis signed a peace agreement that has remained in place, to date, for thirty-eight years, was the year in which Iran's rather positive relationship with Israel—built on certain common interests, most obviously that Israel and Iran were, together with Turkey, the only non-Arab, non-theocratic, distinctly Western-looking countries in the region—emphatically came to an end. After two and a half millennia of monarchy, with a brief constitutional monarchic window and briefer democratic window, the new Iran emerged, by referendum, as a theocratic republic: the Islamic Republic of Iran.

The new non-relationship with Israel echoed Iran's changing course with the United States, Israel's most obvious and powerful ally. Two weeks after Khomeini's arrival, the US Embassy was seized, primarily by militant students—but they soon thereafter withdrew at Khomeini's insistence. Shortly after the Shah was admitted to the United States for medical treatment, the embassy was seized a second time in protest of his ties to the US, on November 14, and this time, fifty-two hostages were taken.

In the United States, with Carter already struggling to hold the White House against the onslaught of Ronald Reagan, the absence of progress on releasing the hostages for over a year helped guarantee a Reagan victory. Soon after the election, Reagan's vice president, George Bush the Elder, former director of the CIA, was apparently able to begin—rather suddenly—serious negotiations that led to the freeing of the hostages on January 20, 1981. In the interim, Saddam Hussein—functionally at that moment a US ally—invaded Iran on September 22, 1980, thus initiating the eight-year-long war between Iran and Iraq. By the time Iran agreed to the UN resolution to end that war, some 750,000 Iranians had perished in the conflict. The following year, a decade after the Islamic revolution, the Ayatollah Khomeini died and was succeeded by the Ayatollah Khamenei as Supreme Leader.

Gradually, in the decades since, there has been a slight diminishing of the intensity with which religious figures reign, but relations with the United States have not necessarily improved. The American government imposed an absolute ban on trade with Iran in 1995, claiming as cause extensive Iranian support of terrorism and the regime's pursuit of nuclear power. But two years later, with the election of reformist Muhammad Khatami as president, cultural and economic exchange was reinitiated. Another two years later, students at Tehran University held demonstrations demanding greater freedom of expression.

By the dawn of the new millennium, the presidential elections taking place every four years began to offer some meaning with regard to Iran's relationship to itself and to the world around it, as opposed to being a completely meaningless exercise undertaken in the shadow of an autocratic religious regime—although the tension of that dual-leadership dynamic has remained in place. The *majlis* elections of 2000–2001 took political control from the conservatives and put it in the hands of reformers—although in April, the judiciary passed a law banning the publication of sixteen reformist newspapers. Khatami was reelected in 2001, and the following year President Bush the Younger declared Iran part of "the axis of evil"—as, later that year, Soviet technologists defied American protests in aiding Iran to build its first nuclear reactor.

It is this last issue, together with the question of how extensively Iran has been involved in sponsoring terrorism—most obviously, but not limited to, support for the development and expansion of Hizb'Allah—that marked out Iran's place in the region and the world over the following decade and a half. In June 2003, the UN nuclear watchdog gave Iran several weeks to prove that it was not pursuing an atomic weapons program; Iran claimed, in November, that it was suspending its uranium-enrichment program and allowed tougher UN inspections of its nuclear facilities—the inspections yielded no evidence of a weapons program. Two years later, after conservatives had regained control of the *majlis*, but after Iran agreed to suspend most of its uranium enrichment, it resumed uranium conversion at its Isfahan plant, albeit only for peaceful purposes.

That same year Mahmoud Ahmadinejad, Tehran's ultraconservative mayor, was elected president. The following year, in February 2006, Iran resumed uranium enrichment at a second site, Natanz; the UN Security Council demanded that by August 31 the program be discontinued. In December, Iran hosted a Holocaust conference; Ahmadinejad was becoming an increasingly vocal Holocaust denier. The Security Council voted to impose sanctions on Iran's trade in nuclear technology and material—and, not surprisingly, Israel was becoming increasingly vocal regarding the threat that Iran posed to the Jewish State, as well as to the region and the world.

In the decade since, discussion has revolved around the nuclear question and Iran's instablity, and with it, the validity of the existential threat to Israel and to everyone else. This issue surfaced most fiercely in the hotly contested election that, in 2009, brought Ahmadinejad into a second term, but amidst serious claims of vote rigging. Supporters of rival candidates took to the streets in protest, yielding over one thousand arrests and more than thirty dead. Iranian leaders blamed foreign governments—particularly Britain—for the protests. There remains no unequivocal proof that the alleged vote rigging actually took place, but it is still a source of major contention in Iran.

Within Iran, hard-liners who were disinclined to seek rapprochement with the West—and part of whose ideology is the denial of Israel's right to exist— became more firmly entrenched in power than ever, controlling all aspects of infrastructure and often partaking in flagrant corruption. Iran has also become a consistent supporter and funder of terrorist organizations, including Hamas, Islamic Jihad, and Hizb'Allah. And despite signing the international antinuclear proliferation treaty, Iran was seeking every opportunity to develop a nuclear weapons program up until a recent agreement with the Obama administration, claiming that its isolation during and after its war with Iraq required it to develop its own sources of nuclear power in order to function effectively. This claim was not found to be credible by most outside observers and the development of Iranian nuclear power is considered by Israel to pose a fundamental threat to its existence.

The threat that Iran posed (and poses) to some Israelis—specifically Prime Minister Netanyahu and his supporters—was being felt by Saudis, as well. The elimination of Iraq as a viable power in the aftermath of the American-led removal of Saddam Hussein, and its dissolution into a de facto Kurdish state and pockets of unstable Sunni and Shi'i Arab rule—positioned Iran, as previously noted, to become a more powerful presence in the region. The counterweight of Iraq was and is gone. The outcome of this has been the frequent and friendly behind-closed-doors discussions between the Israelis and the Saudis.

This trend was further reinforced when the United States, under President Obama, demonstrated increasing interest in pursuing serious diplomatic engagement with Iran, signaling an about-face from Bush the Younger, under whom the United States had been openly hostile to Iran and had pursued a raft of sweeping sanctions as late as October, 2007. With the Obama administration's slow turn, both Israel and Saudi Arabia concluded that they could not count on the United States where Iran was concerned.[219] Despite a US intelligence report in December 2007, which played down the perceived nuclear threat posed by Iran, it wasn't evident to everybody that the time was ripe for American-Iranian repositioning. The *majlis* was dominated by conservatives in the 2008 legislative vote and, during this time, Iran test fired a new version of the Shahab-3, a long-range missile potentially capable of hitting targets in Israel, which Ahmadinejad continued to speak of his desire to eradicate. But in retrospect, one might see the gradual US turn toward pursuing a diplomatic, rather than military option in the note of congratulation sent to Barack Obama by Ahmadinejad after the 2008 US Presidential election, to which the new president responded with an offer of unconditional dialogue regarding Iran's nuclear program.[220]

A few months after Ahmadinejad's 2009 reelection Iran testfired a series of medium- and long-range missiles and acknowledged the construction of a uranium-enrichment plant near Qom, insisting, however, that it was strictly for peaceful purposes. A series of other actions prompted the UN Security Council to impose another round of sanctions in June 2010, but in December, talks in Geneva between Iran and key world powers led to another round of talks at the beginning of the New Year. Let us keep in mind, too, that in early October 2011, Iran's Ayatollah Khamenei completely rejected the Palestinian bid for state-status representation in the UN because to do so would implicitly acknowledge Israel's right to exist, as it would imply an acceptance of a two-state solution. As Khamenei commented at a conference on the Palestine issue, "any plan that seeks to divide Palestine must be totally rejected [by Iran]."[221] Thus, counterintuitively, Iran was supporting Palestine by rejecting its bid for internationally recognized legitimacy.

Meanwhile, as the pendulum continued to swing back and forth on the nuclear issue, in June 2012, the United States exempted seven key customers from sanctions in return for their cutting imports of Iranian oil; in July, the EU imposed an oil embargo and in October announced further sanctions. In April 2013, Iran announced that it had begun operations at two uranium mines and a uranium ore-processing plant. However, contrary to these trends, two months later, the reformist-backed cleric, Hassan Rouhani, was elected president. Three months after his election, he asserted to an American news reporter that Iran would never build nuclear weapons, and in an address to the UN General Assembly he extended an offer for serious talks with key nations to assure this. In keeping with this promise, two months hence, Iran agreed to allow UN inspectors better access in exchange for sanction relief.

More interesting still was the offer made by President Rouhani in June 2014 to assist the (Shi'i-led) Iraqi government in its battle against extremist Sunni insurgents. (Oh, and by the way, *Hamas* was at that point in danger of losing Iranian support because it was supporting the Sunni insurgents.) The next month, a sixth round of negotiations between Iran and the P5+1 group (the five permanent members of the UN Security Council—China, France, Russia, the United Kingdom, and the United States—plus Germany) began in Vienna; in November, Russia agreed to build as many as eight nuclear reactors in Iran, presumably to diminish Iran's sense of needing its own uranium enrichment.

The debate on ending sanctions in exchange for assurances from Iran continued to expand over the following eight or nine months. The discussion in the United States was fast and furious; among other things, it was splitting the Jewish community over whether to support an end or a continuation of hostilities. This culminated with the unprecedented invitation extended to Israeli Prime Minister Netanyahu to address Congress, without presidential approval—an invitation that Netanyahu took up, speaking on March 3, 2015, in eloquent condemnation of any treaty. Not surprisingly, the same voices that pushed for the 2003 war in Iraq echoed that of Netanyahu regarding Iran.

Speculation also developed in 2015 in some quarters that the Israelis might attempt a strike against Iran's reactors without American support—the rising tension could be likened to that of the Cuban missile crisis of nearly fifty-five years ago. While President Obama acceded to bipartisan pressure to allow

Congress a say on the emerging Iran deal, the Iranian *majlis* chose to await the decision of the American Congress before weighing in with its own vote.[222] Congress ended up approving the deal in September 2015, and exactly a year after the Vienna talks began, world powers reached an agreement with Iran on limiting nuclear activity in exchange for the lifting of sanctions; in February 2016, reformists fared well in the latest round of elections to the *majlis*.

As of July 2016, the Iranians, "defying the expectations of the deal's most vociferous critics, gave up 98 percent of their nuclear material. They dismantled thousands of centrifuges . . . By January, even Israel's top military officer said he was impressed . . . ,"[223] albeit little larger progress toward moving Iran into the international mainstream has been made. The internal growth and relations with terrorist groups remain areas with large question marks attached to them.

Questions remain around the future of Iranian-American relations. Will the agreements arrived at in 2015 continue to hold under the Trump administration? Will the relationship between the two countries expand and flourish or wither? Will the role of Iran in Syria and through *Hizb'allah* in Lebanon become more or less problematic? How will that impinge on Saudi Arabia (and Qatar)—and Israel, as well Turkey? Virtually every month, an article appears referring to some aspect of this morass, whether the issue is increasing doubt among the Iranian populace regarding the deal or ongoing concerns in America or any of these other countries.

The condition of Iran is linked to that of Iraq and in turn to that of Saudi Arabia (in particular in that Iran backs the Houthis in Yemen, whom the Saudis are desperately trying to dislodge), Jordan, Syria (particularly in that key combatants in the Syrian civil war are proxies for the Iranians—as others are for the Saudis), and ultimately to that of Israel (in which, interestingly enough, between 2006 and 2016 a growing series of quiet voices actually began to consider the idea that regional peace and stability in the region might be better served by nuclear parity than disparity)[224]—regardless of the outcome of the Israeli-Palestinian problem. Iran's internal political swings are a microcosm of the unpredictable shifts in the region in general. Its relations with others in the region interweave relations with key powers in the outside world.

It is also important to remember and reflect on the distinct role of the United States. We are the power that, in spite of our shortcomings, still has the most capacity to effect positive change in the region. That role was tested in July and August 2016 by the sudden presence of Russia in Iran, using Iranian military bases to fire rockets against ISIS—and after about two weeks of that surprise development (Iran had not permitted a foreign military presence on its soil since World War II), Russia was asked to remove its forces from those bases, on the presumed grounds that it had been too vocal to the rest of the world regarding its presence.

Russia has recently also begun to warm relations with Turkey. And indeed, one of the subtler ways in which the American role in the region is also being currently tested may be seen, in the Turkish demand made, in late July 2016—not for the first time in the past several years—that we extradite the Turkish Sufi theologian and political philosopher, Fethullah Gülen, back to his country. That demand came from the current president of the Republic of Turkey, Recep Tayyip Erdogan, in the aftermath of an alleged coup attempt on July 15 that he claims to have thwarted and has asserted was fomented by followers of Mr. Gülen.

Turkey in general and Mr. Erdogan in particular—and, for that matter, Mr. Gülen—are a significant knot within the tangled web of the Middle East and have been important across the region's history. Like Iran, Turkey is not Arab; unlike Iran, which is mainly Shi'i Muslim, Turkey is mainly Sunni—although that category does not begin to explain the religious complexity of the country's Muslim personality, much less account for other aspects of its cultural and religious history.

In the area that we now call eastern Turkey, a number of cultural forces emerge to our awareness in the Middle Bronze Age, culminating with the development of the Hittite Empire that dominated most of what is now Turkey by the Late Bronze Age (ca. 1600–1200 BCE). Two noteworthy aspects of the Hittite period, for our purposes, are first that the Hittite language was Indo-European, which suggests the origins of the people themselves—related to both the Greeks and the Persians. Second, that the Hittites had a good deal of interaction with New Kingdom Egypt, including a major battle—the Battle of Kadesh in 1274 BCE—that led to the first recorded treaty between former enemies.

After massive population migrations that marked a gradual transition from the Bronze Age to the Iron Age, the empire splintered into a number of small kingdoms: Lydians, Lycians, Luwians, Phrygians, and others. But eventually, most of the region would ultimately be swallowed up by the expanding Achaemenid Persian Empire in the sixth century BCE. Then, with the arrival of Alexander the Great and the collapse of the Achaemenid Empire, Anatolia—as the area is often called, thanks to the Greeks (it means "rising up," a reference to the fact that, being east of Greece, it is the place from which the sun rises up)—became part of Alexander's realm. It was again divided after Alexander's death among various successors and their successors, some parts also eventuating into Parthian hands until the advent of Rome as a power throughout the

Mediterranean and Middle Eastern worlds brought much of it into the ambit of the West.

In the aftermath of the collapse of the Western Roman Empire, in 476 CE, Anatolia was left, among other things, with more Greek archaeological remains than there are in Greece, and more Roman remains than there are in Italy, to go with extensive Hittite, Assyrian, Babylonian, Persian, and even Egyptian remains. But Anatolia was, by then, the remnant Eastern Roman Empire: Byzantium. A rich Christian history—centered on the tradition that the Virgin Mary ended up in Ephesos, attended by John the Evangelist, and on Paul of Tarsus's preaching path across much of its western and central landscape—flourished through the millennium of Byzantine history, but by the era of the Crusades Byzantium was in political danger from two directions.

The first came from the incoming Seljuks, a Turkic people from south-central Asia, and the second came from the Christian West. The animist Seljuks, as they moved into the region, embraced the religion of the Muslims they conquered and in 1071, as we have earlier noted, defeated the Byzantine army at Manzikert.[225] This provoked a cry for help on the part of the Byzantine emperor, Alexios I, to the Pope—a somewhat problematic matter, since the great schism of 1054 had emphatically separated the Western Christians from their Eastern coreligionists, largely over the question of fidelity to the Pope as supreme mediator between God and Christendom.

The West delayed its response—an entire generation—using Manzikert as one of the alleged bases for undertaking the First Crusade in 1095–96. In the long run, however, Byzantium was pillaged, not saved, by Western crusaders during the Fourth Crusade in 1199–1204: the pillagers asserted that the Byzantine Christians were heretics, no less a threat to proper Christianity than the Muslim and Jewish Infidels, so in fact they never even attempted to continue beyond Constantinople to the Holy Land at that time. The ever-shrinking Byzantine Empire reached the end of its line with the conquest of Constantinople by the Ottoman Turks in 1453—the Ottomans, like the Seljuks, having embraced Islam along the way—and in the next nearly five centuries Turkey is the central area of the much larger and longer Ottoman Imperial history.

For our purposes, one of the more important late developments in Ottoman Turkish history is the pair of *tanzimat* (reorganization) reforms introduced by Sultan Abdul Meced I in 1839 and 1856. In both instances, the idea of the *dhimma* was addressed and in effect eliminated, officially removing the limitations to Christians and Jews within Ottoman society and government. Interestingly, those who most objected to these reforms at the time were members of the Greek Orthodox community, which stood on the highest rung of the *dhimmi* ladder, for they feared losing that relatively advantageous position.

A second key development that we have earlier noted was the emerging Arab pushback against the Ottoman Empire by the late nineteenth century, referred to as *intifada*—"throwing off"—of a group viewed by the Arabs as a colonial outsider even after six hundred years in the region. A third development, after World War I and the demise of the Empire, was the failure of the British and the French to crush Mustafa Kemal Atattuerk's attempt to create a modern—secular—Turkish state.

The history of Turkey since the inception of the Republic in 1923, by way of the July 14 Treaty of Lausanne, offers a handful of noteworthy elements to bolster our discussion. A 1925 law formally separated religion and politics; in 1928–29, the Latin alphabet was introduced; in 1933 universal suffrage—giving women the vote—was embraced.[226] Turkey began as a neutral in World War II (a good number of Jews from Nazi-occupied lands took refuge there) and then joined the allies; the country was a cornerstone of the 1947 Truman Doctrine: the outcome of a speech delivered by the president to the US Congress in which he specifically asked for aid appropriations to Turkey and Greece as part of the means for limiting Soviet influence in the Middle East and East Mediterranean.[227]

By 1950, the political landscape within Turkey had expanded, with the development of a multiparty system and the first real elections. There are two particular aspects of the decades that follow that are important if one is to understand the events of the past several years with some clarity. One is the parliamentary structure of the Turkish government. While the president, who serves a five-year term, is nominally the head of state, the actual executive power resides with the prime minster and the council of ministers; the legislative branch is the 550-member parliament elected in eighty-five districts; the judiciary is independent of both. The second aspect of particular note is that between Atatürk's death in 1938 and 2003 there were several attempts to subvert the government. Interestingly, each time that happened, the army intervened, effecting a coup—in 1960, 1971, 1980, and 1997—but then stepped back once a democratic government was firmly in place. The last of these was noteworthy for the fact that a more secular government was returned to power after a brief period defined by a more Islamist leadership.

During those decades, Turkey joined NATO, became engaged in a long-lasting series of conflicts with Greece over the divided Greek-Turkish island of Cyprus, was riven internally by struggles with its Kurdish population—a Kurdish political party (the PKK) was formed in 1984—and maintained a muted but cordial relationship with the State of Israel. Turkish Jews flew to and from Israel with some frequency. Turkey in two obvious respects mirrored Iran—in its secular leadership and its relationship with Israel—all three nations the only non-Arab as well as nominally church-and-state separate countries in the region.

On the other hand, particularly in the last decade or so of the twentieth century and the first decade of the new millennium, Turkey seemed positioned to become a more central part of the Arabo-Islamic world and also to offer a bridge between that world and the West.

This last, potentially important aspect of the recent history of the region seemed to be coming to a particular and fruitful denouement in the first years of the twenty-first century with the election of Recep Tayyip Erdogan as prime minister in 2003. Erdogan, former mayor of Istanbul—which he had very successfully brought into the present as a modern center of culture and business that attracted Western tourists and investors—presented himself as both an Islamist and a modernist.

During his first two terms of office, he was both extremely popular and apparently successful on various political and economic fronts. Turkey's economy was booming; its relations with the Arab world, in large part based on the strong Muslim personality that Erdogan was imprinting on his country, were blossoming, as were relations with Europe. The Turkey that had, a century earlier, been the object of *intifada* animosity was being largely embraced; on the other hand, Turkey found itself for the first time under serious consideration to be a member of the EU. It appeared likely that the vigorous republic would indeed play that key role as a bridge between Europe and the Middle East.

As recently as 2011, Turkey was viewed across the Arab world as having played the "most constructive" role in the events of the 2010 Arab Spring, and Erdogan was the most admired leader in the region. Support for this can be found in the 2011 edition of the annual "Arab Public Opinion Survey" conducted by Shibley Telhami of the Brookings Institution in Washington, DC. The survey interviewed three thousand individuals from Egypt, Morocco, Jordan, Lebanon, the United Arab Emirates, and Saudi Arabia. Egyptians, for instance, in the aftermath of the coup that removed Hosni Mubarak from power, were asked what leader they would prefer the next Egyptian president to resemble; 38 percent cited Erdogan—the next closest leader, Iran's Ahmadinejad, was cited by a mere 11 percent of respondents. Asked which political system they wanted their country to resemble, 44 percent cited Turkey—France was next, at 10 percent.

Not long after this study was published, both Erdogan and his position in the Arab world; the wider region; and the world in general began to change, and not necessarily for the better. Before Egypt's political situation resolved itself in the assumption of power through a military coup under General Abdul Fattah Al-Sisi, things were still in flux under the uneasy leadership of the post-coup elected president, Muhammad Morsi, a scion of the *Muslim Brotherhood*. During this precarious period, Erdogan flew to Cairo and offered to advise the Egyptians but was told that they didn't need his advice. He returned home empty-handed, unable to play the sort of constructive mediating role for which, shortly before, he'd seemed uniquely qualified.[228]

Shortly thereafter, as Syria began to fall more significantly apart, and diverse groups of rebels pitted themselves against Bashar al-Assad, Erdogan—who had an apparently close relationship with Assad, which has since dramatically soured—advised the Syrian leader to desist during the holy month of Ramadan from the intense bombing that was producing so much death among Syrian civilians. Assad agreed—and then proceeded to increase the intensity of the bombing. The swift and significant diminishment of Erdogan's influence in the Arab world was particularly noteworthy since one of the instruments of increasing his influence had been to turn Turkey's relations with Israel 180 degrees in a negative direction.

That turn was gradual but hit a distinct and rapid twist in May 2010 when a small flotilla of six Turkish boats traveled toward Gaza from Turkey into Israel's territorial waters, with the presumed goal of bringing supplies to Gazans who had by then been enduring a blockade imposed by the Israelis to keep weapons out of the hands of *Hamas* in the aftermath of months of rocket attacks into southern Israel. Interestingly, while Turkey protested vehemently and all but ended its diplomatic relationship with Israel, other major Arab countries barely uttered a word—and the Turkish spiritual leader who was gradually becoming an important critic of Erdogan's increasingly difficult political behavior, Fethullah Gülen, spoke out defending Israel's right to protect its territorial boundaries. Much later, Erdogan was known to have played an important role in fomenting the Gaza flotilla catastrophe that left nine people dead and relations between Turkey and Israel in tatters.

These relatively rapid external developments coincided with an internal deterioration most apparent in the increasing vigor with which Erdogan sought autocratic power. General problems of human rights became most conspicuous in the treatment of the press—seventy-six journalists were jailed in 2012 alone, making Turkey the most media-unfriendly country in the world—and in relations with the Kurds, which despite prior signs of some sort of peaceful conclusion, began in that year to move backwards.

In retrospect, this backward movement was accompanied by a broader turn toward not just autocratic but paranoid behavior that expressed itself as early as 2008, such as in the infamous Ergenekon case. Erdogan launched an extensive campaign against the secularist military, alleging that it was poised to carry out a coup against his government. In the witch hunt that ensued, a quarter of the country's generals and admirals were jailed—but the case also targeted Erdogan's secular political opponents, and his critics in the media and in civil society at large, including academics and journalists. Hundreds of individuals ended up in jail, but the prosecution never produced a legitimate account of the coup plot. Soon after the military's top brass resigned en masse in 2011, yielding to Erdogan's power, the country's higher courts began throwing out the indictments—but the lesson this affair offers is that any criticism of Erdogan is now taken by him to be tantamount to treason.

In 2013, Erdogan quickly began plans to develop Gezi Park in Istanbul, an action that would have involved cutting down age-old sycamore trees and removing a green area favored by the city's inhabitants while handing substantive construction contracts to his friends. This resulted in a large protest demonstration throughout the Taksim area. Instead of responding with an offer to discuss the matter, Erdogan brought in a heavy police response, with resultant chaos, violence, and injuries. Two years later, his third term as prime minister having ended, Erdogan copied a page out of Vladimir Putin's playbook, achieving the presidency—but then turning it into a position of genuine power, an unofficial, undeclared but clear Executive Presidency, functionally subverting the Turkish democratic system that typically accords that real political power to the prime minister and the Parliament.[229]

But perhaps most significant is the witch hunt in which Erdogan has been engaged since around 2013—the year of the Gezi Park protest disaster. When, after a succession of inept governments, Erdogan first came to power in 2003, he gained the support of Fethullah Gülen, who saw in Erdogan someone who could help pull the country into the modern era while restoring its sense of an Islam-based identity. Gülen has been living in eastern Pennsylvania since 1999. He came to the United States to deal with a heart ailment, and also because he was accused of trying to foment a coup against the Turkish government at that time. He was exonerated of all charges by the Turkish courts. And what is it that Gülen is all about? He is a cleric inspired by Sufism and in particular by mystics like the thirteenth-century poet, Jalaluddin Rumi, who was both an emphatic Muslim and a profound universalist. Gülen believes that Turkey lost its soul when it became emphatically secular under Atatürk but he also believes that the way forward is for a Muslim Turkey to be completely open to other faiths as well as to nonbelievers, and that a better future will only come about through dialogue engaged by members of diverse faiths, cultures, ethnicities, and races.

As Mr. Erdogan became more comfortable and confident, he saw less and less need for the support of Mr. Gülen and his followers. Late in the prime minister's third term, a clear schism had opened between the two, but with ambiguous motivations. Either Erdogan had been clever enough to mask his true intentions and ambitions all along, so that not only was Turkey duped, but so was Gülen; or the power that he achieved gradually corrupted him, breeding an unslakable thirst for *more* power and an increasing distaste for anyone who might stand in the way of its acquisition. The growing split led Erdogan to hound and attack the *hizmet* movement—*hizmet* means "service" and it is the term used by those inspired by Gülen to describe their affiliation with one another as they go out in the world and do good works. He had gone so far in 2015 as to accuse the group, which he has come to see as the most serious threat to his demagoguery, of seeking to shape a "government within the government."

At the same time, he committed a succession of acts that demonstrate how desperate he has become to assert and maintain authority. Beyond the extraordinarily heavy-handed response to the Gezi Park protests, one might note the recent major corruption scandal in which Erdogan spirited hundreds of millions of Turkish citizens' dollars into his own pockets. In November 2015, his son was recorded asking him, by telephone, where to place several million that couldn't be hidden away quickly enough, as the massive thefts were being discovered and reported. A clear expression of this egregious graft is the enormous, multimillion-dollar palace that Erdogan had built for himself soon thereafter. A further example of his shift into textbook authoritarianism can be found in Erdogan's handling of a mining disaster in Eastern Turkey, which occurred during the same period and led Erdogan to hurry to the area, where he proceeded not to commiserate with but to lambast the miners. When an old man objected to this cruel rhetoric, Erdogan slapped him in the face, exclaiming that it is forbidden to object to the president's words.

Along the way, while he has subverted the rights of Turkish citizens on the one hand and all but destroyed Turkey's relationship with every country with which it had decent relations in the Middle East on the other hand, Erdogan has very publicly tried to look the part of a pious man, praying where he can be seen, and he has with increasing vehemence continued to attack Fethullah Gülen and anyone believed to be associated with Gülen. He has abrogated Turkish law in order to shut down *hizmet*'s schools—secular schools, that have always followed government guidelines with regard to curricula and conduct—*hizmet*'s newspapers (in particular, *Today's Zaman*) and other media outlets and, periodically, members of the professional Turkish world who support *hizmet*.

A climactic flash point of this was the failed "coup" of July 15, 2016, which was quickly suppressed by Erdogan and then baselessly attributed to Gülen and his followers. Except that there was apparently no leadership behind it, no organization to it, no substantial numbers who were part of it; it was carried out at the height, for Istanbul, of the rush hour, rather than the middle of the night, with no key political leaders pulled out of their beds and taken into custody—the oddest coup in Turkish history.

It also runs contrary to Mr. Gülen's manner of being in the world, to his teachings, preachings, writings, and expressed hopes for Turkey and the planet. He has steadfastly asserted that one must work with and through governments and never try to undermine them.[230] Put simply, Gülen has consistently articulated civil Islam; Erdogan has been a consistent exponent of political Islam. The allegedly Gülen-led or Gülen–inspired coup has, however, offered Mr. Erdogan a pretext to arrest tens of thousands of allegedly politically active opponents. He has demanded Mr. Gülen's extradition from the United States.[231] Rather than using the "coup" to bring Turks together, he has used it to track down anybody of even small consequence who might object to his style of governance—inviting Turks to report on family members and neighbors to the authorities in a manner reminiscent of the Nazi and Soviet regimes at their worst. The democracy that was touted not so long ago has been deformed into a reign of terror.

As I write, the demand for Gülen's extradition, accompanied by threats that constitute no less than blackmail regarding American use of air bases in Turkey and Turkey's general role as an ally in the region, have received no answer. To add to the usual repertoire of complications to which, as we have seen, the region is always subject, Erdogan's heavily damaged relationship with Russia and with Vladimir Putin has offered distinct manifestations of repair, following the "coup" and its aftermath. Thus, renewed involvement—interference—in the region from a longtime adversary of the West has again tangled matters.

The United States finds itself in the unenviable position of feeling obliged to publicly cooperate with Mr. Erdogan and tout his role in saving a democracy that he now continues to steadily subvert. Turkey is a long-term member of NATO and an essential ally, due to geography, in our ongoing struggle with the likes of ISIS.[232] There is, however, troubling evidence that suggests that Erdogan was earlier aiding and abetting ISIS while claiming to be the first line of defense between it and Europe.[233] At the moment of this writing, Turkey's role in the struggle with ISIS or in the possible fate of Iraq and Syria is unknowable in any definitive manner.

All of this leads us back to the Arab world and specifically to two major moments in the last twenty-five years that have been pivotal and uniquely transformative. In momentarily returning our focus toward the Palestinians, it is fair to say that the Arab world has varied as to whether it has ignored or championed this most "internal" of regional issues. The Saudis have spent millions of dollars on the Palestinian cause; on the other hand, the Kuwaitis threw out thousands of Palestinian workers during the first Gulf War, eliminating an important means of Palestinian socioeconomic infrastructure—albeit one not located within Palestine itself.[234] Moreover, this entire narrative has exploded in the past generation well beyond the bounds of the Middle East: on 9/11, it reached halfway around the world. The stakes, to say the least, have broadened exponentially. It's not just about Israel and the Palestinians and it's not just about the Middle East but about the world at large.

The theology that pitted Islam and Christianity against each other in the Medieval *reconquista* and Crusades, and that focused both faiths in the postmedieval struggle between the Ottomans and Europe, became an oil-based interest in a politically and socially backward Near East over a century ago on the part of the Prussians and thus the British and the French. The ensuing competition led to the First World War. That oil-based focus from the outside world into the world of the Middle East is continued most obviously in our own era by the United States. It is American oil interests that primarily governed our intervention in the Persian Gulf more than two decades ago and certainly did again in 2003, and that motivates our continued presence in and relationship with Saudi Arabia.

Our success at pushing Soviet influence all but out of the region—in part because of the collapse of the USSR by the 1990s and in part because in that same decade, George Bush Sr. crafted such an effective alliance within and outside the region against Saddam that was followed by Bill Clinton's effective diplomatic role with the Israelis, Palestinians, and Jordanians—has led, by 2017 to an ever-enlarging role for Russia and its increasing involvement in Syria and perhaps Turkey and Iran. On the other hand, China has also reasserted a claim for influence in the region, particularly through the expansion of its involvement in the production and consumption of oil from the New Iraq. Sometime after the dust began to settle from the 2003 American invasion, China began to pour about $2 billion a year and hundreds of workers into the country. The Chinese have also demonstrated a willingness to accept lower profits from their contracts with the new government,[235] and to limit the effectiveness of American-led sanction policies toward Iran, as well as to engage with Israel.

It is the American presence in the Arabian peninsula, however, that so enraged Bin Ladin and those like him: Muslim fundamentalists spiritually descended from Wahhabi Sunnis who gnash their teeth at the notion of all those infidel feet striding back and forth across the soil bearing "the two holy mosques" (Makka and Madina), while also ostensibly fretting at the oppression of too many Saudis by the we-take-it-all-for-ourselves royal family.

At the same time that our troops are in effect protecting not only our own oil interests but the Saudi royal house, the members of that house are necessarily performing a tightrope walk. How do or don't they support our government's attempts to form a coalition like that assembled by the Senior President Bush: one that would pit moderate Christians and Muslims against fundamentalists, and "legitimate" governments against terrorists. Nonetheless, America's potential to serve as a positive regional influence remains great, even with all the flaws of our involvement up to this point. One can observe this from the detailed discussion of those wishing to be associated with American culture as it pertains to Israel by Israeli journalist-historian, Tom Segev, in his *Elvis in Jerusalem*, just as one can observe it from a personal story related in a public lecture by Fareed Sarouq.[236]

Sarouq is a South African Sunni Muslim, an activist in the anti-apartheid movement, who studied for eight years in the very *madrasa* in Pakistan that later became best known for producing Taliban fighters. He was in a position to witness the following moment that he described in his lecture: while a Taliban leader was being interviewed by the media, one of the Taliban body guards quietly pulled an American television cameraman aside to ask him how he could get a visa to the United States and a green card. Sarouq's point at the time was how pervasive American TV is: that the market-driven expression of what America is had captured even this most implacable enemy of America. For the purposes of this discussion what is significant is simply how we capture the world. America's potential to serve as a positive regional influence therefore remains great, even with all the flaws of our involvement up to this point.

This yields several questions. First and foremost: what *are* we Americans? At our best, we offer hope regarding the possibility of improving one's condition in the world, regarding individual rights and communal responsibility and respect for differences between individuals and among communities with respect to religion, race, ethnicity, and a host of other attributes. At our worst, we are arrogant and overly certain of our ability to dominate the world. In the years that have followed the attacks of September 11, 2001, the aftermath of which began with so much sympathy for America on the part of the world, we have been beyond arrogant in our assumption that we can operate as lone rangers.

This sensibility pertains both to words and actions: When George W. Bush, in finally responding to the events of 9/11, continued—five times within a short period of time—to use the word "crusade" in referring to how the United States would engage the terrorists from the Middle East, the very term carried with it the same sort of association to Arab and Muslim ears that Western ears would carry were they to hear a leader from that part of the world refer to opposition to America in terms of *jihad*.

Which United States will move forward toward the future? This is a difficult question to answer. Over recent years, my response to it has evolved
with developments on the ground, particularly the clashes of vision between
those who have competed for the American presidency—first Bush versus
Kerry, then Obama versus McCain and Obama versus Romney, and then most
recently, Clinton versus Trump. The wide variations between the visions this
woman and these men have offered reflect the complex realities that dictate
any response to this question, and which have become only more complex in
these early days of the Trump administration.

15

UNFINISHED EPILOGUES—HOPE AND DESPAIR; MEMORY AND FORGETTING

I remind the reader that my primary emphasis has been on the complexities of the past and not on the present, though there is no place in the world where the present more quickly and emphatically *becomes* the past than the Middle East. Between the time when I began to write this book and its publication, many changes small and large in the region, and the world focused upon the region, will have altered the political, economic, and cultural terrain.

The future of the region depends on many different things, especially in an era where the world is more interconnected than ever before, in which a desperate madman hiding in the mountains of Afghanistan can effect the destruction of the two towers of the World Trade Center without ever leaving his cave. With this in mind, it behooves us to consider a handful of outstanding issues within our narrative, as well as to reflect on what will be required to overcome the obstacles and assumptions of the past.

The issue of Israel-Palestine is, as we have observed, fundamentally complicated by aspects of the problems of definition and aspiration. Key among those aspects is the functional distinction among three groups of Palestinian Arabs, as we have seen: those who dwell east of the Jordan and have been citizens of the Kingdom of Jordan for seven decades; those caught in the aftermath of the first Arab-Israeli war who have been dwelling in Gaza and the West Bank who are most frequently the typical reference point of the word "Palestinian;" and finally those who remained or returned to the State of Israel after that war who, since 1949, have been most frequently referred to as Israeli Arabs.

For Palestinians in the West Bank and Gaza, we can derive hope from entities like *Windows*, a nonprofit joint Israeli-Palestinian grassroots peace organization that, since 1991, "has promoted acquaintance, understanding and conciliation between people from both nations, through educational programs, media and art," and which "ignore[s] the ups and downs of the political arena, . . .overcome[s] the sadness and anger that acts of violence make us feel, and . . . keep[s]. . . busy doing the work we know how to do—creating constructive and equal dialogue between Palestinians and Jews."[237] Such an organization is part of the vanguard of the struggle to write the future history of this corner of the region in terms very different from those of the past.

In a different but related way, we may derive hope from an array of often unheralded artistic enterprises, both those that reflect cooperation across the Green Line and those that simply reflect the will to shape the positive and the creative within the morass of so much negativity and destruction—or on the other hand to use art as a means of addressing issues beyond the realm of political and military discourse. To this end, I recall catching my eye on two 2009 articles by Daniel J. Wakin in back-to-back issues of *The New York Times*. One focused on sixteen-year-old Dalia Moukarker and others like her, in the West Bank city of Ramallah, who have been drawn to and managed to study—assiduously—Western Classical music. The other focuses on eighteen-year-old Shehade Shelalde, also of Ramallah, who turned his natural motor skills in the direction of music: he has his own musical instrument repair shop in a garage. "In a place all too familiar with the sounds of gunfire, military vehicles and explosions, he said, '*Al Kamandjati* ["The Violinist"], a school founded by Ramzi Aburedwan, a French-trained violist raised in a Palestinian refugee camp taught us to hear music.'"[238]

Another extraordinary story of such a use for art—and economics—is found in a September 12, 2008, *New York Times* article by Ethan Bronner, "A West Bank Ruin, Reborn as a Peace Beacon." The article talks of "a quiet revolution . . . stirring in [Jenin, in the northern part of the West Bank], once a byword for the extremes of violence between Israelis and Palestinians," where "[c]ivilians are planning economic cooperation—an industrial zone to provide thousands of jobs, mostly to Palestinians, and another involving organic produce grown by Palestinians and marketed in Europe by Israelis."

This revolution involved, in August 2008, a Bible-Qur'an contest for high school students—in which twelve teams of two players each (one Jew and one Muslim) were asked questions in Hebrew and Arabic about their sacred texts—together with a joint ballet performance. The project was intended to serve as a microcosm and a model of what, in terms of mutual recognition and embrace, *could* eventuate on a larger scale in the Israeli-Palestinian relationship. One of the keys out of the morass is the recognition and respect of the *humanity* of the Other. This is what so many Israelis and Palestinians—and Arabs and Kurds, and Persians and Arabs, and Turks and Armenians, and Shi'is and Sunnis, and Muslims, Christians, and Jews—have had difficulty doing.

Music, which requires no words in the myriad languages that populate the region, is among the most magnificent of the carriers of our humanity, and among the most poignant of the articulators of hope. Another is the cinema. As Eric Alterman observes in an opinion piece in *Moment* Magazine, there have been recent Israeli movies that, "boldly go where few politicians dare."[239] Two films that Alterman particularly notes are *For My Father*,[240] which tells the story of Tariq, "a would-be suicide bomber, who falls in love with an Israeli girl estranged from her Orthodox family"; and *Lemon Tree*,[241] "based on the true story of a Palestinian widow who defends her lemon tree grove when a new Israeli defense minister moves into a house adjacent to her land . . . " and his advisors "decide that terrorists could take cover among the aromatic trees and declare the grove a safety threat." It is as if Chekhov's *The Cherry Orchard* has been squeezed through a dying process and come out a completely new color. Neither film ends happily. Both offer a range of competing interests, but the bottom line is that one sees a suicide bomber through a sympathetic lens and the other sees the "vaunted Israeli justice system as a kangaroo court when it comes to the Territories"—and both think outside political convention.

More recently, a museum devoted to the presentation and discussion of the Holocaust opened in April 2009—on Holocaust Memorial Day—in an apartment in Na'alin, a Palestinian village better known at that time for the weekly protests taking place within it against the Israeli security fence that divides the village in half. One of the residents of Na'alin and a leader of the fence protesters, Ibrahim Amira, commented at the time of the museum exhibition opening that "if leaders on both sides know and remember what Hitler did, maybe we'll have peace."[242] And he might have added: protagonists on both sides of the fence need to think about the real suffering of those on the other side.

An important issue within the larger tensions of Israel-Palestine derives from the inherent and definitional identity complications for Israeli Arabs, which necessarily escalated as a complication in the course of the decade that leads from Oslo to the present.[243] Having to one degree or another come to recognize themselves as Israelis after nearly sixty years of citizenship, their sense of identity as Palestinians, rather than—or in addition to—their sense of identity as Israelis suddenly began to take shape both in the hopeful era of the seven-year-long peace process and in the seventeen-year-long reversion to violence between the end of the peace process and the present.

How exactly to feel and define belonging has become intensified by the events of this period. There is irony here, since what I am describing echoes in large part the condition of many Jews just over a century ago, when confronted

by the birth of Zionism and by the ongoing question of how to define themselves vis-à-vis the host countries of which they had been more or less full citizens for the century since Emancipation—France, England, Austro-Hungary,
even to a more limited extent, Prussia—and how that self-definition was being
affected, ca. 1900, by the shaping of a Jewish nationalist movement.[244]

With such unresolved complications in mind, it is encouraging to encounter organizations within Israel such as *Shalom Akhshav* (*Peace Now*) that,
among other things, works to promote cooperative efforts involving Jewish
and Muslim/Christian Arab Israeli communities and individuals on a range
of cultural, social, economic, and political fronts; or such as *Seeds of Peace*,
which seeks to change the mentality of fear and distrust in the next generation
by intense cooperative programs that target Jewish, Christian, and Muslim,
Israeli, Palestinian, and other Arab youth in various countries in the Middle
East and bring them for an extensive period to a camp in Maine. There their
interaction can be nurtured away from the immediate difficulties of their
native environments.[245]

There are also organizations such as the joint educational and coexistential
institution, *Givat Haviva*, which has flourished for decades now—since 1949.
Its purpose has been to engage Israeli Jews and Israeli Muslim and Christian
Arabs, among others, in a series of active programs of cooperation and active,
rather than merely passive, peaceful coexistence. A similar ideology—of cooperation and ongoing proof of how feasible it is for members of the two communities to live together side by side while remaining committed to their specific
cultural and religious roots—has shaped *Neve Shalom/Wahat as-Salam* ("Oasis
of Peace") since the 1970s.

It is worth noting that in the aforementioned film, *Lemon Tree*, the cowriter,
Suha Arraf, is an Israeli Arab, and the star, Hiam Abbass, is a renowned Israeli
Arab actress. The film is by definition a joint Jewish-Arab (i.e., Muslim) Israeli
enterprise. Similarly, we should recognize the importance of an institution such
as the Barenboim-Said Foundation, established by the Israeli conductor and
pianist, Daniel Barenboim, who has long been a vocal advocate for Palestinian
rights; and Edward W. Said, the Palestinian-born American intellectual. The
Foundation opened a center in Ramallah in 2006 to provide lessons there and
coaching in nearby towns and villages. On the other hand are the complications:
that some Palestinians perceive the idea of an orchestra made up of Israelis and
Palestinians trained through the Foundation's schools and teachers inherently
off-base because of the political reality of the Israeli-Palestinian relationship.
Even threads of hope in this tapestry are not colored simply.

Other stories surface in the media from time to time, such the account of
a Gazan manufacturer of sweaters whose primary distributor was an Israeli.

Shortly before the 2009 Operation Cast Lead catastrophe, the Israeli put in a large order and sent a substantial amount of cash as advance payment. Both parties knew that the borders were moving toward closure and that it might be difficult to get the sweaters into Israel—which is what transpired. But the Gazan made and boxed them, and has them stored and ready to transmit them as soon as it is feasible; the Israeli meanwhile had to turn unhappily to a Chinese manufacturer. "Cheaper," he notes, "but of lower quality," and he trusts that those Gaza-manufactured sweaters will arrive as soon there is a loosening up of border-crossing restrictions. There are surely other instances of active trusting business dealings across enemy lines that offer hope that if the guns could be silenced, normal lives that benefit from mutual cooperation could ensue.

There is also the story of the victory by the Arab Israeli Bnei Sakhnin team in the Israeli State Cup soccer championships in June 2004. This meant that Bnei Sakhnin would represent Israel in the European UEFA Cup Tournament. More to the point, "'this is what's called the New Middle East and this shows the Arabs are here and they are an integral part of Israeli society,' said Bnei Sakhnin's Arab Chairman Mazin Ghanim after his team beat HaPoel Haifa 4–1 in Ramat Gan Stadium before 30,000 cheering fans."[246] The article reporting this story goes on to observe that "Bnei Sakhnin is seen as a model of coexistence with six Jewish players mixed among the Arab players—joined by four players from four different countries." Moreover, "for most Israelis, Sakhnin is known as the town which hosts annual 'Land Day' commemorations for six Arab Israeli demonstrators killed by the police during protests against land confiscation in 1976. It was also in this town of 23,000 that 13 Arabs were killed by the Israeli police during demonstrations of support for the Palestinians in the early days of the *intifada*, three-and-a-half years ago. But with last week's game these incidents have faded to the back burner." In the late night celebrations, Jews and Arabs were joined together, their sports heroes common property.[247]

The story of the Bnei Sakhnin soccer team brings to mind the dictum that I offered at the outset of this narrative: that the key to a transformation of the Arab-Israeli arena from a nonstop war cauldron to a zone of peace is the ability to engage in two acts simultaneously. The first is *not to forget and to acknowledge* the long history of agony that each side has experienced in general and at the hands of the other. The other is *to forget every ounce of it*; to remain cognizant of the past while abandoning it as a shackle to our abilities to build from present to future, so that we *can* build, unshackled. The Arab martyrs of Bnei Sakhnin will not cease to be remembered, but if the memory of the ugliness that led to their martyrdom can be moved to the side of the stage in favor of beautiful moments such as this one—for sports, like music, can help us transcend particularized language—then ". . . a lot of good can come out of this."[248]

The Bnei Sakhnin story also brings to mind another issue. The use of the phrase "The New Middle East" evokes discussions such as that by Daniel Pipes, back in November 1998 of "The Real 'New Middle East'."[249] Pipes observed how, in the aftermath of the collapse of the Soviet Union and the advent of the Peace Process signaled by the Oslo Accords, the matter of "who is my enemy" and "who is my friend," including "my enemy's enemy," became reconfigured. In his account—which included Greece by way of Cyprus, in his definition of the "Middle East," reminding us that our very terminology is subject to change— "if all goes as scheduled, Russian ships will begin delivering $400-million worth of advanced surface-to-air missiles, CAM-300s to Greek Cyprus in late November. Greek Cypriots insist that they must have this powerful weapon to balance Turkish air superiority over the island." The Turks warned the Greeks that they would prevent deployment by force, if necessary; Athens, in turn, warned the Turks that it would come to the aid of the Greek Cypriots if the Turks carried out their threat; the Turkish foreign minister asked then-Israeli Prime Minister Binyamin Netanyahu for help in preventing the missiles from reaching Greek Cyprus; the Greek Cypriots asked the Russians to exert pressure on Israel not to get involved.

At the same time, Greece itself solidified its ties to Russia as well as with Syria, Armenia, and Iran—none of which had been a natural ally of the others in the past—and offered increasing support to the PKK (Kurdish Workers Party), the leftist movement whose terrorist activities had led to the death of at least thirty thousand Turks between 1984 and 1998. Meanwhile the Turks, aside from reinforcing relations with Israel, augmented their military ties to Jordan and moved troops toward the Syrian border. Pipes goes on to observe that the potential for further allies for the Turkish-Israeli-Jordanian alliance could include Kuwait and the United Arab Emirates as well as groups exiled from Syria, Iran, Iraq, and Libya, and furthermore Christians in Lebanon and Sudan. Conversely, the Greek-Syrian-Iranian alliance could also include the Palestinian Authority, Muslims in Lebanon, and possibly even Iraq, with whom "relations are even improving, [although Iraq] has nearly always been on bad terms with Syria and Iran alike, and the same holds true for relations with Libya and Sudan."[250] As for the Kurds, depending upon their country of residence, their alliances would likely vary.

The two main points that Pipes makes are that the reconfiguration extends connections beyond what has for most of the past century been thought of as "The Middle East," and that "the logic of 'my enemy's enemy' can override even such powerful fundamentalist factors as shared religion or ideology."[251] Here we might recall that the very terminology that labels the Near or Middle East as "Near" or "Middle" has itself undergone change since the beginning of the last century, when British colonial vocabulary still understood the "East" as having three zones—far, middle, and near, in which India and its environs constituted the "Middle East," and that it was from India that the troops arrived to defend British prerogatives in Mesopotamia in both World Wars. Yet now we hardly think of that neighborhood as part of the Middle East at all. The Muslim world might extend as far as the Philippines, but the Middle East peters out in our current thinking beyond Iran—or at least beyond Afghanistan. So reconfigurations that extend beyond where current or recent vocabulary leads is not really so surprising in the discussion of this region.

One might also note that whereas Pipes's discussion ends with both negative and positive conclusions—increasing arsenals and shrinking incomes, hardened attitudes toward Israel and intensification of Islamic fundamentalism, new rogue regimes on the one hand; a new Turkish-Israeli-Jordanian alliance on the other hand—in principle the fact of reconfigurations where other than ironclad religious or political or ethnic ideology governs positions is a reminder of the hope that under the proper conditions, individuals and peoples can think outside entrenched views of fear and mistrust.[252]

To whatever extent Pipes may or may not have been correct in his article, between then and now there have been even more significant reconfigurations, particularly where Israel and Turkey are concerned, as we have seen. Thus the flotilla debacle of 2010 tore apart the frayed relationship between these two countries but—in large part through Obama's mediation and in spite of the bellicose personalities of both Erdogan and Netanyahu—they have gradually inched back toward each other.

From Turkey's perspective, there are at least three reasons for Erdogan's willingness to inch back in that direction. One was the development of an important economic relationship between Israel and Greek Cyprus that grew out of the discovery of petroleum deposits off the Greek Cypriot coast and the fact that Israel has the technology to access it, which the Greek Cypriots do not. Turkey's sense of responsibility for the Turkish Cypriot community and therefore to be concerned about how the resultant oil might be apportioned to the island communities pushed Erdogan in a slightly more conciliatory direction toward Israel.

Moreover, the role he anticipated playing as a leader—or *the* leader—of the Arabo-Islamic world, for which he was willing to sacrifice the prior Turkish-Israeli relationship, never developed as planned. This has been further complicated for Turkey by the combustion of Syria and Iraq, which has meant that the overland route to the gulf and the transport of Turkish products to that market has been significantly compromised, leaving a route across Israel and Jordan as the only viable alternative. However, conveniently for Erdogan, it is now in all parties' interests to seek a rapprochement, as both Israel and Jordan have also been threatened by the fallout from conflict in Syria and Iraq. The three nations also share a parallel concern about the rise of ISIS, which has served both to inundate Turkey and Jordan with refugees and has directly threatened security for all three nations.[253]

There is also, arguably, the matter of Iran. While Israel and Saudi Arabia have been much more obviously concerned about the rise of Iran and, specifically, its potential nuclear development program, the fact is that Turkey, largely Sunni Muslim, finds itself at a natural loggerhead position vis-à-vis Iran's Shi'i population. This is no doubt further reinforced by the fact that there is a substantial Alevi minority in Turkey that is nominally more aligned with Shi'i than Sunni ideology—albeit not specifically Iranian Shi'i ideology.

An interesting development that presents a complex but hopeful connection between Iran and Iraq, on the other hand, also challenges the assumptions of several of our earlier comments. Up to this point, we have presumed that the New Iraq, as a Shi'i-dominated polity, might draw very close to Shi'i Iran. But there have been suggestions that Iraq's Grand Ayatollah Ali as-Sistani, whose geopolitical center is Najaf, and who is seen as the highest spiritual authority for many of the Shi'i Muslims across the world, was pushing in 2015 for the sort of direct elections that would put the country in the hands of politicians, not clerics.[254]

He would thus be taking a very different course from that of Iran's theocracy. This emulation of a "quietist" tradition, in which his own role is relegated to that of an *eminence grise* is presumably designed to help stabilize the post-Saddam Iraq on its own terms—although by paradox, his very presence within political discourse, worrying about corruption and encouraging young men to serve Iraq in taking up arms against ISIS, suggests a variation on the familiar theme of religion-politics interpenetration. He is, it seems, interested in *rapprochement* with Iran, but not a connection that could lead to domination from Tehran—or from Qom, Iran's holy city.

If there is a truism regarding the Middle East, it is its unpredictability. Nobody but a divinely inspired prophet would have predicted the shaping of such alliances discussed by Pipes a few years before he wrote his article. If we backtrack further, two or three years before 1993, nobody could have anticipated the Oslo Accords or the progress made—and almost made—in the seven years that followed. Nobody could have imagined, in the aftermath of the War of Attrition that led up to the 1973 Yom Kippur War and the aftermath of that war, that Anwar Sadat would visit Jerusalem just a few years later and begin a peace dialogue with Menahem Begin—much less that the two would develop such a strong personal relationship.

Who would have thought, for that matter, that in the aftermath of the June 1967 war, with the Israeli victory over the Arabs, a course for further conflict was being set from two directions and two forces that played relatively minor roles in the conflict up to that point, but which became the two most salient sources of conflict between that time and now? I am referring to the revolutionary Palestinian guerilla movement on the one hand and the Jewish national-religious movement on the other, both of which have provided the lion's share of the extremists who have made a final peace so elusive in that particular corner of the Middle East.

Considering another primary flash point in the region—Iraq—I love the following small historiographic irony. Barely had Joseph Braude finished writing his book, *The New Iraq*, and by the time it was actually published—he must have finished it in 2001 or 2002, as it was published in 2003—the Second Gulf War was being planned and then begun by the Bush-Cheney administration.[255] Braude's narrative addresses the question of how to rebuild the country in the aftermath of the first Gulf War, not only for the benefit of its own inhabitants, but of the entire region and the world, both the West and the East.

Braude's text begins with the words "This book is not about Saddam Hussein." It goes on to discuss the rich ancient, medieval, and modern history of what we now call Iraq; the complications of maintaining the richness of that identity during the twenty-three years of Saddam's power; and a formula for reconstruction based on a combination of inherent, internal historical elements of identity and judiciously applied lessons from outside. The book eloquently and cogently fulfills its promise to be a book about Iraq apart from and in spite of Saddam, about "an Iraq beyond Saddam Hussein, an Iraq that preceded him and that will remain long after he has been relegated to the margins of history."[256]

The irony is that the invasion being planned unbeknownst to the author virtually while he was shaping his narrative would indeed relegate Saddam to the margin of present-tense and future-tense history and make the question of how to fashion a non-Saddam Iraq—a post-Saddam Iraq—a reality with just the sort of questions being raised by Braude. It is almost as if the author *was* engaged in the sort of prophecy to which I referred a few paragraphs back. His discussion became in a sense *more* relevant than it was when he composed it.

The disposition of a new Iraq remains open and unclear, after the capture and execution of Saddam and the various levels of transformation to which Iraq has been subject—including the very notion of trumpeting a national sense of "Iraq"ness by many of its inhabitants and their leaders that was inconceivable even a generation ago. It remained open and unclear in the aftermath of the transition to a new American administration in 2009 and continues to do so in the months currently leading up to another new American administration.

Consider again, that Iraq has essentially reverted to its pre-British, Ottoman-dictated composition as functionally three provinces, excluding the southern part of the southernmost of these three, which remains the independent Kingdom of Kuwait. Thus the Kurds, in the northwest, function more or less independently, and the Sunni-dominated northeast remains largely separate from the Shi'i dominated south—and the Sunnis worry that the Shi'is will undertake some alliance with the Iranian Shi'is, with the goal of shrinking or overrunning or eliminating the Sunnis. Iran itself remains a complicated, not finally answered question, even if the easing of tensions between Iran and the world has opened up positive, peaceful possibilities.

If nuclear development is the most obvious, dominant feature of the discourse regarding Iran and between Iran and the rest of the region as well as the West and the world at large, it is not, as we have seen, the only one. The spawning of ISIS, in large part facilitated by our dismantling of Iraq and elimination of its Sadam-dominated leadership, has led to its spreading through much of Syria and Iraq. With that spreading out, the question of whom the Iranians are supporting and how much—whether rebel groups in Syria, factions of ISIS, *Hizb'Allah* or even *Hamas*—means that the country's role in full international relations remains unclear at this point.

The concerns of and threat to Israel and Saudi Arabia, obviously, but also to the Gulf States and Turkey, as well as to Jordan and whatever might today be called "Lebanon" is palpable. The Syrian civil war twists and turns—the Syrian map is currently really divided into six parts: one large area held by the government, one large and one small area held by the rebels, two substantial areas held by ISIS, and an area held by the Kurds. Indeed, Assad seems to have ceded control of three different areas of the state that he ruled before the conflict began, including, most recently, the northeastern province of Hasaka. Hasaka is now officially and not just *de facto* controlled by the Kurds, after an August 23, 2016, treaty signed by them with the Syrian government.[257] They thus govern two distinct autonomous regions, one in former Iraq and the other in former Syria, while still engaged in a struggle with Turkish authorities; Turkey's opposition to Assad may well change 180 degrees because of this new Kurdish development. And ISIS/ISIL seems to be steadily shrinking its realm of control, in part because of American military intervention and in part, more recently, due to Russian involvement.

Every week, if not every day, new developments occur within and between these countries: on successive days—August 24 and 25, 2016—one front-page *New York Times* article commented on an unusual rally in Istanbul, for post-coup unity, while a second reported on Turkey's air force bombing ISIS/ISIL positions in Syria a few days after a preteen suicide bomber in southern Turkey blew himself up in the midst of a wedding party, killing more than fifty people.

Sudden news shapes may also be noted for other places within and on the edge of the region, such as Yemen, which has been subject since the summer of 2016 to repeated bombings by Saudi Arabia, designed to keep the Houthis—a Zaidi Shi'i movement—at bay, to say naught of the Talibanesque fragments that began to embed themselves there a few years back. The picture constantly re-complicates itself. Indeed, the "New Middle East" of Pipes's description was already old by the first few years of the new millennium, when the winds of hope that were still blowing so strongly at the time of Pipes's article—as the Israeli-Palestinian peace process, among other things, was still inching bravely forward—had shifted. And the "new Middle East" is older still now, in 2017, as the winds have shifted again. The *newer* Middle East has reverted to the cycles of violence and distress that were the staples of the Old Middle East in the decades—or centuries—before 1993 and Oslo. But the potential is enormous, should the positive outgain the negative—should a handful of leaders with vision push forward and help redirect the Middle Eastern peoples toward an *intifada* of the self-destruction that their current leaders seem to favor. The combination of human and natural resources necessary to shape an astounding future is there, but grasping those resources remains as tricky as taking up residence in a windblown sand castle.

But anything can happen and the twists and turns, knots and dissolutions of the tangled threads of the Middle East are unpredictable, so without being sanguine one has the right to hope. If misunderstanding can give way to understanding without supposition of solution, then fear and mistrust can also give way to fruitful dialogue. Antipathy can be replaced by empathy, and peace is not absolutely beyond reach. To return to the Socratic-Platonic reference in the beginning of our narrative, it is by constant cross-examination and dialogue that we may be able to come closer to the truth of peace.

AFTERWORD

When I began piecing this history together, in the early autumn of 2004, large questions of hope and despair lay before the American people regarding the upcoming elections. Thirteen years have passed since then, but as I review my text, it seems as relevant now as when I began, since the lion's share and primary purpose of the narrative was and remains to disentangle a tangled historical web toward coherence.

Although there have been obvious and important changes in the region in the past thirteen years, none of them affects either my historical sweep or my limited prescriptions toward a hopeful future, though my thinking has evolved in several places. For example, in my discussion of what Israeli Prime Minister Sharon might do from his side, two obvious developments have affected that discussion from the Israeli perspective. One might have anticipated Sharon's unilateral decision to withdraw his troops and his settlers from the Gaza Strip, since even though that move seemed surprising to many, to others it reflected that truism regarding the Middle East: the only thing predictable about it is its unpredictability. More difficult to have anticipated or to digest was Sharon's sudden withdrawal of himself from the stage of history due to a stroke that left him virtually comatose. In the wake of that event, Ehud Olmert was elected by the Israelis, pushing forward a political stance that asserted its reflection of a new Sharonist agenda of concerted unilateral efforts toward peace with the Palestinians, should bilateral efforts continue to shrink rather than grow. But now Olmert, in turn, is gone, and Bibi Netanyahu has once more ascended to the prime minister's office with an avowed preference for negating the idea of a Palestinian State.

In fact, Netanyahu has now been elected four times and has now been prime minster longer than anyone, including Ben-Gurion, in Israel's history.

His most recent reelection highlights a number of issues where he is concerned and regarding where one might hope or expect Israel to go with respect to the Palestinians and the region at large. As the time of this last election day approached, it appeared possible that Netanyahu was going to lose, in part because the Israeli Arab population, perhaps for the first time in its history, was making a concerted effort to be part of the electoral process, and he was clearly not the candidate for which they would be voting.

In the last week before the election, he pulled out all the stops with respect to fear: security issues in general and most specifically, the notion that "the Arabs are going to take over." The outcome was a narrow victory for his party, but the price was to pull to the surface the ugliest side of human nature—a side with which Jews have been long familiar through the prejudice to which they have been subject for many generations in many places. Netanyahu's victory, moreover, seems to have been viewed by him as offering the mandate to build more settlements, push back ever more waspishly against Obama and, in general, to harden his stance against real, active negotiations with the Palestinians. The culmination of this might be seen in his visit to the United States and his speech before Congress in which he sought to derail the evolving new relations with Iran. This has not impinged on the quiet, behind-the-scenes discussions with the Saudis, nor on the eventual return to some sort of normalized relationship with Turkey—thanks, on the one hand, to the shared concerns regarding Iran and on the other hand to concerns regarding Syria and ISIS.

Similarly, in the aftermath of Chairman Arafat's death, the Palestinian side of this equation has sustained two obvious question-inducing developments. The first is the inability of Arafat's elected successor, Mahmud Abbas (Abu Mazen), to stem the ongoing mood on the part of enough Palestinians to respond to the Israeli withdrawal from Gaza—even when Sharon was still alive, well, and leading the Israeli State—with their own peace initiative, rather than with more anti-Israel violence. Thus, while waiting to see whether and what the Israelis might have in mind to further extend the process of withdrawal from pre-1967 Palestinian territory, the Palestinian Arabs have seemed determined to demonstrate that they simply have no interest in peaceful coexistence with Israel.

This general tone was reinforced by the Palestinian elections of 2007, which brought *Hamas* into official political power in Gaza, and with *Hamas*, a significant upsurge in violence vis-à-vis Israel—but also, more recently, vis-à-vis Egypt. Is this apparent preference for violence simply due to unwillingness to think in any other way? Is it due to frustration with what the Gazans perceive as Israeli obtuseness and American one-sidedness? Is it a function of feelings developed since 2000, or since 1967, or since 1948 pertaining to an existential sense of despair? Has *Hamas* held the Gaza Strip hostage since 2007 or do Gazans want *Hamas* and its ideology in charge—in defiance of Israel, the Arab world, the world at large? At what point does defiance for its own sake become a synonym for self-destruction?

To date, there has been little to suggest a desire on the part of *Hamas* to shift from being a revolutionary force—calling for the destruction of Israel on religious grounds and trying to effect that destruction through violent activity—toward being a political partner in dialogue. That disinterest in dialogue has, in fact, shown itself even within the Palestinian context—so that there has been sporadic civil war within the Gaza Strip—and certainly the more so with respect to Israel. Hundreds upon hundreds of rockets have rained down upon southern Israel's towns from Gaza, which activity culminated with a massive Israeli reprisal attack on Gaza with powerful human-cost consequences for the Palestinian Gazans as we have observed. Thus the issue of trust—or rather, of mutual mistrust—to which I referred above could not be more problematic.

Of the immediate past events leading to the present and its myriad complications, there is a peculiar symmetry to the Sharonist unilateral decision nearly a decade ago to build a fence between Israel and its Palestinian neighbors and to withdraw from part of the territory of those neighbors. We have noted how unclear it remains as to where Israel would have sought to go next on both these fronts had Sharon lived, but for the moment that question seems almost moot, since there has been no evidence of pushing the same envelope from the Palestinian side in the last dozen years.

On the other hand, the matter of Israel's security and survival once again reared its head during that period, in a different way—in the form of the 2006 kidnapping of three Israeli soldiers: one on June 25 by *Hamas*, and the other two on July 12 by *Hizb'Allah*;[258] and the war between Israel and *Hizb'Allah* that ensued following the kidnappings. That war has yielded further food for thought on several fronts.

The notion of a well-armed and well-trained force that is not a state, dedicated to the destruction of Israel, offers a new spin to an old question: with whom does one negotiate a peace? Also, the fact that *Hizb'Allah* was being armed by Iran and arguably Syria suggests general and not merely localized complications and underscores the idea that the instability of the region has far-flung sources. If, on the one hand, the previous Iranian president offered a fairly consistent flow of neo-Hitlerian rhetoric where Israel and the Jews are concerned, on the other there *were* suggested hints of Syria's willingness to return to the negotiation table after an absence of more than eight years— though this is also currently moot, given the events of the "Arab Spring."[259] It is also not clear as to how far the Lebanese themselves are willing to go with regard to pushing for a peace with Israel and/or a relationship with *Hizb'Allah*.

It should also be noted that whereas most sources report these kidnappings as a provocative pair of acts yielding Israeli responses, at least one Arab American source, Rashid Khalidi, asserts something quite contrary:

> [*Hamas*] for eighteen months observed a cease-fire in the face of . . . [various] provocations (other factions were not so restrained, firing rockets into Israel). However, after a major spike in Palestinian civilian deaths and the particularly provocative Israeli assassination of militant leader Jamal Abu Samhadana, whom the [*Hamas*-led Gazan] PA had just named to a security post, *Hamas* finally took the bait and responded with the capture of one Israeli soldier [Shalit] and the killing of others. The predictably ferocious Israeli response . . . finally provoked *Hizb'allah* (or perhaps gave *Hizb'allah* and its allies, Iran and Syria, the presumptive opportunity they had been searching for)."[260]

Thus Khalidi ascribes the rocket-fire into southern Israel to groups other than *Hamas*, and views the conflict with *Hizb'Allah* in Lebanon in 2006 to be tied to Israeli actions in the wake of the *Hamas* electoral victory in the Gaza Strip, rather than provoked by the kidnapping of Goldwasser and Regev. His perspective offers a counterpoint from that of many others, and it is difficult to ascertain with any objectivity the facts of the matter, as in so many aspects of this tangled region.

In 2009, the endpoint of many of these events was not yet clear. Binyamin Netanyahu, in his capacity as the new prime minister of the State of Israel, had very emphatically called for the then-current Pope—Benedict XVI, who had just visited the Middle East in early May 2009—to speak out more strongly against the continuous calls by Iran's president for Israel's destruction. On the one hand, Netanyahu's urging resonated back to the time of the Holocaust, when Pope Pius XII failed—as many, but not all, historians argue—to speak out against Hitler's avowed plan and execution of that plan to destroy all of European Jewry. This resonates particularly given that then-Iranian President Ahmadinejad's consistently denied that the Holocaust happened and frequently referred to the destruction of Israel. On the other hand, the brief conversation between Pope and prime minister, and the urging made immediately public, had followed on the heels of the Pope's visit to a Palestinian refugee camp and his call for the creation of a Palestinian state. Thus, Netanyahu's statement may be understood as a demand for even-handed papal statements.

Shortly after the Pope's visit to Israel, Palestine, and Jordan, Netanyahu himself traveled, visiting the White House for a meeting with President Obama. That visit prompted an array of public responses from American Jewish groups and their leaders, ranging from expressions of dismay that the new president might stray from the policies of the Bush-Cheney administration in the Israeli-Palestinian situation to those encouraging a distinct departure from them.[261]

Since that time, the so-called Arab Spring that began in late 2010 has caused direct repercussions from Tunisia and Libya to Egypt, and from Syria to Yemen, and indirect repercussions just about everywhere else in the region. The phrase "Arab Spring" is a coinage inspired both by the spate of revolutions across Europe in 1848—referred to in standard European historiography as "the year of revolutions," but also sometimes called "the Springtime of Nations"—and by the so-called "Prague Spring" of 1968. Commentators using the phrase envisioned a sweep of democratic renovation throughout the region. Alas, this has only been the case, thus far, in the country where protests by the people first took place.

In Tunisia—in the aftermath of and response to the December 2010 self-immolation of an impoverished roadside-fruit-stand vendor, Muhammad Bouazizi, when his wares were confiscated by a government inspector—longtime President Zine El Abidine Ben-Ali was deposed on January 14, 2011, and fled to Saudi Arabia. Tunisia, after a difficult transitional period, became a parliamentary republic in October 2014 and has appeared fairly stable since then.

In Libya, Mu'amar Qaddafi was deposed but the aftermath is still fractured, including among the protagonists, a branch of ISIS; and over forty thousand people have died in the six years since Qaddafi's demise. In Egypt, after huge protests beginning on January 25, 2011, long-term President Mubarak was deposed in February; democracy prevailed for a brief period, only to be later subverted by a military coup and, with General Sisi in charge, things are back to where they were before the initial protests began: stable but autocratically controlled.[262]

In Syria, the attempt to overthrow Bashar al-Assad that began with protests on January 26, 2011, has led to a civil war that is still in its endlessly-seeming throes, in which ISIS/ISIL is an active participant—and in which well over three hundred thousand people have perished. In Yemen, the Houthis managed to depose president Ali Abdullah Saleh in February 2012—culminating a campaign that began with protests on January 27, 2011—but the Saudis are still pushing vigorously to restore his presidency. To date, well over ten thousand people have died in the ongoing conflict.

Other countries across the region have been affected as well. In Algeria, large crowds of street protestors in late December 2010 and early January led to the lifting of the nineteen-year-long state of emergency. In Jordan, following a spate of protests against the government in January 2011, King Abdullah replaced the prime minister three times in the following year and restructured the parliament to offer a more reformist body.

Similar concessions were made by Sultan Qaboos in Oman in response to protests extending from January 17 through May, 2011. So too, King Habad of Bahrain, who is Sunni, granted economic concessions, freed political prisoners, and opened discussions with Shi'a representatives in response to protests from mid-February to mid-March, 2011.[263] In Kuwait, the prime minister resigned and parliament was dissolved after protests that extended from February 2011 through December 2012.

King Muhammad VI of Morocco also responded to protests taking place between February 20, 2011, and April 2012 by granting political concessions and offering a referendum on constitutional reforms. After protests in mid-March 2011, Saudi Arabia's King Abd'Allah granted economic concessions, offered new (male only) municipal elections in late September—and then announced that women would be allowed to both vote and run for office in the municipal elections in 2015.[264]

Even in Iraq there were protests from February 12 through December 23, 2011, that led to Prime Minister Nouri al-Maliki's announcement that he would not seek a third term, and to the resignations of many provincial governors and local authorities. That which was formerly Iraq, of course, remains a trio of volatile fragments; the reference to protests really only refers to the Shi'i-governed portion.

Meanwhile, during these same last six years or so, Iran has arrived at a new position and place in the world; Turkey has been rocked by internal and external issues; ISIS, as we have seen, has come into being and helped reshape the chaos of Iraq and Syria. A string of military victories has gradually been turned back by those allied against ISIS, but the organization has either ramped up or managed to inspire a growing array of terrorist acts outside the region.

Bibi Netanyahu has continued to build settlements on the West Bank, while arguing that the Palestinians are not interested in peace; the United States has moved past the Obama years and is defined by uncertainty as the Trump administration continues to shake up the political landscape and its apparent chief strategist, Steve Bannon, has expressed to Conservative Republicans his ambition of sowing more chaos. Russia, under Putin, has begun to pursue a more substantive role in Middle East developments, particularly in Syria— for better and for worse. At the same time, during this period, Pope Benedict stepped down in a virtually unprecedented papal abdication, and a very different sort of figure, Pope Francis, has entered the fray of environmental concerns, human rights, and political issues that include our region.

But to return to the question of the American role in sliding toward a solution to the problematic of the Middle East: There did not appear to be great hopes for a positively nuanced American involvement as recently as a year or two ago, since whatever credit may have been built up with the Arabo-Islamic world in different ways—through the alliance organized by the first President Bush during the period of the first Gulf War and the efforts made by the Clinton administration to bring the Israelis and Palestinians toward peace, and even in pure sympathy terms in the aftermath of the 9/11 catastrophe—was squandered by the second President Bush.

The latter's extraordinarily ill-conceived push into Iraq to depose his father's erstwhile enemy—without having completed the "mission" in Afghanistan, where the Taliban was *not* fully dismantled, and is again on the rise—coupled with an outpouring of misinformation, fed both to the American people and to the rest of the world, all but erased that credit. Nearly nine years out from the Bush-Cheney era, we are still challenged with regard to how precisely to regain standing while rebuilding a leadership role that can appeal to the various sides of the various conflicts that define the region.

Who can truly gauge how many tens or hundreds of thousands have died in the pursuit of the dual chimeras of objects and ideas that were never in Iraq in the first place—such as Weapons of Mass Destruction and ties to the Taliban or to al-Qaeda—and in the assertions that redirecting our efforts away from the unfinished business of Afghanistan and the pursuit of Usama Bin Ladin *there* would make us safer or the inhabitants of the Middle East more free? By turning so many erstwhile friends and neutrals into enemies, both within and outside the country, both within and beyond the Middle East, the Bush administration effectively eliminated its capacity, at least for the time being, to be part of the solution to a diverse and far-reaching problem.

By pretending—or, perhaps, in simple, spectacular ignorance, genuinely imagining—that the questions of the Middle East and of our relationship with it have a simple, weapons-based answer, we have created problems where there weren't any before, or at least expanded smaller ones into larger ones, enabled many of those who are part of the problem to speak and act as if they are not, and licensed many to act as if the problem is simply Israel and the Palestinians and the uneven position of the United States in that *part* of the conflict. Most obviously, by eviscerating Iraq we have empowered Iran—to repeat—to the potential destabilizing detriment of the entire region and potentially the world: we opened a door through which Iran and its former venom-spewing president strode, to assert a power-wielding role in the region, with no intact Iraq to threaten that role.

The Obama Administration, for a number of reasons, offered some hope that the time of positive American involvement may have returned. At the very least, there was a window of opportunity through which President Obama seemed eager to climb. This was most directly evidenced by his early visit to the Middle east where he made a strong speech in Cairo, obviously directed to the Arabo-Islamic world and to assuring it of America's desire to be evenhanded in understanding and interfacing with the region in general and the Israel-Palestine dilemma in particular; and in his late, successful push to reestablish relations with Iran. Alas, as of 2017, that hope of a major American role in solving the dilemma and helping stabilize the region remained largely unfulfilled and that window of opportunity less open than it appeared in 2008. Obama's political opponents spent most of his two terms seeking to undermine him—in part by promoting the myth that he was turning against Israel. That myth has ended up harming both Israel and the Palestinians by helping to maintain a distance from a final peace between the Jewish state and all of its neighbors.

At this point, conditions have once again changed; there is a new administration in Washington that, thus far has offered an unusually high level of volatility and chaos with regard to every issue, domestic and international. Where the Middle East is concerned, the jury is not yet in. Will Mr. Trump attempt to dismantle the fragile relationship with Iran and the agreement that sustains that relationship? What will be the influence of the Russians and Mr. Putin on Mr. Trump's thinking and/or conduct with regard to Turkey, Syria, Iraq, or half a dozen other regional hot spots? What of the already twice-repeated effort through a pair of Executive Orders to ban Muslims from seven—or six— countries from entering the United States—and the already well-documented claims that incoming or returning Muslims, including American Muslims, are experiencing harassment at the hands of the our border authorities? What are the repercussions?

Where Israel and Palestine are concerned, Trump offered an absurdly casual observation to Bibi Netanyahu in the latter's first visit to the new White House that perhaps the Two-State Solution might be dropped, without proposing an alternative. He has also chosen an individual with strong ties to Israel's far right for our ambassador to that nation, hardly suggesting an interest in evenhandedness in Israel's relations with the Palestinians and others. There are certainly reasons to be concerned but, for those who enjoy mental gymnastics, there are opportunities to ruminate about the next phase in the ongoing transition of Israel-Palestine from past to future, and not merely to despair.

On the other hand, where this last key-but-not-singular issue—the Israeli-Palestinian issue—is concerned, there continue, even since 2004, to be small signs of hope that receive few headlines. I was privileged to attend a conference held in Jordan at the end of 2005 that brought mostly Israeli and Palestinian women—with a large outsider population from Europe, the Americas and other parts of Asia, and among these, a handful of men—to articulate a call for Israeli-Palestinian peace. A range of viewpoints was put forth. Disagreements were aired vociferously. Emotions were not held in check or angers suppressed. But most of the three hundred delegates to the conference *listened* to one another, recognizing that to have their own stories heard they needed to hear those of others.

Perhaps the most hopeful element within the varied hopeful elements was the presence of a group of mothers from both sides of the fence who have lost children to the conflict—Palestinian children killed by Israeli soldiers; Israeli children killed by Palestinian suicide bombers—who have determined that their children's memories can only be honored by their becoming the cutting edge of peaceful coexistence; that an endless cycle of vengeance and bloodletting will yield nothing; that their common enemy is all of those individuals and groups on both sides who stand in the way of peaceful coexistence. They are a fragile plant, but a tough one. Their convictions must prevail if there is to be a future and not just a continuous reshuffling of an endlessly pain-filled past.

But one cannot and should not forget the mantra with which this text opened: the complications of the Middle East extend well beyond the problems of the Israelis and Palestinians, or even the Israelis and the Arabs at large. As the vast literature covering the myriad aspects of the region, its problems, its continuum of pasts, presents, and futures, continues to expand at breakneck speed, we must continue to doubt those who offer black-and-white encapsulations and overly simple solutions.[265] We must continue to question ourselves and one another and continue to hope for a day when the unpredictable might take positive shape. And we must begin to untangle the threads, one by one, even as we recognize that such an onerous task may never come to an end.

APPENDIX 1:
EGYPT AND THE ARAB
SPRING[266]

As Egypt approaches its next elections and those who thought that the revolution that overthrew Hosni Mubarak would lead to a simple, direct path to democracy have realized that it *won't* or still hope that it somehow, maybe, still *will*, one might consider how this narrative fits into history, the definition of terms, and the problems that remain in the wake of revolution.

As by now others besides me have also noted, "spring" was an inappropriate term for the anti-Mubarak revolution—unless one assumed a scorching summer to follow it. What transpired might more appropriately be labeled "The Fourth Arab Awakening." The first arrived at the very beginning of the nineteenth century, in the person of an *outsider* named Mehmed Ali, an Albanian claiming Arab descent, who served successfully in Egypt as an army officer under the Ottomans during the Napoleonic period. He realized, once the French forces had withdrawn, that he was far enough away from a weak Sultan Selim III that he could establish an independent regime.

Mehmed Ali might be called the father of modern Arab Nationalism. He instituted military, political, and cultural refoms, founded the first indigenous Arab press, and nurtured the beginnings of an Arab literary renaissance. As such, several aspects of his process are of particular note. One, he removed potential competition from the indigenous Mamluk nobility by inviting them to a dinner party and slaughtering them there in 1811. In order to validate his political position, he also turned to religion, as so often happens in history, establishing an alliance with the fairly new Wahhabi movement. When his position was sufficiently secure, he turned on and slaughtered them in 1817. However, he could not in the long run generate enthusiasm for a pan-Arab identity, as opposed to a more localized tribal and familial one; his polity lasted as long as he and his charisma and skill lasted—the mid-1840s.

By that time, the seeds of a *second* Arab Awakening were being inadvertently sown, in part through the activities of French Catholic and American Protestant missionaries. Hoping to transform Muslim Arabs into Christians, they established schools during the middle of the century in which this might be effected. The consequence was the growth of a Christian Arab population with an intensified consciousness of the glorious history of Arabic language, literature, and culture.

Christian Arab leadership in the person of Butrus al-Bustani, Nassif al-Yazigi, and others at first championed the cause of Arab cultural awareness within Ottoman-ruled lands: writing Arab encyclopedias, forming literary and scientific societies from Beirut to Istanbul, and clamoring for the right to teach their children about their heritage. This movement eventually morphed in a more political direction toward an interest in Arab independence from Ottoman control. The Arabic term, *intifada*—meaning "throwing off"—was coined in this anti-Ottoman context toward the end of the century.

Sultan Abdul Hamid II was indeed cast off his throne, in 1908—but by Turkish officers, the "Young Turks," not Arabs. That officers' corps had been created for the Sultan by the Prussians, who within six years of his overthrow would be engaged with the Ottomans and the Austro-Hungarians against the British and the French, and eventually, the Americans in the Great War. The War was mainly fought over the Middle East and control of its quickly developing resource: petroleum. The aftermath of the war saw a reconfiguration of the entire region in favor of British and French colonial and economic needs. New Arab states were shaped, and were eventually led by a succession of Arab leaders with rarely more than lip-service concern for the Arab populations they ruled. Such leaders formed the *third* awakening as they gradually threw off their British and French mentors.

In Egypt, this came when a military leader, Gamal Abdel Nasser, helped overthrow the descendants of Mehmed Ali in 1952—two centuries after the family had ceased to lead armies, and three generations after they had become the puppets of the British colonial power—to create a new, independent autocracy. A few years later, as president, Nasser outlawed the *Muslim Brotherhood* (founded in 1928) and briefly tried a version of what Mehmed Ali had forged: a United Arab Republic that put Egypt and Syria under one political and military roof. That project lasted less than four years, from 1958–61.

Not long after Nasser died in 1970, his successor, Anwar Sadat, another military leader who like his predecessor expended his military energy in failed wars against Israel, came to Jerusalem and signed a peace treaty with the Jewish state in 1979—the same year in which the faux-military Shah was formally deposed by the Islamic revolution in another, non-Arab part of the region. Sadat commented on the absurdity of Egyptians "fighting all these wars on behalf of the Arabs." Of course, the definition of "Arab" is more complicated than one might suppose from the way the word is typically used, and dependent upon whether one's criteria are linguistic, ethnic, cultural, or political.

The *fourth* Arab Awakening, from Tunisia to Egypt to Syria and elsewhere, has directed itself toward leaders like Mubarak, Sadat's successor. It is the first Arab awakening *both from within and against those who rose to rule from within.* This leads to the question of where the Fourth Arab/Egyptian Awakening will lead. How will it operate toward non-Muslim minorities? How will it affect the most obvious non-Muslim state in the region, Israel—and the Palestinians? How will it affect intra-Muslim issues, such as relations between Sunnis and Shi'is? How might it spill out of the Arab world elsewhere within the region—or how has it—toward the diverse Kurdish populations, say, or toward Turkey or Iran?

Where Egypt is concerned, those who led this Awakening, including the *Muslim Brotherhood* and its leader, Morsi, were eaten by it. Those grassroots organizers, called *Tamarod*, who, in pushing Morsi to hold new elections, helped the military devour the Brotherhood, were either in turn devoured or have been subverted by the military leadership: of the five creators of *Tamarod*, three are now well-fed spokesmen for the army. The spring awakening has been moving through a long, parched summer.

But Egypt's condition is hardly a surprise when it is examined from within not just its own history, but world history. Those who guillotined Louis XVI were themselves guillotined not long thereafter, and it took more than a century for the French Revolution of 1789 to finally produce a democratic France. Tsar Nikolas was overthrown by Kerensky and the Mensheviks, who were cut down nine months later by Lenin and the Bolsheviks—and a century after the 1917 Russian Revolution, who would assert seriously that democracy is in place in Putin's Russia? Unlike these, the American Revolution was uniquely shaped, offering unique promises. But we have good cause to ask where, from Cairo and Damascus and Jerusalem to the computer drives of the NSA, our own Revolution and its principles have been leading in the last half century—and to hope that it's not toward a long, harsh winter.

APPENDIX 2:
THE TURKISH COUP
THAT WASN'T

Nobody who has watched Recep Tayyip Erdogan degenerate into demagoguery could believe his story about the recent so-called "coup" attempt, or imagine that Fethullah Gülen was behind it. Erdogan came to power as prime minister a decade and a half ago, following inept and/or corrupt leaders who had pushed Turkey back toward social and economic oblivion. He gained the support of Fethullah Gülen, who saw in Erdogan someone who could help pull the country into the modern era while restoring its Islam-based identity.

As Erdogan became more comfortable and confident, he saw less need for the support of Mr. Gülen and his followers. By the end of the prime minister's third term a schism was opening between them. One of two things seems to have occurred. Either Erdogan had been clever enough to mask his own true ambitions all along, or the power that he achieved gradually corrupted him, breeding an unslakable thirst for *more* power and increasing distaste for anyone who might stand in the way of its acquisition.

The growing split has led Erdogan to attack the *hizmet* (service) movement inspired by Gülen in a manner recalling Hitler's targeting of Jews in 1933–35, accusing the group of seeking to shape a "government within the government." Meanwhile, a succession of actions has demonstrated how desperate he has become to maintain his authority.

A few instances: the corruption scandal—in which he spirited hundreds of millions of dollars into his own pockets. (Did the funds for the multimillion-dollar palace that he built for himself come from heaven?) The role he played in helping to create the Gaza flotilla catastrophe that left nine people dead and relations between Turkey and Israel in tatters. The manner in which, moving toward the end of his third term as prime minister, he manipulated the political system to become president, and to elevate that role to an executive authority rather than one in service to the parliamentary legislature—a page out of Putin's book.

As he has subverted rights of Turkish citizens and all but destroyed Turkey's relations with every country across the Middle East, he has attacked Gülen and anyone believed to be associated with *hizmet*. Nothing but extermination, however, will apparently satisfy Erdogan's animosity for a man and a movement that stand for everything he is not. So: a "failed coup"—one without apparent leadership, without organization, with no substantial participation, no arrests of political leaders, at the height of day, not the middle of the night—the oddest military coup in Turkish history or any country's history . . . and Erdogan has accused *hizmet* of fomenting it.

Gülen, *hizmet*'s inspiration, has been living in eastern Pennsylvania since 1999. He came here to deal with a heart ailment. He was also accused of trying to foment a coup against the Turkish government, of which charges he was fully exonerated. And what is Gülen about? He believes that Turkey lost its soul when it became so secular under Attaturk—but also that the way forward is for Muslim Turkey to be completely open to other faiths (including atheism); and that the way forward toward a more perfect world is for members of diverse faiths, cultures, ethnicities, and races to engage in dialogue. He preaches civil Islam, not political Islam.

I have read most of what Gülen has written and the prior thinkers who have influenced him—such as Rumi, the thirteenth-century Sufi poet who, while Muslim, wrote eloquently of God's equal embrace of all faiths. I have spoken with Gülen—and his mystic's need to eliminate his ego in order to be filled with God could not be more evident. I have met scores of individuals affiliated with *hizmet*—and unless they are all going to the same acting school, they really *walk* and don't just talk of seeking a better world by working across sectarian lines with not mere tolerance but embrace.

Hizmet people are the opposite of everything that Erdogan represents in his ego-ridden, tyrannical, crush-anyone-who-disagrees-with me manner of being-in-the-world. They are far less likely to have had anything to do with a "coup" than Erdogan himself, who will do anything to expand his control and to destroy all opposition. Logic suggests this as possibly even an action shaped by Erdogan himself to give him the excuse to arrest tens of thousands in the first forty-eight hours since the "coup" was crushed and to demand Gülen's extradition from the United States.

It is reminiscent of the Ergenekon case, Erdogan's 2008 campaign against an alleged military coup-in-the-making against his regime, that resulted in the jailing of a quarter of the country's generals and admirals as well as academics, journalists, and others—and which, when by 2011 the prosecution had still failed to show any coherent evidence of the so-called plot, the courts were forced to drop the indictments, one by one.

I understand why we may need to pretend with Erdogan that he has saved the democracy that he has subverted—to ignore his similarity to Augustus Caesar, who claimed in his *Last Will and Testament* that he had saved the Roman Republic, while he had actually driven the last nails into its coffin. Turkey is an essential ally, due to geography, in our struggle with the likes of ISIS. But surely we are clever enough not to believe the tale being told or to succumb to Erdogan's attempted blackmail regarding that alliance. But the assertions of someone who emulates tyrants like Hitler, Putin, and Augustus should hardly guide us.

BIBLIOGRAPHY[267]

Abu Ju'ub, Ghassan, and Kurt Schetelig, "The Jordan River: Natural Flow and Current Composition by the Riparian Countries," in Zereini, Fathi, and Wolfgang Jaeschke, eds., *Water in the Middle East and in North Africa.* Berlin: Springer Books, 2004.

Abu-manneh, Butrus, *Studies in Islam and the Ottoman Empire in the 19th Century, 1826–1876.* Istanbul: Isis Press, 2001.

Allan, Tony, *The Middle East Water Question: Hydropolitics and the Global Economy.* New York: I.B. Tauris Publishers, 2001.

Armstrong, Karen, *A History of God: The 4,000 Year Quest of Judaism, Christianity and Islam.* New York: Ballantine Books, 1994.

_____. *Jerusalem: One City, Three Faiths.* New York: Knopf Publishers, 1996.

_____. *The Battle for God.* New York: Knopf Publishers, 2000.

Avineri, Shlomo, *The Making of Modern Zionism: The Intellectual Origins of the Jewish State.* New York: Basic Books, Inc., 1981.

Avneri, Arieh L., *The Claim of Dispossession: Jewish Settlement and the Arabs 1878–1948.* New Brunswick, NJ and London: Transaction Books, 1984.

Bahramitash, Roksana and Eric Hoogland, eds., *Gender in Contemporary Iran: Pushing the Boundaries.* Abingdon: Routledge, 2011.

Ball, George W. and Douglas B. Ball, *The Passionate Attachment: America's Involvement with Israel, 1947 to the Present.* New York & London: W. W. Norton & Co, 1992.

Barbati, Gabriele, "World Water Wars: In the West Bank, Water is Just Another Conflict Issue for Israelis and Palestinians," *International Business Times,* July 12 2013.

Barnett, Michael N., *Dialogues in Arab Politics*. New York: Columbia University Press, 1998.

Bar-On, Mordechai, *The Gates of Gaza: Israel's Road to Suez and Back. 1955–1957*. New York: St. Martin's Press, 1995.

Beker, Avi, *The United Nations and Israel: From Recognition to Reprehension*. Lexington, MA: Lexington Books, 1998.

Benjamin, Medea, *Kingdom of the Unjust*. New York: OR Books, 2016.

Bergstraesser, Gotthelf, *Introduction to the Semitic Languages*. Winona Lake, Indiana: Eisenbrauns, 1983.

Berkovits, Eliezer, *Faith After the Holocaust*. New York: Ktav Publishing House, Inc, 1973.

Bill, James A. and Robert Springborg, *Politics in the Middle East*. Third Edition. New York: HarperCollins, 1990.

Blook, Mia M., "Palestinian Suicide Bombing: Public Support, Market Share, and Outbidding," *Political Science Quarterly* 199.1 (2004): 61–88.

Braude, Joseph, *The New Iraq: Rebuilding the Country for Its People, the Middle East, and the World*. New York: Basic Books, 2003.

Bryson, Thomas A., *American Diplomatic Relations with the Middle East, 1784- 1975: A Survey*. Metuchen, NJ: The Scarecrow Press, 1977.

_____. *Tars, Turks, and Tankers: The Role of the United States Navy in the Middle East, 1800–1979*. Metuchen, NJ: The Scarecrow Press, 1977.

Burke, Edmund, III and David N. Yaghoubian, *Struggle and Survival in the Modern Middle East* (Second Edition). Berkeley: University of California Press, 2006.

Carey, Roane and Jonathan Shainin, Eds., *The Other Israel: Voices of Refusal and Dissent*. New York: The New Press, 2002.

Chafets, Ze'ev, *Heroes and Hustlers, Hard Hats and Holy Men: Inside the New Israel*. New York: William Morrow & Co, 1986.

Cleveland, William L., *A History of the Modern Middle East* (Third Edition). Boulder, CO: Westview Press, 2004.

Cole, Peter and Brian McQuinn, eds., *The Libyan Revolution and Its aftermath*. New York: Oxford University Press, 2015.

Curtis, Michael, Ed., *People and Politics in the Middle East*. New Brunswick, NJ and London: Transaction Books, 1971.

Davis, Moshe, Ed., *The Yom Kippur War: Israel and the Jewish People*. New York: Arno Press, 1974.

Dothan, Shmuel, *A Land in the Balance: The Struggle for Palestine 1918–1948*. Tel Aviv: MOD Books, 1993.

Ebaugh, Helen Rose, *The Gülen Movement: A Sociological Analysis of a Civic Movement Rooted in Moderate Islam*. New York: Spring Books, 2010.

El-Nawawy, Mohammed and Adel Iskandar. *Al-Jazeera: The Story of the Network that is Rattling Governments and Redefining Modern Journalism.* Boulder: Westview Press, 2003.

Field, James A. Jr., *America and the Mediterranean World 1776–1882.* Princeton, NJ: Princeton University Press, 1969.

Finnie, David H., *Pioneers East: the Early American Experience in the Middle East.* Cambridge, MA: Harvard University Press, 1967.

Fisher, Eugene M. and M. Cherif Bassiouni, *Storm over the Arab World: A People in Revolution.* Chicago: Follett Publishing Co, 1972.

Fleischner, Eva, ed., *Auschwitz: The Beginning of a New Era? Reflections on the Holocaust.* New York: Ktav Publishing House, Inc., 1977.

Foad, Dr Baher, *Islamic Concepts: Evidence from the Qur'an.* Cincinnati: Zakat and Research Foundation, 1989.

Friedman, Thomas, *From Beirut to Jerusalem.* New York: Doubleday, 1990.

Fromkin, David, *A Peace to End All Peace: The Fall of the Ottoman Empire and the Creation of the Modern Middle East.* New York: Henry Holt & Co, 1989.

Gabriel, Richard A., *Operation Peace for Galilee: the Israeli PLO War in Lebanon.* New York: Hill and Wang, 1985.

"General Assembly Votes Overwhelmingly to Accord Palestinians 'Non-Member Observer State' Status in United Nations," *UN Department of Public Information.* UN Sixty-Seventh General Assembly, November 29, 2012.

Geyer, Alan, *Piety and Politics.* Richmond, VA: John Knox Press, 1963.

Gibb, H. A. R., *Mohammedanism.* Oxford: Oxford University Press, 1962; paperback edition of the 1949 original.

Goitein, S. D., *Arabs and Jews: Their Contacts Through the Ages.* New York: Schocken Books, 1974.

Goldschmidt, Arthur, Jr, and Lawrence Davidson, *A Concise History of the Middle East* (Eighth Edition). Boulder, CO: Westview Press, 2006.

Halabi, Rafik, *West Bank Story: An Israeli Arab's View of Both Sides of a Tangled Conflict.* New York: Harcourt Brace Jovanovich, 1981.

Handy, Robert T., ed., *The Holy land in American Protestant Life, 1800–1948.* New York: Arno Press, 1981.

Harkabi, Yehoshafat, *The Bar Kokhba Syndrome: Risk and Realism in International Politics.* Chappaqua: Rossel Books, 1983.

Hasan, Sana, *Enemy in the Promised Land: An Egyptian Woman's Journey into Israel.* New York: Pantheon Books, 1986.

Hertzberg, Arthur, Ed., *The Zionist Idea.* New York: Atheneum, 1970.

Herzog, Chaim, *The Arab-Israeli Wars: War and Peace in the Middle East from the War of Independence through Lebanon.* (Revised Edition) New York: Random House, 1984.

Heyman, Philip B., *Terrorism and America: A Commonsense Strategy for a Demo- cratic Society.* Cambridge: MIT Press, 2001.

Hitti, Philip K., *History of the Arabs.* New York: Palgrave Macmillan, 2002; Tenth Edition.

Hoch, Gary, "The Politics of Water in the Middle East," in *Middle East Insight.* 9.3 (1993), 17–21.

Holt, P. M., *Egypt and the Fertile Crescent 1516–1922: A Political History.* Ithaca: Cornell University Press, 1969.

Hourani, Albert, *A History of the Arab Peoples.* Cambridge: Harvard University Press, 1991.

Huntington, Samuel P., *The Clash of Civilizations and the Remaking of the World Order.* New York: Simon & Schuster, 1996.

Indyk, Martin, *Innocent Abroad: An Intimate Account of American Peace Diplomacy in the Middle East.* New York: Simon & Schuster, 2009.

Karetsky, Stephen and Peter E. Goldman, Eds., *The Media's War against Israel.* New York: Steimatsky/Shapolsky Press, 1986.

Karin, Michael and Ina Friedman, *Murder in the Name of God: the Plot to Kill Yitzhak Rabin.* New York: Henry Holt & Co, 1998.

Kark, Ruth, *American Consuls in the Holy Land, 1832–1914.* Jerusalem: Magnes Press, 1994.

Khalidi, Rashid, *Resurrecting Empire: Western Footprints and America's Perilous Path in the Middle East.* Boston: Beacon Press, 2004.

_____. *The Iron cage: The Story of the Palestinian Struggle for Statehood.* Boston: Beacon Press, 2007.

Khouri, Fred J., *The Arab-Israeli Dilemma.* Syracuse: Syracuse University Press, 1977.

Kliot, Nurit, *Water Resources and Conflict in the Middle East.* London: Rout- ledge, 1994.

Kurtzer, Daniel C. and Scott B. Lasensky, *Negotiating Arab-Israeli Peace: American Leadership in the Middle East.* Washington, DC: US Institute of Peace Press, 2009.

Kurzman, Dan, *Genesis 1948: The First Arab-Israeli War.* New York and Cleve- land: New American Library, 1970.

La Guardia, Anton, *War Without End: Israelis, Palestinians and the Struggle for a Promised Land.* New York: St. Martin's Press, 2003.

Laqueur, Walter, ed., *The Israel-Arab Reader: A Documentary History of the Middle East Conflict.* New York: Bantam Books, 1970; revised and enlarged edition.

_____. *A History of Zionism.* London: Weidenfeld & Nicholson, 1972.

Latourette, Kenneth, *Missions and the American Mind.* Indianapolis: National Foundation Press, 1949.

Lee, Robert D., *Religion and Politics in the Middle East: Identity, Ideology, Institutions, and Attitudes*. New York: Westview Press, 2013.

Lewis, Bernard, *The Arabs in History*. New York: Harper & Brothers, 1960.

_____. *What Went Wrong? Western Impact and Middle Eastern Response.* New York: Oxford University Press, 2002.

Lowi, Miriam R., *Water and Power: The Politics of a Scarce Resource in the Jordan River Basin*. Cambridge: Cambridge University Press, 1993.

Lunt, James, *Hussein of Jordan: Searching for a Just and Lasting Peace*. New York: William Morrow & Co, 1989.

Makdisi, Ussama, *Artillery of Heaven: American Missionaries and the Failed Conversion of the Middle East*. Ithaca, NY: Cornell University Press, 2008.

Manor, Yohann. *To Right a Wrong: The Revocation of the UN General Assembly Resolution 3379 Defaming Zionism*. NYC: Shengold, 1997.

Mansfield, Peter, *A History of the Middle East* (Second Edition, revised and updated by Nicolas Pelham). London: Penguin Books, 2004.

Matthews, Elizabeth G., *The Israel-Palestine Conflict: Parallel Discourses*. Abingdon: Routledge, 2011.

McLaurin, R. D., Mohammed Mughisuddin and Abraham R. Wagner, *Foreign Policy Making in the Middle East: Domestic Influences on Policy in Egypt, Iraq, Israel and Syria*. New York and London: Praeger Publishers, 1977.

Mearsheimer, John J. and Stephen M. Walt, *The Israel Lobby and U.S. Foreign Policy*. New York: Farrar, Straus and Giroux, 2007.

Memmi, Albert, *Jews and Arabs*. Chicago: J. Philip O'Hara, Inc, 1975.

Merlin, Samuel, *The Search for Peace in the Middle East: The Story of President Bourghuiba's Campaign for a Negotiated Peace Between Israel and the Arab States*. Cranbury, NJ: Thomas Yoseloff, Publisher, 1968.

Miller, Aaron David, *The Much Too Promised Land: America's Elusive Search for Arab-Israeli Peace*. New York: Bantam Books, 2008.

_____. *The PLO and the Politics of Survival*. The Washington Papers/99; Washington, DC: Center for Strategic Studies, Georgetown University and Praeger Press, 1983.

Morris, Benny, *Righteous Victims: A History of the Zionist-Arab Conflict, 1881-2001*. New York: Vintage books, 2001.

Naghibi, Nima, *Rethinking Global Sisterhood: Western Feminism and Iran*. Minneapolis: University of Minnesota Press, 2007.

Ochsenwald, William and Sydney Nettleton Fisher, *The Middle East: A History* (Sixth Edition). New York: McGraw-Hill, 2004.

Oren, Michael, *Power, Faith and Fantasy: America in the Middle East, 1776 to the Present*. New York: W. W. Norton & Co., 2007.

_____. *Six Days of War: June, 1967 and the Making of the Modern Middle East*. Oxford: Oxford University Press, 2002.

Palmer, Leonard R., *Descriptive and Comparative Linguistics: A Critical Introduction*. London: Faber & Faber, 1972.

Pappe, Ilan, *A History of Modern Palestine: One Land, Two Peoples*. New York: Cambridge University Press, 2007; Second Edition.

Peters, Joan, *From Time Immemorial: The Origins of the Arab-Jewish Conflict Over Palestine*. New York: Harper & Row, Publishers, 1984.

Pollack, Kenneth, *The Persian Puzzle: The Conflict Between Iran and America*. Washington, DC: Brookings Institution, 2004.

Porath, Yehoshua, *The Emergence of the Palestinian-Arab National Movement, 1918–1929*. London: Cass, 1974.

Quandt, William B., *Camp David: Peacemaking and Politics*. Washington, DC: Brookings Press, 1986.

Rabinovich, Itamar, *The Road Not Taken: Early Arab-Israeli Negotiations*. New York: Oxford University Press, 1991.

Ro'i, Yaacov, *From Encroachment to Involvement: A Documentary Study of Soviet Policy in the Middle East, 1945–1973*. New York: Halsted Press, 1974.

Ross, Dennis, *The Missing Peace: The Inside Story of the Fight for Middle Eastern Peace*. New York: Farrar, Straus & Giroux, 2004.

Roucek, Joseph S. and Michael V. Belok, *The U.S. and the Persian Gulf*. Malabar, FL: Robert E. Krieger Publishing Co, 1985.

Rubenstein, Richard, *The Cunning of History: The Holocaust and the American Future,* New York: Harper and Row, 1975.

Rubin, Barry, *The Tragedy of the Middle East*. Cambridge: Cambridge University Press, 2002.

Sacher, Howard Morley, *The Course of Modern Jewish History*. New York: World Publishing Co., 1958. An updated edition was put out by Vintage Books in 1990.

Salinger, Pierre and Eric Laurent, *Secret Dossier: The Hidden Agenda Behind the Gulf War*. New York: Penguin Books, 1991.

Segev, Tom, *Elvis in Jerusalem: Post-Zionism and the Americanization of Israel*. New York: Henry Holt & Co, 2002.

_____. *One Palestine, Complete: Jews and Arabs under the British Mandate*. New York: Henry Holt & Co, 2000.

_____. *The Seventh Million: The Israelis and the Holocaust*. New York: Hill & Wang, 1993.

Shehadeh, Raja, *Occupier's Law: Israel and the West Bank*. Washington, DC: Institute for Palestine Studies, 1988.

Shipler, David K., *Arab and Jew: Wounded Spirits in a Promised Land*. London: Penguin Books, 2001.

Shlaim, Avi, *Collusion across the Jordan: King Abdullah, the Zionist Movement, and the Partition of Palestine*. New York: Columbia University Press, 1988.

Silberman, Neil Asher, *Between Past and Present: Archaeology, Ideology, and Nationalism in the Modern Middle East*. New York: Henry Holt & Co, 1989.

Silberstein, Laurence J., Ed., *New Perspectives on Israeli History: The Early Years of the State*. New York & London: New York University Press, 1991.

Sinai, Anne and Allen Pollack, Eds., *The Hashimite Kingdom of Jordan and the West Bank*. New York: American Association for Peace in the Middle East, 1977.

Soltes, Ori Z., *Embracing the World: Fethullah Gülen's Thought and Its Relationship to Jalaluddin Rumi and Others*. Clifton, NJ: Tughra books, 2013.

Stauffer, Thomas, *Water and War in the Middle East: The Hydraulic Parameters of Conflict*. Washington, DC: The Center for Policy Analysis on Palestine, 1996.

Stern, Jessica, and J. M. Berger. *ISIS: The State of Terror*. New York: HarperCollins, 2016.

Stillman, Norman A., *The Jews of Arab Lands: A History and Source Book*. Philadelphia: The Jewish Publication Society of America, 1979.

Tamir, Major-General Avraham, *A Soldier in Search of Peace: An Insider's Look at Israel's Strategy in the Middle East*. New York: Harper & Row, Publishers, 1988.

Telhami, Shibley, *The Stakes: America and the Middle East; the Consequences of Power and the Choice for Peace*. Boulder: Westview Press, 2002.

Thomas, Lewis V. and Richard N. Frye, *The United States and Turkey and Iran*. Cambridge, MA: Harvard University Press, 1952.

Tibawa, A. L., *American Interests in Syria, 1800–1901*. Oxford: Oxford University Press, 1966.

Timerman, Jacobo, *The Longest War: Israel in Lebanon*. New York: Random House, 1982.

Tyler, Patrick, *A World of Trouble: The White House and the Middle East—from Cold War to the War on Terror*. New York: Farrar, Straus & Giroux, 2008.

Vogel, Lester, *To See a Promised Land: Americans and the Holy Land in the Nineteenth Century*. University Park, PA: Pennsylvania University Press, 1993.

West Bank and Gaza: Assessment of Restrictions on Palestinian Water Sector Development. The World Bank: Middle East and North Africa Region Sustainable Development, April, 2009.

Williams, John Alden, *The Word of Islam*. Austin: University of Texas Press, 1994.

Wolf, Aaron T., *Hydropolitics Along the Jordan River*. Tokyo: United Nations University Press, 1995.

Ye'or, Bat, *The Dhimmi: Jews and Christians under Islam*. Cranbury, NJ: Associated University Presses, 1985.

Zeitlin, Solomon, *The Rise and Fall of the Judaean State*, (vols I and II); Philadelphia: Jewish Publication Society, 1962.

Zipperstein, Steven J. and Ernest S. Fredrichs, Eds., *Zionism, Liberalism, and the Future of the Jewish State: Centennial Reflections on Zionist Scholarship and Controversy*. Providence, RI: The Dorot Foundation, 2000.

INDEX

ENDNOTES

Preface

1 In addition to the works that I shall mention as my narrative moves forward, each of which focuses on a discrete aspect of the region and its issues, there is a number of significant texts, much longer than this one, which cover much of the wide sweep that I am seeking to cover, but in a manner different from mine. Let me mention five of these, although there are always more. One of them is *A Concise History of the Middle East*, by Arthur Goldschmidt Jr. and Lawrence Davidson. It differs from my narrative in four ways. It is obviously much longer, thus presenting the reader with a more arduous journey to arrive at an understanding of the region. (It is worth the journey if one has the time and the energy.) It nowhere offers a straightforward summary account of where the complications reside (as I believe I do in my introduction); it requires the reader to infer that summary. It reduces what I believe is a crucial story with ramifications continuous until today—that of the Crusades—to a mere three pages, thus underemphasizing its importance. Finally, I find it skewed: the Jewish presence in the Middle East seems suddenly to emerge with colonial Europe in the late nineteenth century, and that presence is not treated in an evenhanded manner (for example, on page 279, the British during the period of the mandate "tended to back Zionist aims because of Jewish *pressure* on London," [my italics], while at the same time they "favored the Arabs, often influenced by concern for Muslim *opinion*..." [my italics]. The consistent usage (this is only one example) of terminology that is subtly different in nuance cannot but leave the reader with a skewed perspective.

Nonetheless, the book is, on the whole, an excellent and clear one, offering a majestic sweep of the region and its history.

William Ochsenwald and Sydney Nettleton Fisher's monumental *The Middle East: A History* was first published in 1979 and has been reissued in a number of subsequent editions, and is even more sweeping and in some respects more comprehensive than the volume by Goldschmidt and Davidson. It seems to me to suffer from the same sort of flaws. Thus it lacks a summary account that will guide the reader before s/he plunges into nearly 750 pages of text; so, too, the Crusades are minimized and no connection between them and the vast coverage of Ottoman history is offered. Finally, I find the anti-Jewish bias even more obvious: the Jews are virtually invisible in the coverage of antiquity—or misconstrued. Thus page 11 offers a historically inaccurate reference to King David's "expanding Jewish state." It was an Israelite state, which is something different; the word "Jewish" did not yet exist, and would not exist for more than another one thousand years. That inaccuracy will have repercussions for the [mis] understanding of the religious relationship among Judaism, Christianity, and Islam. The index suggests that the Jews in antiquity are discussed on pages 17 and 18, but they are not—they are mentioned, again with historical and theological inaccuracy, in half a line on page 17. More distressing is the fact that the Jews appear out of nowhere in chapter 36, but on page 448 we read that "the earlier development both of Jewish Zionist national feeling and of Arab nationalism were discussed in Chapter 27" when in fact only Arab nationalism is discussed there, so nowhere does one gain a sense of the complexities and layers of Jewish nationalism to balance one's understanding of nationalism among the Arabs. Similarly, the brief account of the Arab refugee problem that resulted from the First Arab-Israeli War hardly seems to share the unhappy credit for the problem between the two sides. Once again, however, this is a very useful book, provided the reader is aware of these drawbacks.

Peter Mansfield's much shorter *A History of the Middle East*, revised and updated after his death by Nicolas Pelham, is rife with fundamental definitional and terminology errors (once more we read that King David founded a Jewish kingdom, an even more profoundly anachronistic turn of phrase than that which refers to the Hebrews, not the Israelites coming out of Egypt under Moses's leadership); and imbalances—in this case most apparent in the discussion of the period leading from the assassination of Rabin to the beginning of the Second *Intifada*. While the book acknowledges that the details of the collapse of Israeli-Palestinian peace negotiations "remain shrouded in recrimination," (on page 360) it clearly places the responsibility on Israeli shoulders—the subhead is entitled "Israel's Missed Opportunity for Peace"—treating Mr. Arafat as blameless; Mansfield refers without footnote to post-Oslo "pogroms against Palestinians in Jerusalem" (on page 356) with neither a source nor an explanation for just what that means, and nary a word about Palestinian suicide bombers. This easily read book is in fact disturbingly lacking not only in evenhandedness—even its "further reading" section, when one arrives at the section on Israel, is profoundly skewed toward those *critical* of Zionism or of the state!—but also in footnotes: there are none.

Struggle and Survival in the Modern Middle East, edited by Edmund Burke III and David N. Yaghoubian differs from my narrative, as the title suggests, in focusing mainly on the modern era. It does so, moreover, by offering a series of biographies of a range of different everyday inhabitants from the region, thus presenting social history in large part through the perceptions of those being studied. Once again, I cannot help but be disturbed by an obvious shortcoming in an otherwise fascinating and illuminating volume: the only Jew among the individuals depicted is a settler in the West Bank. Certainly June Leavitt and what she stands for must be understood if we wish to understand the Israel-Palestine part of the Middle East's problematic, but it hardly seems legitimate to offer only that perspective as the representative of the Jewish and Israeli side of the equation. Moreover, this American whose "unconventional blend of spirituality and nationalism" (page 387) is not that unconventional within the settler population, although its basis in "her own somewhat secular formulation of Judaism" is certainly not the formulation that one encounters every day, is thereby less representative even of the "settler movement" than one might suppose. By comparison, the very sympathetic presentation of the Palestinian woman, "Ghada: Village Rebel of Political Protestor?" furthers a prejudicial picture of untainted sympathy for the Palestinians and unmitigated criticism of the Israelis.

Finally, William L. Cleveland's *A History of the Modern Middle East* is an extremely incisive work that effectively digs beneath the varied surfaces of the region's problematic. The reader will already have recognized from this lengthy endnote that I find prejudicial perspectives most obvious in writers' discussions of the Israeli-Palestinian or Israeli-Arab focus of various books—more often than not, prejudiced against the Jewish/Israeli side of the equation—as is the case with varied obviousness or subtlety in the four other works I am discussing here. Cleveland's discussion of that aspect of the region shows evenhanded sympathy for the complications, successes, and ideological or moral failures of both sides. His book differs from mine most obviously in the narrower chronological band of its focus and its therefore more limited discussion of all the threads that interweave themselves in the tangled web.

I have belabored my discussion of this handful of books—and there are others that will be found in the bibliography, even as no bibliography can keep pace with the expanding number of them (in fact, I wrote these comments in 2004, and by now, 2017, many more books could be discussed)—in order to underscore what I hope will be recognized as the validity of my *elengkhos*. I hope that my narrative is both evenhanded and uniquely, if concisely, comprehensive.

Introduction
2   See the discussion of this in Shibley Telhami, *The Stakes: America and the Middle East*, 98–100.

Chapter 1
3   One might note that even the question of whether to use the phrase "Near East" as opposed to "Middle East" offers a double-definitional issue. We have inherited our terminology from the British colonial era, in which context the area under discussion was referred to as the Near East, and between that region and the Far East lay the Middle East—India and its environs. More recently, though, and since for current political and related purposes India (but not, most recently, Afghanistan!) is a separate matter from the region under discussion, it is fairly common for an "updated" perspective to refer to the region formerly called the "Near East" as the "Middle East." The latter phrase, strictly speaking, seems to have first been suggested—coined—as far back as 1902 by the American naval theorist, Alfred Mahan. One could, as I am wont to do, use the first phrase to refer to the area that extends from Egypt to Iraq and the second to include Iran and its nearest neighbors (thus perhaps including Afghanistan but stopping short of Pakistan and India—or at least India). One might also note that in French, the phraseology was and remains "Middle East" (*Moyen Orient*). Conversely, in German, it is Near East (*Naeher Oste*).

Of course all three languages also use versions of "the Levant," as well, (meaning "rising,"—as in where the sun rises, in the east, and therefore "eastward"). Then again, some use that term only to refer to the area between the Mediterranean and Mesopotamia—i.e., what is now geopolitically defined as Israel, Palestine, Jordan, Lebanon, and Syria.

The entire discussion of the previous paragraph, it should be noted, reflects changing details in what is in any case a Euro-American perspective.

To India or China, the region that is our subject could surely be called the Near West! One could almost call it Western Asia or Southwestern Asia, except that this would leave out Egypt and the other North African countries from Sudan to Morocco, which can sometimes (Egypt always) be considered part of the region. Check the Internet, in fact, and you will find half a dozen different geographic parameters for "map of the Middle East." Definitional issues dog the process of understanding this arena of history and geography from beginning to end.

4   Simply put, not all Jews are necessarily traceable to the Middle East, period, much less to its "Semitic" parts. Aside from the general matter of occasional conversion or more frequent rape as dual methods of creating Jews from non-Jewish "stock" throughout the past fifteen centuries or so, there is the story of the Khazars. From the area just northeast of the Black Sea, they were a Turkic people said to have converted to Judaism en masse (or at least the upper classes did) in the late eighth century. With the destruction of their empire by the early eleventh century and subsequent putative migration north, up into Slavic lands, one could argue that a compelling percentage of Eastern European Jews are their descendants. Not all scholars, it must be noted, agree on this version of Khazar/Jewish history.

Chapter 2

5   Until about thirty years ago, for reasons I cannot certainly explain—probably because they followed the pronunciational lead of the Ottoman Turks and their successors, who "Turkified" the Arabic words that Turkish absorbed into its vocabulary over the centuries—it was the norm for Anglo-American scholars to make no effort to render Arabic sounds as effectively as possible in English. The Arabic vowel system is based on a-i-u; "o" and "e" don't exist. Therefore the more correct transliterations are Muslim, Muhammad, Qur'an, Makka, Madina, *hijaz*, Hashimite, Nasir, etc.

6   The Arabic-language name, *'Allah*, is a crasis of *al'Illah*—and cognate with Hebrew *El*. Too often, Islamic scholars will say "Allah" when speaking to a general audience, which tends to obscure the fact that the term simply means "God"—in other words, Muslims use the same term as do Jews and Christians, but in prayer and Qur'anic recitation, they are likely to use the Arabic term, as Jews will the Hebrew and many Christians the Greek or Latin, (among others), rather than the vernacular.

7   Note the impropriety of calling Muslims "Muhammadans" or Islam itself "Muhammadanism." Christianity derives its name from *khristos* (Greek for Hebrew *mashiah*; the two words are anglicized as "christ"

and "messiah" respectively), which word came to express the belief that Jesus as the Messiah was God in human form. But Muhammad is never regarded as more than a prophet, albeit the *ultimate* prophet.

8   It is symptomatic of how every detail within this narrative finds itself subject to definitional debate that, while the standard Muslim understanding of why Yathrib became al-Madina is as I have stated it—more precisely, that its full name was *Madinat al-Nabi* ("the city of the Prophet")—many Western scholars assert that the Jewish agriculturalists who first settled Yathrib (long before the Prophet arrived on the *hijra)* first gave to the expanding oasis the name al'Madina. See, for example, Norman A. Stillman, *The Jews of Arab Lands*, 9.

9   See *Ibid*, 9: "They [the Jews] formed the majority of the population and were organized into tribes. The three most important were the Banu 'I-Nadir, the Banu Qurayza, and the Banu Qaynuqa' . . . Medina [*sic*] was also inhabited by two large confederations of pagan Arabs—the Banu Aws and the Banu Khazraj . . . A long struggle for dominance ensued in which the Nadir and Qurayza sided with the Aws, while Qaynuqa' allied itself with the Khazraj."

10   See below, 28.

11   The plural of *sura* is *suwar*.

12   Others would disagree, even as to the precise timing of things: they would say that the conquest of Makka took place by 628, largely through choking the city by blocking her trade routes—and that Muhammad therefore lived another four years, so that the argument that he was punished by 'Allah is specious.

13   The word is cognate with the Hebrew *miqra'*, a term that Jews often use to refer to the Torah.

14   Certainly Genesis, the first twenty or so chapters of Exodus, significant passages in Leviticus and Numbers, and all of Deuteronomy represent fairly coherent narratives; between these narrative parts are sandwiched the extensive legislative elements of the Torah.

15   But this seems a particularly strong issue in at least parts of Islamic time and space. One might recall the account in T. E. Lawrence's *Seven Pillars of Wisdom* of how great an effort was required to gain active assistance for various actions from Muslim Arab associates who were more likely to consider events to be unchangeably "written" by God. To be more precise, the two primary theological perspectives in Sunni Islam disagree on the matter of free will and therefore disagree regarding the degree to which God exercises an absolutely predetermining will: the Mu'tazalites contend that humans have free will and that God chooses not to interfere in ways

that would abrogate that attribute; Ash'arites, on the other hand, contend that we essentially have no free will, since everything is predetermined by God. There is far more that might be said about this issue, but a larger discussion falls outside the scope of this narrative.

16 With the incredibly rapid spread of Islam in the seventh and eighth centuries, it soon became apparent that some so-called *hadiths* were not legitimate, but creations of individuals with their own political motives for representing them as telling about or ascribed to Muhammad. The work of examining and compiling legitimate, reliable collections included, among early efforts, that of Muslim (ca. 821–75). He gathered some nine thousand *hadiths* into a compilation so revered that it is known as *Sahih Muslim*: "[the] authentic Muslim [collection]." Ultimately Hadiths fall into different categories with regard to how "reliable" they are—how strongly or weakly the linkage is considered to be between a statement or story and the Prophet himself or those in his immediate circle.

17 The Arabic word *din* is the analogue of the Hebrew word *din*, but does not quite mean "judgment," as the latter does. It is more like the Hebrew word *dat*, which is usually translated as "religion" but that includes the connotations of "judgment" and "law." *Iman* is cognate with Hebrew *emunah*.

18 The Jewish calendar is lunar-solar; it also shifts about ten or eleven days every year vis-à-vis the Gregorian calendar but is adjusted by the interpolation of an entire leap month (*Adar* II) every fourth year to send it back to where it began.

19 The spilling of blood in the context of doctrinal differences is, of course, not unique to Islam. In Christian history, for example, both the centuries following the East-West schism of 1054—and even more so the Reformation/ Counter-Reformation period in the West, from the 1520s to the early eighteenth century—were marked by considerable bloodshed.

20 Because word of mouth is unreliable, the *shi'is* assert, how do the *sunnis* know that they are not interpolating customs not sanctioned by the prophet? They, the *shi'is*, know what Muhammad did and did not sanction since he spoke specifically to Ali, who transmitted the legitimate orthodox traditions (the *sunnis* consider themselves orthodox and call the *shi'is* heterodox) from Muhammad through a line of divinely inspired *imams*. The Ayatollah Khomeini was to his followers such an infallible, divinely inspired *imam*. He represented the largest of the *shi'i* sects, the *imami*—one of three major *shi'i* groups. Today, about 86 percent of Muslims are Sunni, and about 14 percent are Shi'i.

21 See below, 121–22, for further discussion of *jihad*.

22 Thus, for example, 6:07, 16:82, 21:07–109, 88:21–22, 64:12, 60:8, among others.

23 However, one might understand the Hanafis (found over time mostly in India, Central Asia, and Turkey) as the "Rationalists"; the Malikis (found mostly in North and West Africa) as the "Traditionalists"; the Shafi'is, (found mostly in Egypt, East Africa, and Indonesia) who developed as a kind of compromise between the Hanafis and Malikis in the tenth century, as "Rationalist-Traditionalists." A fourth group of Sunnis, the Hanbalis (found in Saudi Arabia), might be labeled "Fundamentalists."

24 By the time of Muhammad, Judaism had already absorbed into itself the Christian tradition of angels and demons—which still prevails folkloristically in Jewish literature, although it is neither originally nor logically Jewish.

25 The most historically significant of these is probably the Fatimid Shi'i ruler Al-Hakim, See below, 42 and nn 33, 34. As a separate but related or at least interesting issue, one might wonder: if Muhammad had claimed descent from the House of David, and that therefore he was the *mashiah*, might he have been accepted in the long run by the Jewish tribes of Yathrib? But he claimed to be the last prophet, (and to even suggest otherwise is to speak as a non-believer rather than a believer: for believers, Muhammad claimed to be a prophet because that is what he *was*) and that was surely anathema to them—since prophecy was assumed to have disappeared by (or shortly after) the time of Ezra, not to return again *until* the time of the *mashiah*. It is perhaps even more complicated than this: the Jews of Yathrib apparently initially perceived him as asserting a role as *mashiah* (which I don't believe he did) but, since he was not descended (didn't claim to be descended) from the House of David he could not be the *mashiah*. So ultimately he and they parted spiritual and political ways (to use an overly gentle turn of phrase; the parting was not overly friendly).

26 The standard Muslim understanding of the collapse of good relations between Muhammad and the Yathribian Jews is that it was a function of the Jews's decision to turn against the Prophet and ally themselves with his enemies. Even this little detail has implications for the development and history of Islam and for the evolution of the relationship between Muslims and Jews. At issue is a pair of divergent interpretations of events for which there is no absolute and concrete record of how they played out.

27 One can, of course further subdivide. What Catholics and Orthodox Christians call Intertestamental or Deuterocanonical texts (Susannah, Judith, Maccabees I and II, Tobit, The Wisdom of Solomon, Ecclesiasticus,

et al) Protestants term apocrypha; like Jews, Protestants view these as other than God's word.

28 Both Jews and Christians embrace this idea, although the two groups interpret the significance of Abraham's offering of Isaac differently from each other. Muslim scholars debated for centuries both the question of whether it was Isaac or Ishmael whom Abraham offered and whether it took place on that hill in what later became Jerusalem, or elsewhere, on a hill outside Makka. The vast majority of Muslims today understand the son offered by Abraham to have been Ishmael.

29 The account of the *'isra* and *mir'aj* have a starting point in *Sura* 17:1 of the Qur'an, which merely refers to the Prophet's night journey to "the far mosque" (*al-masjeed al-aqsa*); the detailed account of the *mir'aj* and discussion of Muhammad's exchanges both with prior prophets, especially Moses, on the way up and down, and with God is found in a series of h*adith*s.

Chapter 3

30 See below, 66–7 and 69–73.

31 "Judaea" in the narrow sense was more or less the geopolitical area that was a lineal descendant of what had survived the Assyrian destruction of the Israelite north (722–21 BCE), and that subsequently resisted but was ultimately defeated by the Babylonians (586 BCE), and to which territory those who returned from the Babylonian exile came back with the Medo-Persian defeat of the Babylonians (538 BCE). That area eventually achieved independence under the Hasmonaeans (ca. 140 BCE), and was in turn swallowed up by Herod the Idumaean (37 BCE). By the time of Jesus's birth a "Greater Judaea" encompassing Samaria and Galilee as well as additional territory had been achieved through military and diplomatic successes first by the Hasmonaeans and then by Herod, the latter as an important client and ally of Rome. For an excellent and detailed discussion of this, see Solomon Zeitlin, *The Rise and Fall of the Judaean State* (especially volume I and the first one hundred pages of volume II.

Chapter 4

32 "Animist," in brief, means that they worshipped many different gods embodied in the forces of nature.

33 To further complicate the historical picture, it should be noted that al-Hakim's mother was Christian. Having chosen his father's faith, his antagonism to Judaism and Christianity and attempts to force-convert

Jews and Christians raises interesting psychological questions beyond the scope of this study.

34   Al-Hakim's disappearance led his followers to develop a cult around his memory the adherents to which asserted that he would return at some indeterminate future date. Those followers, who diverged from, while remaining rooted in Islam, became the Druze. Mostly dwelling in northern Israel, Lebanon, and Syria, they are another population whose cultural, spiritual, and political concerns offer a challenge to defining who is who even within that subregion of the region at large. Of course, this leads to yet another definitional matter: who and what really *are* the Druze? In brief, they are the descendants of followers—Arab followers— of al-Hakim. More properly called *Muwahiddun* ("monotheists"; they call themselves *Ahl al-Tawhid*, which in Arabic means "People of the One"), the group is popularly known as Druze after the eleventh-century preacher Darazi who, together with the mystic, Hamza ibn Ali ibn Ahmad, was one of the first to proclaim al-Hakim to be the Incarnation of God. (The notion that the *mahdi*—whoever he might be according to whichever Muslim group—is divine, constitutes an absolute heresy for Islam; Darazi was ultimately excommunicated and executed for his distortions of the message). Strictly speaking it was al-Hakim's associate, Baha al-Din, who led the group after al-Hakim's disappearance. The *Muwahiddin* consider themselves bearers of the core of the Muslim message, but Muslims don't regard them as Muslim, since they do not maintain the Five Pillars as a guide to spiritual and/or everyday life and because of their notion of a divine *mahdi*. Politically speaking, having been granted autonomy by the League of Nations in 1921 they were shortly thereafter swallowed up by the French Mandatory power and never again regained that autonomy. Today they total somewhere between 350,000 and 600,000, (depending upon whose count), dwelling mostly in Lebanon in the vicinity of Mount Hermon; there are communities in Syria and Northern Israel and also about 75,000 living in Jordan.

35   In fact, the sack of Jerusalem by the Khwarizmian nomads was followed by one of the most disastrous of battles for Christian Crusaders in the course of all of the Crusades: the Battle of Formie, near Gaza, in which Templars, Hospitaliers, and Teutonic Knights and their Syrian and Bedouin allies were cut to ribbons by the Mamluk Sultan Baybar's forces of Egyptians supplemented by Khwarizmians.

36   To an already extant railway line from Istanbul to Damascus, Abdul Hamid added a section connecting Damascus to Madina—which is as far as the project got by the time World War I intervened to force its discontinuance.

37 The insurgents came to be known as the "Young Turks."

Chapter 5

38 "Mehmet" is, incidentally, a Turkish version of the Arabic-language name, Muhammad.

39 If one considers the matter of "oriental" carpets, so diverse in style, with each style derived from a particular tribal group, and then one further understands that each of those tribal groups possesses fierce familial loyalties and cultural, social, and political identities that distinguish them emphatically from other tribes, one begins to understand how profound the issue of tribal, as opposed to national or broadly ethnic political thinking is.

40 To be precise, the first American Protestant missionaries, ahead of the main chronological curve, were Levi Parsons and Pliny Fisk, dispatched from Boston in 1819 by the American Board of Commissioners for Foreign Missions. Parsons arrived and stayed briefly in Jerusalem in 1821, primarily distributing Bibles, but died the following year on a journey to Alexandria, Egypt—at not yet thirty years of age. Fisk focused more on language studies, so that he could preach, and began to do so in 1825—but died on October 23 of that year on a trip to Beirut at age thirty-three.

41 For example, the printing press set up by the American Eli Smith as early as 1827.

42 One recalls that Mehmet Ali was an Albanian, and thus not indigenous to the region—and he spoke no Arabic—although his ancestry was presumably from the 'arav.

Chapter 6

43 The proposed bill actually failed at that time; too many British Christians were not yet ready to accord equal civil status to their Jewish neighbors. But this first raising of the issue set the stage for later Emancipation success.

44 Note that the Hapsburg decree refers to the Jews as a nation, whereas the French edict is based on an understanding of Judaism as a religion. As discussed above, that definitional problem has yet to be solved in our own time.

45 Duehring was a German socialist whose book, *The Jewish Problem as a Problem of Race, Morals and Culture*, published the previous year, espoused a biological view of the world, in which the German/Nordic "type" was superior to all others, and the Jews—their depravity an innate function of their biology—capable of any and every sin and crime, represented a

threat to the future of that race. He argued that Prussia must be purified of its Jews, by racial war, if necessary. At the very least and as a start, laws needed to be passed that would eliminate Jewish influence in education, the press, finance, and business.

46 Herzl was actually born in Budapest and only moved with his family to Vienna in 1883 when he was eighteen years old. There he became a lawyer to satisfy his parents' concern (and perhaps his own) that he have a financially viable profession, but he identified as an Austrian not a Hungarian (and not per se, as a Jew, which, in the unassimilated corners of the Austro-Hungarian, Hapsburg world, would have been separate from either Austrian or Hungarian identities). He aspired to success as a playwright and journalist, rather than as a lawyer, writing in German (again, rather than in Hungarian) since that language was the primary language of both the Austro-Hungarian Empire and most of Middle Europe.

47 See Theodor Herzl, The Jewish State, of which there is any number of English-language editions. I am quoting from the translation by Sylvie D'Avigdor used in Arthur Hertzberg's The Zionist Idea.

48 He is referring to the hard-fought gains of Emancipation, according to which, in most central and western European countries Jews had achieved a degree of theoretical socioeconomic, cultural and political parity with their Christian neighbors by the late nineteenth century—although it must be remembered that it was the shock of the Dreyfus Affair and what it meant for the actual insufficiency of that achievement that prompted Herzl to write his pamphlet.

49 This last statement is as close as Herzl gets to actually acknowledging the presence of Arabs and others in the area where he envisions his State. He is very much a European, a child of his time, who views any and every imposition of Europeanism on any and all indigenous populations as drawback resistant and positive. See my further comments below.

50 I have not quoted all of these passages in the order in which Herzl offered them. His comment about "mud huts," etc., comes from chapter one and the references to the work of the Society and the Company as well as that regarding "benefits to neighboring lands" from chapter two of his pamphlet.

51 A further aspect of this American Christian interest in shaping the Middle East is reflected in the number of Civil War veterans who went to Egypt in the late 1860s and 1870s to train soldiers. This training program soon became a program of teaching reading and in turn offering broader education that would include civic values and shape nationalism and patriotism—with obvious political implications for the Ottoman Empire's

waning ability to control its Arab provinces. See Michael Oren's excellent book, *Power, Faith and Fantasy: America in the Middle East, 1776 to the Present.* On the other hand, American policy with regard to the Ottomans between about 1850 and World War I turns out to have been largely based on the briefings provided to our State Department by several key figures among the many, mainly Congregationalist, missionaries active throughout Ottoman territory during this period. A fine discussion of this will be found in the not-yet-published Georgetown University Liberal Studies PhD dissertation by Elizabeth Worth Shelton, *Setting the Stage: Nineteenth-Century American Protestant Missionaries in Turkey and Their Influence on American Foreign Policy, 1840–90.* It may be obtained from Georgetown's Lauinger Library.

52 For a brief summary of this, see Howard Morley Sachar's *The Course of Modern Jewish History*, chapters 9, 10 and 13.

53 See above, 2, 34. There is irony here in the adoption—or perhaps, adaptation—of an ethno-racial category for "Jew" that Wilhelm Marr had introduced into European discourse two generations earlier and that Hitler was embracing at the same time.

54 See below, 88, regarding the "Balfour Declaration."

55 This phrase is quoted from a letter of protest written by a handful of German rabbis at the announcement of the impending conference. The entire text may be found in the Central Zionist Archives, 4 Zalman Shazar St. Jerusalem.

Chapter 7

56 At least four cities—Safed, Tiberias, Jerusalem, and Hebron—had a continuous Jewish presence since antiquity; about another twenty-five had Jewish inhabitants again by and since the medieval period, including Gaza, Jaffa, Caesarea, Haifa among others. By 1880, there were about twenty-four thousand Jews in Ottoman Palestine; by 1914, that number had grown to about ninety thousand. By contrast, the non-Jewish Arab population went from about forty-seven thousand to five hundred thousand during that same thirty-four-year period. How much of this was from influx and how much from birthrate has not been documented to my knowledge.

57 That is, the British created the state of Transjordan as a kingdom for the Sharif, carving it out of the eastern portion of "Palestine."

58 Yemenite Jews, for example, began to come in large numbers to *Eretz Yisrael* in 1881—impelled not by Zionist fervor but by messianic hopes. The passage in Song of Songs 7:8—"I will ascend to the date palm tree"—was interpreted by their spiritual leaders to refer to ascent of the anointed

one to the Holy Land in the year of the palm. The latter was deduced by deconstructing the three consonants (*t-m-r*) that comprise the word "date palm" (*tamar*) as signifying the equivalent of the year 1880. (The Jewish year dates itself from the putative beginning of the world. In September 2008, we entered the year 5769, which is where we will still be with the arrival of the Gregorian year 2009.) The year 1880 would have been 5640 in Jewish accounting. Every consonant in Hebrew has a numerical value, and thus the year 5640 is rendered with the Hebrew letters *t-r-m*, which equal 640, the "5" of five thousand being assumed. Another twist gave, instead, 1882, for "*in* the year of the date palm" would add the Hebrew "*b*," which means "in" and equals "2," therefore yielding the equivalent of 1882.

59 See below, 182.

60 Technically the descendants of Mehmet Ali remained in charge of Egypt for a century after his stepping down from power in July 1848; the death of his son and successor, Ibrahim, four months later; and his own death in 1849. The eleventh and last ruler in their dynasty, Fouad II, was deposed by the revolution of 1953 that brought Muhammad Naguib and shortly thereafter, Abdel Gamal Nassir to power, but the British were in fact virtually in control after 1882. To this might be added (among other complications) the fact that theoretically Mehmet Ali and his dynastic successors answered to the Ottomans (in actuality they did not) until 1914 with the beginning of the collapse of the Ottoman Empire at the outset of World War I; they answered more unequivocally to the British until the 1953 revolution. This is another tangled web within the larger web that could invite its own book-length discussion.

61 The term "Hashimite" reflects the assertion that the family descended from the Quraish tribe and indeed from Muhammad himself by way of his grandson, Hussain, (hence: "*Hashimite*") who was the son of Fatima (the Prophet's daughter) and 'Ali.

62 Note the turn of phrase "the British permitted": even in raising an army to support British interests, the Arab nationalists were neither accorded full authority by the British nor were they in a position to assert it without British acquiescence.

63 The full text of the letter with the full text of the British Cabinet statement may be found in Laqueur's *The Israel-Arab Reader: A Documentary History of the Middle East Conflict*.

64 See Michael Oren, *op citum*.

65 Regarding the Kurds, see below, 112 and nn 201, 202.

66 Once more let us consider some of the further complexities in this part of the larger picture. It was the second son of Sharif Hussain, 'Abd'Allah,

who became his father's foreign minister and political adviser after the latter assumed the title of King of the *Hijaz* with British support in 1916. 'Abd'Allah's younger brother, Faisal, was proclaimed King of Syria, whence he was expelled by the French in 1920. 'Abd'Allah assembled troops for the purpose of marching to Damascus to restore his brother's throne but the British prevailed on him to go no further than Amman. Eventually the British made Faisal king of Iraq—from which throne his grandson, Faisal II, was removed by assassination in the coup of 1958 in which Saddam Hussein was a participant (although it would take Saddam twenty more years to assume full power in Iraq). 'Abd'Allah, the British-imposed Emir of Transjordan in 1921, took the title of King in 1946 and in turn became King of Jordan in 1949, changing the name of the country after his annexation of the West Bank. He was assassinated in the al-Aksa Mosque by a Palestinian follower of the Grand Mufti of Jerusalem (see below, 98, 100) on July 20, 1951. The recently deceased King Hussein was 'Abd'Allah's grandson. Hussein's son and successor and Jordan's current ruler is 'Abd'Allah II.

67   For the purposes of the discussion of statehood within western Palestine— and really, during the entire discussion of Arab nationalism—I am again using the word "Arab" in the common parlance sense to exclude Jews and encompass primarily but not exclusively Muslims, even though I have been at pains to demonstrate that, in the larger historical context, this is at least an oversimplification and at most an inaccuracy. The ease with which we necessarily slip into such small but not insignificant inaccuracies is discouraging.

Chapter 8

68   One of the now-forgotten but extensively thought out plans around that time was to establish a Jewish enclave along the Kimberley Plateau in the province of Western Australia. The beginnings of the Kimberley Project were rooted in the Uganda Proposal of 1903, at which time the Jewish Territorialist Organization was formed to consider non-Middle Eastern possibilities for Jewish colonization. The project was reborn on July 26, 1935, with the formation in London of the Freeland League for Jewish Territorial Colonization. In seeking a site for Jewish refugee settlement, the League decided upon the East Kimberley region, in 1938. Both the elaboration of the project and the campaign to convince the Australian government to embrace it continued through mid-1948, when it was finally abandoned through a combination of Zionist opposition—and Israel would in any case declare its independence in May of that year—and

Australian fears that the enclave would bring in too many Communists and/or seek independent status. See *This Australia*, Vol 6, No 2, March 1987 (Melbourne: Greenhouse Publications), and Isaac Steinberg's *Australia—The Unpromised Land* (London: V. Gollancz, 1948).

69 See the Report of the *American Christian Palestine Committee*, 1947, 8–12, 17–21.

70 See ACPC, 17 and MG, 165

71 MG, 155

72 See Richard Rubenstein, *The Cunning of History: The Holocaust and the American Future*, 16–21 and in particular his quote (on 17) from Lord Moyne, British High Commissioner in Egypt in 1944, regarding the possibility of saving a million Jews through Adolf Eichmann's "blood for trucks" offer: "What shall I do with those million Jews? Where shall I put them?" Palestine as an answer to that question was less viable to the British government than mass extermination (providing the Germans did most of the dirty work).

73 From a speech by David Ben-Gurion delivered on February 28, 1940. See the Central Zionist Archives, 4 Zalman Shazar St, Jerusalem.

74 See below, 103, but see also 232.

75 *ACPC*, 5

76 I am referring, most obviously, to Samuel P. Huntington's strident thesis, expressed in his *Clash of Civilizations and the Remaking of the World Order* (which appeared in essay form in *Foreign Affairs*, Summer, 1993, 72(3), 22–49 and subsequently in book form); and to a less severe extent to the viewpoint expressed by Bernard Lewis in his *What Went Wrong? The Clash between Islam and Modernity in the Middle East.*

77 See above, 52.

78 As I shall point out shortly, that did not in the end deter Begin from signing a peace with Anwar Sadat or prevent Yitzhak Rabin from signing agreements with Yassir Arafat and King Hussein. See 128, 159 and nn 105, 124.

79 "Yishuv" ("settlement") refers to the community of Jewish inhabitants of Palestine before 1948. The term came into common Jewish use in the late nineteenth century with the expansion of that population during the proto- Zionist and early Zionist period.

80 The matter of Jewish leaders, particularly Zionist leaders, as complicit with the Nazis has a painful history within the pained history of the Holocaust. The most prominent moment in that narrative surrounds the name of Rudolf Kastner, formerly a leader of the Hungarian Jewish community, which community went with surprising silence into the Destruction

Camps toward the end of the war. When by the mid-1950s Kastner was a member of Ben-Gurion's *Mapai* party, he was accused of having negotiated with Eichmann to allow a small group of Jews—his family and friends—to escape to Palestine in exchange for spreading the necessary fictions regarding where Jews were all being sent by the Nazis in order to maintain calm acquiescence from the community at large. I don't believe that the absolute truth on this issue is known or will be known in the near future.

81 See Tom Segev, *Elvis in Jerusalem: Post–Zionism and the Americanization of Israel*, 100–101: "Over and over people asked survivors how they had survived. By implication they were asking not how but why, and the question contained an insinuation of guilt. Ben-Gurion said: 'Among the survivors . . . were people who would not have prevailed had they not been what they are—hard, bad, and egotistical. . .'" Also see Benny Morris, *Righteous Victims: A History of the Zionist-Arab Conflict, 1881–1999*, 162: "If I knew it was possible to save all [Jewish] children of Germany by their transfer to England and only half of them by transfer to *Eretz Yisrael*, I would choose the latter—because we are faced not only with the accounting of those children but also with the historical accounting of the Jewish people." See also the book-length focus of Tom Segev's *The Seventh Million: The Israelis and the Holocaust.*

82 See Segev, *Elvis*, 100: "Many were ashamed of the Jews' weakness; some were ashamed of the Zionist movement's inability to save them. Some blamed themselves for not doing more."

83 Fackenheim is quoting here from Walter Laqueur, *A History of Zionism*, 593.

84 Emil Fackenheim "The Holocaust and the State of Israel: Their Relation," in Eva Fleischner, ed., *Auschwitz: Beginning of a New Era? Reflections on the Holocaust*, 209–210.

85 See 76.

86 See above, 53.

Chapter 9

87 I am ignoring as tangential to this particular discussion (but not to the problematic of human history or even to that of the Middle East considered broadly enough) the driving out, forced relocation, and/or genocide of perhaps a million Christian Armenians by the Ottomans in 1916, in the midst of World War I, but that matter is not easily forgotten in Armenia, just as many Greeks have not yet forgotten their quarrels with the Turks that go back to the early nineteenth century and the Greek struggle for

independence against the Ottoman Empire, which animosity still lives on actively on the island of Cyprus. There are also Greeks who refer to the expulsion of 1.5 million Hellenes by the Turks in 1923 (see the reference to this in the 2007 resolution of the International Association of Genocide Scholars) in a forced population exchange that also brought tens of thousands of ethnic Turks into Turkey proper from Greece.

The fact of continued distrust or hostility on both of these fronts offers another potential complication for the larger Middle Eastern picture. But it is interesting that in a May 25, 2009, article in the *California Courier*, Harut Sassounian reports that the then-Turkish Prime Minister, (currently President) Recep Erdogan "admitted for the first time that the expulsion . . . was a 'fascist' act. Reuters reported . . . [that] Erdogan [also] made an indirect reference to the tragic fate of other groups, such as Armenians, in Turkey." As usual in the context of such a declaration, there are those who praise Erdogan's conciliatory remarks as historic, while others immediately jumped in to question the level of his sincerity and commitment to back up his words with "the restitution of rights to those who have been expelled, the return of confiscated properties, or compensation." Aside from the obvious fact that it is too soon to know what the long-term consequences are of Erdogan's remarks, we may also see parallels to the Israel-Palestinian situation, where similar sorts of actions are discussed regarding Palestinians displaced from what is now Israel.

88 The relationship began in the form of granting a franchise to the United States'-owned Trans-Arabian Pipeline Company for the shipment of Iraqi oil *through* Syria to the Mediterranean.

89 Lebanon's large middle-class mercantile population tended to oppose the concept of overall Arab unity, preferring to push its own capitalist system into enriching contacts with the West, and so the Ba'ath party made narrower inroads—it was denied a place on the ballot by President Camille Chamoun when he came to power in 1952. For opposite reasons, Egypt offered an inhospitable environment: Nassir was already engaged in developing his own program of Arab unity and socialism.

90 For a full and very excellent discussion—perhaps the finest in a single volume—see Michael Oren's *Six Days of War*.

91 This was the civil war in which King Hussein was asserting his control and crushing Palestinian resistance—it culminated with Black September, 1970 (that lasted until July 1971).

92 This is the Turkish word for a sub-province; the term *vilayet* refers to an entire province.

93   For example, John Voll, former Director of Georgetown University's *Center for Muslim-Christian Understanding*, in a lecture delivered at an Alumni College on the Middle East for Washington & Lee University in July, 2004.

94   See 142, 213–8, 238–9.

95   See above, 26.

96   By "heavier or lighter" I mean with respect to the manner in which individual *Hadith*s are weighted, depending upon the nature and directness of transmission, back (or not) to attestations ascribable to the first group of companions of the Prophet or to the second generation of his followers, and so on.

97   A similar fate befell 'Abd'allah I in 1951—he was by then king of Transjordan—who was shot three times while praying at the al-Aqsa Mosque, shortly after rumors spread that he was meeting with the Israelis to discuss a permanent peace arrangement. His grandson, Hussein, by his side, narrowly avoided death, and is said to have eschewed peace discussions with the Israelis until the post-Oslo era because he feared suffering his grandfather's fate.

98   See Segev, *Elvis*, 129. Since Za'im was murdered shortly thereafter, the issue for the purposes of the present discussion is not as much that of a lost opportunity and what might have evolved toward an Israel-Arab peace as the principle of selective memory and how the Israelis and Arabs understand each other's behavioral history.

99   Moshe Dayan, "hero" of the Six-Day War, announced to Israelis on the state radio station, "Soldiers of Israel, we have no aims of conquest." To the BBC he said, "The war is over; now we are waiting for a phone call from Hussein." That call never came.

100   Ironically, a version of the phone call from Jordanian King Hussein referred to in the previous note came ten days before the Yom Kippur War, warning the Israelis that Egypt and Syria were likely to attack the Jewish State. The message was ignored, for the Israelis neither conceived of the Arabs being ready for war nor imagined that Sadat, in particular, would be willing to fight a war that the Arabs would lose militarily for *political* gain. The overconfident sense of difference between their own abilities and those of the Arabs that lulled the Israelis was shattered even with the actual eventual military victory of 1973. Paradoxically, the collapse of Israeli triumphalism and the concomitant rise in Arab self-esteem opened a door to peace through which Sadat walked a few years later.

101   See above, 20–21.

102 As we shall shortly see (below, n 155) this is the other side of the view by those religious Jews who see a "Greater Israel"—from the Mediterranean Sea to Mesopotamia—as a God-originated mandate.

103 The interesting manner in which the renunciation was initially made was by declaring the PLO Charter *caduc*—not an Arabic term, but a French one meaning "lapsed." Those distrustful of Arafat argue(d) that this term falls short of a full-fledged renunciation of violence on the one hand and recognition of Israel on the other, analogous to the way in which *sulh* falls short of full-fledged peace (*salaam*).

104 See above, 17, 21, n 16 and also 180–81. This *Hadith* is said to be related by al'Bukhari and Muslim, neither of whom was a direct companion of the prophet. The *Hadith* (quoted in Chapter One, Article Seven of the *Hamas* Covenant) continues: ". . . and until the Jews hide themselves behind a stone or tree, and a stone or tree says: 'Muslim or Servant of God, there is a Jew behind me; come and kill him. . .'" The *Hamas* Covenant may be found in English translation, among other places, on the Internet.

Chapter 10

105 See above, 98.

106 These different organizations were very much still in play in the 1980s, between the time of the Israel-Egypt Peace Treaty and the developments leading to the Oslo Accords. PLO means "Palestine Liberation Organization;" it was officially established (at a conference in the Ambassador Hotel in Jordanian-controlled East Jerusalem). One might call the PLO's central core the group that Yassir Arafat had founded with a small circle of friends in Kuwait in 1959 when Arafat was working as an engineer in the emirate's public works; it is (or was) called *al-Fatah* ("the opening" or "conquest"). PFLP stands for "Popular Front for the Liberation of Palestine" and emerged as Fatah's primary rival within the PLO or apart from the PLO by late 1967. DFLP stands for "Democratic Front for the Liberation of Palestine" and split off from the PFLP in 1969; DFLP-GC means "Popular Front for the Liberation of Palestine—General Command" and it also split off from the PFLP, but in 1968. *Saiqa* ("the Thunderbolt") was a Palestinian branch of the Ba'ath Party created by the Syrians in October, 1968; and ALF stands for "Arab Liberation Front" and was created by Iraq in order to counter Syrian influence within the PLO but with a more pan-Arab than merely Palestinian makeup and agenda. Each of these splinters, in fact, has its own agenda. For details, see Aaron David Miller's excellent small book, *The PLO and the Politics*

of Survival, especially 40–65. If by now, many of the particular details are moot, the general issue of fragmented negotiating partners is not.

107 The Americans pushed the Likud Party Israeli prime minister, Yitzhak Shamir, to the Madrid Peace Conference in October 1991, after which the infant peace process might have died a crib death, but when in 1992 Yitzhak Rabin and his Labor Party were elected, the process gained the momentum that brought it to Oslo the following year.

108 See above, 2, 34.

109 Both passages are quoted in Eliezer Berkovits, *Faith After the Holocaust*, 17. There are other similar quotes from other individuals quoted by Berkovits, the sum of which would make one despair of any future for Jewish-Christian relations were there not antidote passages during the Holocaust and since. More recently, Steve Martin's documentary film, *Three Theologians and Hitler* tells the chilling story of how three prominent German Lutheran theologians used their engagement of the Bible and other Christian texts to validate Hitler and used the power of their position as religious leaders to garner support for him and his cause.

110 See above, 76–8. Echoes of this are heard in between these eras, as well, of course. Thus at the time of the birth of Israel, the Chief Rabbi of Iraq, Sassoon Kliadouri, denounced the creation of a Jewish state—he continued to espouse that view as late as 1969 even when Iraq hanged several Jews, as well as some Muslims and Christians for "spying" for Israel. Whether in both cases this was due to religious conviction of the sort to which I have referred above or as an act of survival in a dicey political environment is difficult to say with certainty.

111 See the discussion of this by the Catholic theologian, Eva Fleischner, in her 1974 paper that was part of a conference, "Auschwitz: The Beginning of a New Era?" held at the Church of St. John the Divine in New York City, and inspired by the events of the Yom Kippur War. Other papers by Christian theologians from that conference, notably those by Gregory Baum, Aarne Siirala, and Johannes Christiaan Hoekendijk, are also of interest and were all gathered in the volume of that name edited by Fleischner. The letter to the conference from Gabriel Habib is also significant both for what it suggests regarding the relationship between the Holocaust and the Israeli-Palestinian conflict and for what Habib fails to understand with regard to the overall content of the conference. Most recently, this issue of a double standard presented itself in January 2009 when the entire world seemed up in arms regarding the Israeli attack on Gaza but with nary a comment or a reference to the hundreds upon hundreds of rocket attacks from Gaza into southern Israel that provoked

the Israeli attack, nor any reference either to the cynical use by Hamas of mosques, hospitals and, in general, civilians, as hideouts, arms-storage facilities, and shields; of their massacres of their political opponent fellow-Palestinians; or of the lengths to which the Israelis went to warn civilians of impending attacks on buildings they understood to be containing Hamas fighters or arms caches. I am not debating the issue of how appropriately or inappropriately large the Israeli response was, but commenting on the general media failure to consider these other aspects of the situation. Interestingly, the most notable exception to this was the Arab leadership and its media, which reacted far less strongly to the Israeli attacks than one might have expected.

112 Barbara Amiel reported that French Ambassador Daniel Bernard had made the comment at a party at her home. It was reported in the *London Daily Telegraph* and subsequently elsewhere. I first saw it cited in the *National Review* in a January 10, 2002, article by Tom Gross.

113 See above, 76–7 and 131.

114 The concept was first floated by the young New York City journalist, John L. O'Sullivan in 1839, although he first used the actual phrase in a pair of articles in 1845.

115 This should, incidentally, make those Americans who are critical of the settler movement less self-righteous about it: critical, yes, but not self-righteous, since our own American history—our secular Christian American history—did on an exponentially larger scale in North America what the settlers are seeking to do in the West Bank. And on the other hand it should reinforce criticism of the settlers since the imagery of American injustice toward Native Americans stares us in the face as a sufficiently reasonable comparative experience to that evolving in Israel-Palestine.

116 In the first case, he went on to refer to that "victory" as one producing "a spark of hope"; in the second case there is some debate as to what he actually meant in the larger context of his remarks.

117 Did he *hail* the withdrawal or *adjudge* the withdrawal as a victory for *Hizb'Allah*? If the former, and depending upon what he meant by "enlarging the sphere of resistance," then what were the options facing the Israeli courts? (I am asking this straightforwardly and not rhetorically.) What would happen to a US congressman who made comparable statements? Except that there are no comparable statements simply imaginable, since the United States is not in a comparable position vis-à-vis its neighbors or with regard to internal disaffected groups to that of Israel.

118 More subtly with respect to Arab participation in the Knesset is the fact that the Arab political parties are never invited to become part of the sort of party coalitions—they are barred by tradition from joining coalition governments—that are always part of such a multiparty system. Those who are part of a coalition may often wield some negotiating power for issues dear to their party, even if they are a small party; those who don't participate are virtually powerless. In the January 12, 2009, *Newsweek* article by Daniel Gavron, the writer observes that "Arabs have served in the cabinet, but only if they were members of Zionist (Jewish) parties. On a few occasions, Arab parties have formed temporary blocking coalitions with Zionists, but the Arabs were never allowed close to the center of power." It should also be remembered, on the other hand, that the political voice of Israeli Arabs has become complicated by divisions within the Israeli Arab community both since Oslo and since the beginning of the al-Aqsa *intifada*; and that that voice not only dwarfs that of Jews in any and all of the Arab lands, but most of the of Arabs in most of the Arab countries. See also, below, n 122.

119 The issue was the "new historiography" of the "post-Zionist era" of the past fifteen years in which the historiography regarding the founding decades of the state has been under aggressive review.

120 Ilan Pappe, "A Lesson in New History," *Ha'aretz*, 24 June 1994. He is quoted (on page 140) in the discussion offered in Segev, *Elvis*, 133–56.

121 Haim Nahman Bialek is regarded as the ultimate modern Hebrew poet and commonly referred to by Hebraists as the father of modern Hebrew poetry.

122 I have selected only a handful from the assortment of quotes offered in Segev, *Elvis*, 146–50.

123 Both quotes come from Segev, *Elvis*, 151.

124 *Ibid*, 152–6. Not all Israeli Arabs agree with Smooha's proposals, mainly out of fear that if implemented, they would cement a condition of inferior civil status—turning Israeli Arab Christians and Muslims, in effect, into *dhimmi*. Of those who agree in principle, not all agree on the details. In referring to ultra-Orthodox communities (not all that many, but some) in the United States, I had in mind a place like New Square, New York, an all-Hassidic village in the town of Ramapo in Rockland County, (not far from New York City) that functions in virtual autonomy with regard to the legal—and not just cultural, educational and religious—life of the community.

125 Daniel Gavron, "Israel's Arabs Are the Answer," *Newsweek*, January 12, 2009, 33—and see above, n 115.

126   To be more precise, the Camp David accords brokered by President Jimmy Carter were initiated in September 1978 but, due to several crises, it was not until March 1979 that the full peace treaty was signed. In spite of the relatively cold nature of the aftermath relations between Israel and Egypt, at least since Sadat's assassination in 1981, the treaty has never been abrogated by either side. Perhaps the best—certainly the most thorough—one-volume account of the diplomatic backdrop to the Egyptian-Israeli treaty is William Quandt's *Camp David: Peacemaking and Politics*.

127   Both comments were made by Ta'mari in a 1998 interview with Anton La Guardia. See Anton La Guardia, *War Without End: Israelis, Palestinians, and the Struggle for a Promised Land*, 147.

128   The group's name morphed several times before arriving at "*Islamic Jihad*" and would shortly thereafter become closely allied with Usama Bin Ladin and al-Qaeda. Prior to the assassination of Sadat the group obtained a *fatwa*—a religious ruling—approving the act on theological grounds, from Umar Abdul-Rahman, the cleric later convicted in the United States for his role in the 1993 World Trade Center bombing.

129   I say "fairly consistently" as opposed to "consistently" in order to split a hair. Since Hamas has desisted, at times, from the rocket attacks from Gaza into Israel, and did agree, briefly, to a cease-fire with the Israelis, one could say that even they are not absolutely unsusceptible to the possibility of a peace agreement. Critics of this thought would argue that the cease-fire was abrogated all too quickly, demonstrating complete unsusceptibility.

130   The decision made in 2004 led to Israeli soldiers forcibly evicting 9,840 Jewish settlers from twenty-one settlements in Gaza (and from four West Bank settlements), between August 16 and 30, 2005. Every settlement structure, with the exception of a few synagogues and an array of greenhouses, were bulldozed by the Israelis. The last Israeli soldier formally withdrew from Gaza on September 11, 2005, and the border fence at Kissufim was closed.

131   Seriously. In accordance with an ancient tradition, the group of rabbis, led by Rabbi Yosef Dayan, pronounced the *Pulsa diNoura*—literally, "lashes of fire," in Aramaic—which calls upon the Angel of Death to smite him. The Torah—and with it, the mainstream rabbinic tradition—forbids the act of praying that disaster befall someone; rather, one is enjoined to pray that the evil inclination within a given individual perish so that s/he becomes righteous. I have no doubt that there are many who believe that the stroke that reduced Sharon to a coma and a vegetative

state in early January 2006 was a result of the curse. One keeps encountering additional ways in which religion and politics interweave each other.

132 The question has been raised by some as to whether Sharon was motivated by an interest in peace or a concern for the future demographics of an Israel in which, through the continued absorption of Gaza and the West Bank, Jews end up outnumbered—but then it would make sense to pull out both from Gaza and the West Bank, not just from Gaza.

133 This was the gist of what Ambassador Dennis Ross asserted in a public comment at Georgetown University on September 8, 2016, in a panel discussion (that included Elliott Abrams, Benny Morris, and Natasha Mozgovaya and was moderated by Professor Robert Lieber) focused on an evaluation of the Netanyahu Prime Ministership up to that point. Ross explained that he was in Gaza after Sharon pulled out the settlers and spoke to the Gazans in a public assembly where he beseeched them to show the world that they could build a viable infrastructure, beginning with what the Israelis left behind, but that they failed to do that.

134 See the article by Steve Erlanger in *The New York Times* (July 5, 2005): "Israeli Sttlers Demolish Greenhouses and Gaza Jobs," the headline of which is more provocative than the contents of the article. Erlanger notes, in part, that "[o]f the roughly 1,000 acres of agricultural land that were under greenhouses in the 21 Israeli settlements in Gaza, only 500 acres remain—creating significant doubts that the greenhouses could be handed over to the Palestinians as 'a living business,' the goal cited by the Israeli coordinator of the pullout, Eival Giladi."

135 Thus the unsigned AP report on September 13, 2005, entitled "Palestinians Strip Gaza Greenhouse," comments, in part:

Palestinians looted dozens of greenhouses on Tuesday, walking off with irrigation hoses, water pumps, and plastic sheeting in a blow to fledgling efforts to reconstruct the Gaza Strip.

American Jewish donors had bought more than 3,000 greenhouses from Israeli settlers in Gaza for $14 million last month and transferred them to the Palestinian Authority. Former World Bank President James Wolfensohn, who brokered the deal, put up $500,000 of his own cash.

Palestinian police stood by helplessly Tuesday as looters carted off materials from greenhouses in several settlements, and commanders complained they did not have enough manpower to protect the prized assets.

136   See Greg Myre's November 28, 2005, *New York Times* article, "Gaza Gets
      Ready for a Harvest of Produce and Prmise," in which he writes, in part:

> Less than three months after the Israelis departed, Palestinians
> have repaired scores of greenhouses left by the settlers and planted
> a fall crop, and they are preparing to harvest an estimated $20 mil-
> lion worth of strawberries, cherry tomatoes, sweet peppers and
> herbs and spices. The produce is intended mostly for export to
> Europe, but some will also be headed to Israel, Arab countries and
> the United States.
>
> After overcoming numerous obstacles, the Palestinians said
> their main worry now was the Karni border crossing between
> the Gaza Strip and Israel, critical to moving the produce to the
> markets.
>
> After intense negotiations this month, Secretary of State
> Condoleezza Rice brokered an agreement on the Gaza crossings
> that says Palestinian agricultural exports are to pass through Karni
> "on an urgent basis." But the Palestinians say they remain worried
> about possible delays at the crossing.
>
> Still, the harvest, which begins in about 10 days, will be the
> first tangible measure of development in Gaza, which has been in
> an economic free fall for most of the past five years.

137   Put another way: *Hamas'* record of creating and maintaining a range of
      social services in other contexts was hardly in evidence in the roughly
      two years between their take over in Gaza and the Israeli reprisal attacks.
      I might add, alas, that it has been a consistent policy of *Hamas* to con-
      fiscate materials permitted into Gaza by the Israelis, such as cement and
      steel—intended to build homes, schools, and hospitals—to use them for
      building tunnels into/under Israel in order to further their violent efforts
      against the Israelis.

138   See Maura Pham's August 8, 2014, *World Policy Blog* article, "Terrorism
      and Charity: Defining *Hamas*." The article makes a strong case for the
      social services that Hamas has provided for Gazans but with remarkably
      little detail. Her overall point, that one ought not to two-dimensionalize
      Hamas is, in any case, well taken.

139   The story is still incomplete and being told of that attack, both in terms
      of actual numbers of injured and killed (the Western media almost inev-
      itably accepts the Palestinian statistics which more often than not turn
      out to be exaggerated; the Israeli numbers may be under-exaggerated
      but are typically ignored) and the kind of efforts made (or not) by Israel
      to minimize the "collateral damage"—as well as the role of *Hamas* in

maximizing that damage to public relations advantage—is similarly not often discussed in the mainstream media. Video footage substantiates the claim that Hamas uses human shields—embedding its armories in and around schools and hospitals—to make it more difficult for the Israelis to avoid causing civilian casualties in their military confrontations.

Chapter 11

140   There is considerable irony in the fact that the legal and political tradition to which much of the current political leadership in Israel belongs recognizes the legitimacy of violence—or at least some forms of it—as a means of *intifada* (to borrow a term from Arabic), since that tradition employed it against the British (and the Arabs) nearly seventy years ago.

141   Adi Ophir, "A Time of Occupation," in Roane Carey and Jonathan Shainin, eds., *The Other Israel: Voices of Refusal and Dissent*, 61. As I shall shortly note, this is an Israeli writing, not a Palestinian.

142   Yigal Shochat, "Red Line, Green Line, Black Flag", in Carey and Shainin, 128.

143   Amira Hass, "Are the Occupied Protecting the Occupier?" in Carey and Shainin, 163–4.

144   Rashid Khalidi, *The Iron Cage: The Story of the Palestinian Struggle for Statehood*, XII.

145   It should be noted that the lead-up to that arduous event was that the PLO had lodged itself in Jordan by 1968, and aside from using Jordan as its base of terrorist attacks into the West Bank and pre-1967 Israel, had begun to function as an autonomous "state" within the state of Jordan. There was no central authority and minimal discipline, with various groups, increasingly splintered, functioning separately from one another but all ignoring or denouncing the legitimacy of the Hashimite government. Between mid-1968 and the end of 1969 there were no fewer than five hundred violent clashes between Palestinian guerillas and Jordanian security forces, together with a good number of kidnappings of and violence against Jordanian citizens by armed PLO members. Armed Palestinians established their own systems of visa control, customs checks, and checkpoints in certain Jordanian cities. King Hussein began a campaign against the PLO between February and June, 1970, during which about a thousand lives were lost. By September 15, after several failed attempts to assassinate the king, three plane hijackings by the PFLP and the declaration by the PLO of the Irbid area and its camp as a "liberated region," Hussein declared martial law. To make a long story somewhat shorter, the Jordanian army attacked PLO headquarters in Amman as well as camps in Irbid and five

other areas, supported by Iraqi reserve forces that had been in Jordan since the 1967 war. While Arafat would later claim that the Jordanian army killed between ten thousand and twenty-five thousand Palestinians, other estimates were as "low" as one to two thousand.

146 The most notorious instance of Israeli assistance or acquiescence in the massacre of Palestinians by the Christian Lebanese Phalangist militias came two days after the assassination of President Bashir Gemayil, who came into office with Israeli support and the promise of a peace treaty between Lebanon and Israel. The Phalangists, eager for revenge (for the assassination, but no doubt also driven by the anger that had built up through a decade of an oppressive PLO-led presence), who were supposed to be mopping up PLO fighters on behalf of the Israelis, massacred at least five hundred civilians, including women and children in the Palestinian refugee camps of Sabra and Shatila. (These were post-1970 camps, not camps such as those in Gaza and the West Bank that came into being after 1948–9). The Israelis at least stood by without intervening to stop their allies; at worst they provided illumination for them as day became night became day (in more than one sense).

147 The methodology of suicide bombings would be less evident in the *intifada* that began in 1987 and ended when the Oslo Accords were put into place than in the *intifada* that began when the negotiations that stemmed from those accords fell apart at the end of the 1990s.

148 For those with a technical interest, the religious justification that Amir claimed for his act was *din rodef*—"law of the pursuer"—according to which someone in pursuit of someone else with the intent to kill that individual may/should himself be killed before he is able to do any harm. (Thus Amir's rabbi perceived Rabin as further able to do a good deal of harm should he continue on his path, and thus viewed Amir's bullets as forestallers of such further harm). Of course, even that "law" presumes that all other options for stopping the would-be killer have been exhausted.

149 Among the ironies is that while he was running the infant Palestinian polity he was so obsessive about maintaining personal control over everything that his days, like his desk, were buried in slips of paper: he insisted on reviewing and signing off on every conceivable detail of administrative life—even requests for leave from middle-level administrators were addressed by his signature.

150 Quoted in Anton La Guardia, *War Without End*, 147, from the interview La Guardia had in 1998 with Ta'mari.

151 A good deal has been written in recent years regarding the division of water resources within the region at large and in particular within the area encompassed by Israel, Palestine, Jordan, Syria, and Lebanon. While rainfall is beyond anyone's control and the attempts to direct and otherwise control the water that comes from above-ground rivers and lakes is an obvious way of altering the natural availability of that resource, less obvious is the management and/or manipulation of water found deep *beneath* the earth's surface. The ability to do so depends, in part, on technological capabilities, in part on political control. See Tony Allan, *The Middle East Water Question: Hydropolitics and the Global Economy*; Gary Hoch, "The Politics of Water in the Middle East;" Elisha Kally and Gideon Fishelson, *Water and Peace: Water Resources and the Arab-Israeli Peace Process*; Nurit Kliot, *Water Resources and Conflict in the Middle East*; and Aaron T. Wolf, *Hydropolitics Along the Jordan River*; among other recent discussions of this issue. I have listed a few more in the bibliography.

152 See Jeff Halper's discussion of this on pp 35–6 of his essay, "The Key to Peace: Dismantling the Matrix of Control," in *The Other Israel*. Most commentators seem unaware of Barak's last-minute pullout. Anton La Guardia, for example, credits him with negotiating "with the Palestinians virtually to the last day of his government," by contrast with Sharon. (Anton La Guardia, *War Without End*), 336. Given La Guardia's often imbalanced coverage of the two sides of the coin (he seems to me far more critical of the Israelis than of the Palestinians—but more on this below in footnote 153), his willingness to exonerate Barak of any responsibility for the breakdown in peace negotiations is significant. I would not for a moment wish to minimize the negative role played by both Arafat and Sharon in this horrific drama, but it is larger than they and others have contributed to its tragic quality, including Barak.

153 As always, there is still more than meets the eye. According to La Guardia (*Ibid*, 363), "Arafat himself seemed to have a flash of realization in June 2002. . . when he told an Israeli interviewer that he belatedly accepted the Clinton parameters set out 18 months earlier. . . But by the time he reached this belated conclusion, it was too late. Israelis had lost faith in him." If La Guardia is right—which is difficult to assess, because as usual he gives us no footnote to tell the reader where this information comes from, so we cannot attest to its accuracy, aside from how we might evaluate the interpretation—then Arafat himself remains the main flaw in the flawed process, and the tragedy of mistimed realizations and recognitions achieves an unprecedented profundity given what was lost and where things have gotten since Taba.

154   The 1929 massacre was the culmination of riots fomented by the Mufti
      of Jerusalem as part of his campaign to "defend" Muslim holy sites from
      what he asserted was the threat to them from militant Jews. The mili-
      tant Jews, on the other hand, were mainly focused on gaining control
      of the Western Wall. The dispute over the wall became a series of Arab
      riots in Jerusalem by August in the course of which 133 Jews and 116
      Arabs were killed. The denouement was the Hebron massacre, unique
      because the Jewish population of six hundred was mostly non-Zionist,
      had lived there for centuries and believed that it would not be attacked
      by its long-term Muslim neighbors. They were neither wrong nor right,
      since some Muslim Arabs rioted and attacked and others hid and pro-
      tected. Goldstein's horrific act was the first instance in Israeli history in
      which a Jew carried out a massive and unprovoked attack on his Arab
      neighbors. The majority of settlers elevated him to virtual sainthood; the
      Israeli left and Rabin's government excoriated him.

155   And to repeat and amplify: since 1967, the growth in Israel not only of
      the population of Jews with visions of a Greater Israel which they regard
      as divinely driven but also of secular messianic Jews who share similar
      visions has further complicated the issue of how to configure two states.
      Not only has an expanded range of settlers de facto expanded the bor-
      ders of pre-1967 Israel—and as such, been party to expansionist plans of
      successive governments from both sides of the Labor-Likud fence. Many
      of them have been a recalcitrant and dangerous force at such times as
      the Israeli government has sought to pull back from such expansionist
      plans, because, like their Muslim counterparts, who cannot accept an
      independent *dhimmi* state in the region, these groups cannot accept an
      independent Palestinian state which would deprive them of political and
      religious control of the entire area encompassed by a Greater Israel.

156   See above, n 99.

157   By 2009, Arafat had died in Paris, so that his role in the drama has been
      altered from present and future to past. See above, the final pages of
      chapter ten and below, the last few pages of this chapter.

158   I am for the moment ignoring the larger Middle Eastern arena in which
      President Bush earned Arab distrust and/or enmity toward the United
      States (most obviously, his bankrupt and blatantly imperialist Iraq policy
      and general disregard for the importance of international cooperation
      regarding terrorism), although obviously that is essential as we re-widen
      our focus away from Israel-Palestine to encompass the entire region.

159   The entire text of the Geneva Accord with a map that delineates areas of
      land exchange, may be found online at www.geneva-accord.org.

160 This last issue has at least two aspects to it. One deals generally with the volume of force. The other refers to the volume of "collateral damage" in the form of civilian Gazan, non-*Hamas* injuries and deaths. This second issue also has at least two different aspects. One pertains to whose numbers one believes: there is a long history of inconsistency with respect to injuries and body counts between the two protagonists (as even between the Palestinians and the Jordanians in the aftermath of Black September), and of irresponsibility on the part of the Western media with regard to reporting numbers without any attempt to verify them. The more profound issue is the question of whether and how and the degree to which the Israelis did or did not make every effort to avoid civilian casualties; and whether and how and the degree to which *Hamas* used civilian shields and covers in order to make it impossible for the Israelis to succeed at minimizing civilian casualties.

161 *The Iron Cage*, XIII. I am neither endorsing nor criticizing Khalidi's perspective; I am merely pointing out how important it is to acknowledge and understand his perspective. And he does not deny problematic internal Palestinian issues, referring to the factionalized infighting of Palestinian leaders and their cohorts as offering "an almost criminal level of irresponsibility."

162 The term was first used in 1920 in the context of the post–World War I carving up of the Middle East into British and French areas of colonial administration: the destruction of hopes for Arab unity and independence is referred to as *al-Nakba*.

163 La Guardia, 155. La Guardia's book, by the way, offers a good case of my point regarding books and articles by outsiders who fail to be objective. He certainly *claims* to be objective and for the first two chapters appears to be, but I found myself less and less convinced of this as I read through the rest of its four hundred pages. While ostensibly evenhanded, virtually every comment he made about Israeli actions he presented in a negative manner; no matter how positive an Israeli effort, he sensed a negative nuance to it. I did not find the same negative attitude when he discussed Palestinian actions and efforts. Moreover while quite thorough in delineating negative Israeli actions (such as the demolishing of two small mosques in opening up the area around the Western Wall in 1967) he somehow missed far larger counterpart actions on the other side of the fence (such as the wholesale destruction of every synagogue in Jerusalem's Jewish quarter by the Jordanians between 1948 and 1967). I should add that a four hundred-page book with nary a footnote is troubling, in spite of its impressive bibliography: if one's purpose is to explain

a difficult problem and to educate one's readers, then one ought to provide them with the instruments with which not only to look further but
to examine and even challenge one's interpretations. In spite of these
objections, La Guardia's narrative is an excellent one overall, extremely
detailed, and exhibiting an admirable grasp of both the history and the
sensibility of both worlds.

164   This does not necessarily mean that there are not mad and militant Jews
in Israel who would be happy to pursue a Nazistic, exterminationist path
toward the Palestinians, but fortunately they are relatively few and far
between—and every group of people has its mad militants.

Chapter 12

165   The United States, since the collapse of the Soviet Union, has been—or
has the potential to be—the most influential outside participant in the
Israel-Palestine dialogue. Even if, in 2016, Putin has asserted a role for
his Russia, nobody but nobody in the region—certainly not the Israelis
and Palestinians, and probably not even Turkey—really takes his "trust-
worthiness quotient" of support very seriously compared to that of the
United States.

166   I must also add that, both when I first wrote these words in 2004 and
reviewed them in 2007, and again in 2009, the Israeli and American
leaderships were different from what they are now, in 2017. To wit: Ehud
Olmert was succeeded by Bibi Netanyahu (again)—and Netanyahu was
in turn reelected (in part, alas, by appealing to the fear on the part of
enough Israelis that Israeli Arabs were rushing to the voting booths to
displace him); and George W. Bush was succeeded by Barack Obama.
In the first case, I thought that the change might be a cause for concern,
and I would say that those concerns have been fulfilled as Netanyahu
has shown himself to be inimical to a true peace process (regardless of
how inimical the Palestinians may or may not be); in the second case, I
thought that the change might be a reason for hope, but that hope has
not borne full fruit (in part for the sort of Obama-obstructing issues that
I have discussed above). At this point, of course, we have arrived at the
end of the Obama era and with his erratic successor Donald Trump it is
not clear where the United States will go next with regard to the region.

167   See above, 77. "*Merkaz ha'Rav*" means "the Rabbi's Center"—*the* Rabbi
meaning Rabbi Abraham Isaac Kook.

168   In part his sermon, apparently delivered in great anguished tones, continued: ". . . and where is our Hebron? Do we forget this? And where is
our Shechem? Do we forget this? And where is our Jericho? Do we forget

about this, too?!. . . Is it in our hands to relinquish any millimeter of this? God forbid!!"

169 La Guardia, Ibid, 287. The italics are mine.

170 See above, 72.

171 See the perspective discussion of this last point in Dennis Ross, *The Missing Peace: The Inside Story of the Fight for Middle Eastern Peace*, especially 25–9, 44–5, and 797–9.

172 Telhami, Ibid, 62.

173 The strategy of victimization is discussed with regard to the Palestinians by Ross, op citum, 42, 775–6. As it applies to the Arab world in general, see Albert Hourani, *A History of the Arab Peoples* (Cambridge, Mass: The Beltknap Press/Harvard University Press, 1991). Hourani also talks of the tendency to romanticize one's history as a characteristic particularly endemic to the Arab world. The strategy of victimization—and the tendency to look outward rather than inward for causes of failure and/or disaster—as it applies to the Arabo-Persian, Islamic world at large, is also taken up at length (it is the core theme of his book) by Barry Rubin in his *The Tragedy of the Middle East*, (Cambridge: Cambridge University Press, 2002). Of these three works, Hourani's is the most unassailable, since he is himself an Arab and one of the deans of historiography of Arab culture and history; Ross's will be unassailable by many, given his role in the peace negotiations in which his objectivity was presumably paramount— but as an outsider will be viewed suspiciously by many in the Middle East; Rubin's indictment is the strongest and certainly his absolute objectivity, in spite of his powerful prose and compelling presentation of both concept and detail, the most suspect for some, given that the Global Research in International Affairs Center that he directs is located in Israel. His book reminds me of La Guardia's, but from the other side of the fence and with a larger arena of focus. (And he is quite clear that the Israel-Palestine and Israeli-Arab conflicts are only part of a much bigger morass.)

174 See above, 136.

175 I am well aware of the irony—indeed I intend to be ironic—of raising the issue of the "Jewishness" of the "Jewish" State in this manner, since the debate about that issue has been a constant in Zionist history, from the discussions of Herzl and Ahad Ha'Am and their generation regarding what and where the state should be, to the debate regarding the right to be automatic citizens of Israel by way of its Law of Return, for Jewish children of non-Jewish mothers and Jewish fathers from the former Soviet union, or for converts to Judaism whose conversions were not performed by Orthodox rabbis.

176   *Tikkun olam* means "fixing/repairing the world." It is a rabbinic phrase
      that came to be particularly strongly emphasized in the sixteenth-
      century mystical movement surrounding Isaac Luriya (1534–72) in
      Safed. It enjoins Jews to improve the world, however minimally; each is
      obligated to leave it a better place than it was when s/he was born into it.

177   See the last paragraphs of the article by Kevin Peraino, "How We Got
      to This Point," in the January 12, 2009, issue of *Newsweek*, 34–5. In it
      the author effectively summarizes observations contained in three
      recent books, Daniel Kurtzer's and Scott Lasensky's *Negotiating Arab-
      Israeli Peace*, Patrick Tyler's *A World of Trouble: The White House and the
      Middle East—from Cold War to the War on Terror*, and Martin Indyk's
      *Innocent Abroad: An Intimate Account of American Peace Diplomacy in
      the Middle East.*

178   In the last few years it has become more widely known that Rabin was
      willing to give up the Golan Heights in exchange for a serious peace ini-
      tiative from Syria, so one might even say that there is a precedent of sorts.

179   See, for example, the scurrilous article by Nasi Ahmad in the Palestinian
      Authority daily *Al'Hayat a'Jadida* of November 7, 1998, that begins with
      the words "Corruption is a Jewish trait worldwide, so much so that
      one can seldom find corruption that was not masterminded by Jews
      or that Jews are not responsible for." Or the rhetorical question asked
      in the Egyptian weekly, *Roz al'Yusuf* of August 24, 1998, "Is Israel wag-
      ing chemical and biological warfare against the Arab states and Islam?"
      (by passing on imported blood units infected with AIDS, hepatitis, and
      bilhariza to Arab and Third World nations). Or the nasty article by Dr
      Hassan Ragav in the July 14, 1998, issue of the Egyptian daily, *al'Akbar*,
      asserting that "the Zionist movement is a racist political movement"
      and going on to deny the Holocaust. Or more recently, the anti-Jewish
      rant by the Egyptian Cleric, Muhammad Hussein Ya'qub, broadcast on
      January 17, 2009, on *Al-Rahma* TV across Egypt—which aside from its
      horrifyingly hateful content (" . . . Jews . . . whose ancestors were apes
      and pigs . . . ") also exhibited stunning ignorance both of Jewish ideology
      (". . . the Jews say that Uzair is the son of God . . . ") and of history (". . .
      They [fight and kill us] for the sake of their religion . . . ").

180   While it is true that since the time of writing this narrative, Arafat has
      gone from the scene, this does not mean that the American adminis-
      tration's attitude toward the Palestinian leadership has significantly
      changed. Again, however, that attitude clearly *did* change as we moved
      toward the summer of 2009 and the second one hundred days of the
      Obama administration. The American attitude toward the PA on the one

hand and toward Hamas on the other has remained fairly constant since that time on into 2016.

181 In the first edition of this narrative, in 2009, I wrote at the end of this paragraph: "This will presumably change, now, too, with the Obama administration in its relationship with the new Netanyahu administration." Eight years later, one can see that some things have changed, but not necessarily for the better. Barack Obama managed to regain some of the trust from the Palestinians that George Bush the Younger threw away, but his (Obama's) relationship with Netanyahu became so toxic—and Netanyahu's attempt to go around Obama, for example with regard to a shift in the American relationship with Iran, aided and abetted by members of the Republican party equally eager to undermine the president so ugly—that, while we cannot be accused of being one-sided, members of each side perhaps feel that we are not offering it enough support, the Palestinians toward political self-determination and the Israelis toward survival.

182 At the time I was writing these words, President Obama was about to travel for six days through parts of the Arabo-Islamic Middle East, stopping in Riyadh to meet with Saudi leadership and in Cairo to offer a public address. The outcome of that trip was to significantly improve American standing throughout the region—with the exception of the Israeli political leadership (but not nearly all Israelis)—and to raise "concerns" regarding where the new president stood regarding Israel within the American religious and Republican right.

183 See above, 131 and 133.

184 The discussions of the "dangers" to the United States of an overly influential AIPAC—particularly as and when those discussions ignore lobbies such as the Cuban-American lobby and its success at holding American foreign policy vis-à-vis that Caribbean island hostage—smack of just that sort of implied accusation (double loyalty). The primary text discussing this issue in recent years has been the March 23, 2006, *London Review of Books* article (originally written for the *Atlantic Monthly* but not published by them) and subsequent book by John J. Mearshimer and Stephen M. Walt, *The Israel Lobby and U.S. foreign Policy*. The primary weaknesses of the accusatory thesis are first, that the authors single out AIPAC, rather than presenting it in a comparative framework that, to repeat, could well examine the activities of the anti-Castro Cuban-American lobby with regard to the issue of holding US policy hostage; and second, that they ignore the fact that our political system was designed precisely to give interest groups the opportunity to be heard in the halls of governmental

power, without drawing a line with regard to success at that endeavor. Their thesis places the old wine of the "dual-loyalty" idea in a new bottle.

185 Mordecai Ben-Hillel HaCohen is quoted in Segev, *Elvis*, 52.

186 See above, 60 and n 40.

187 Indeed times and conditions have changed and not changed! One recalls how the British and the French, as Israel's primary allies, collaborated with her in the 1956 Sinai Campaign—who now, for good reasons, are both far too distrusted to be able to exert much influence on her—and how it was pressure from the United States, now more than ever in a position to exert friendly influence on Israel, that at that time caused all three to withdraw from Egypt.

188 The earlier-noted *Geneva Accord* (see above, 110 and note 159) refers, in Article 4.6, to a land corridor linking the West Bank and Gaza, but it doesn't explain in practical terms how the goal "not [to] disrupt Israeli transportation and other infrastructural networks" will be achieved and it was, of course, conceived before Gaza came under the control of Hamas.

189 The eight cities are (south to north), Hebron, Bethlehem, Jerusalem, Ramallah/Jericho, Salfit, Nablus, Tubas, and Jenin. The idea is that the evolving state would grow around these population centers that would feed and be fed by the train infrastructure.

190 The authorial team for "The Arc" included Doug Suisman, Steven N. Simon, Glenn E. Robinson, C. Ross Anthony, and Michael Schoenbaum. The work was part of a two-part study (the other part titled "Building a Successful Palestinian State") the overall title of which is *Helping a Palestinian State Succeed*.

191 At least until the re-advent of Netanyahu: I wrote these words before his reelection, and, although theoretically his stance on this issue has not changed, I don't know where he stands on it, particularly given his fairly consistent efforts to steer clear of any substantive talks with the Palestinians.

192 This is in part what Klaidman, among others, suggests in his earlier-referenced January 12, 2009, *Newsweek* article with regard to refugees and a "law of return."

193 See above, 102, 107.

194 This is also discussed by Klaidman, among others.

195 The May 28 email to *J Street*'s constituents noted that "Clinton said yesterday that President Obama 'wants to see a stop to settlements—not some settlements, not outposts, not natural-growth exceptions.' This is exactly the sort of leadership we need from the President and Secretary of State if we are going to achieve a two-state solution to the Israeli-Palestinian

conflict—the only way to truly secure Israel's future as a Jewish, democratic homeland." The email goes on to urge recipients to "make sure the President knows pro-Israel, pro-peace Americans support his strong line on settlements, both for Israel's and America's sake and security. Click here to send the President a message telling him you support his 'Freeze means Freeze' approach to Israeli settlements . . ."

196   Audiotapes of the dialogue may be obtained from Chautauqua Institution.

197   Gorenberg, a Jerusalem-based journalist—it is significant that he lives in Israel and not the United States, since he cannot be accused of making his comments from ten thousand miles away—among other things noted that hammering the Gaza Strip had the opposite effect from what it had been intended to have: "Among Palestinians, support for the hard-line Hamas grew . . . In Israel, the suicide bombings of the second intifada had a similar effect." And he commented, "For diplomacy to succeed abroad, Obama will need support at home. He'll want the support of the Jews in particular . . . The first time [he] asks something from Israel . . . will [Jewish leaders] have the courage to support an initiative that is essential to Israel's future?" See *Moment* Magazine, March/April 2009, 12.

198   Frum contends that "sometimes in politics, the only thing to do is the dumb thing, not the smart thing. Your neighbor throws a rock at you. The smart thing is to walk over, find out what's bothering him, and see if you can resolve the disagreement without escalating the violence. Then he throws another, bigger rock. And another. And another after that. At that point you have to recognize: I guess we're in a rock-throwing competition, dumb as it is. He hits me, I hit him harder . . . How does this end? I don't know." It is a compelling argument, if one assumes that the conditions that precipitated the Israeli-Palestinian conflict may be reduced to this paradigm—that the Israelis are simply next door to rock-throwing neighbors. A Palestinian might object (and we might debate the objective validity of the objection) that the house in which the Israelis live is one from which the neighbor next door had been unjustly evicted. What then? See *Ibid*, 18.

199   Non-Muslim troops on sacred Muslim soil presented a serious religious problem. *See 201–2.*

Chapter 13

200   It may not be so surprising to learn that the Israelis were initially hailed by the Lebanese as liberators—but they made the error of overstaying their welcome, so that when they finally left, their departure was a source

of joy and offered a sense of victory to the mixed Lebanese-Palestinian array of communities from which Israel departed.

201 The closest the Kurds have come to an independent polity (until recently), interestingly enough, was in 1945. After leading a revolt that went nowhere for two years within Iraq, Sheikh Mustafa al'Barzani led his followers in that year to Mahabad in northern Iran, that had been established with Soviet support as a Kurdish Republic. But when, at the insistence of both the UN and the US, the USSR withdrew from Iran in 1946, Mahabad collapsed; al'Barzani and his followers left for Soviet Armenia. Interestingly—almost, one might say, ironically—the Kurds in northwestern Iraq have again achieved a functionally, if not officially recognized, independent state in the aftermath of the tearing apart of Iraq thanks to the American invasion of 2003. If one downside of that invasion and tearing apart is that we have made it infinitely easier for Iran to assume a position of substantial dominance in the region and for an entity like ISIS/ISIL to develop; one up side, at least from the Kurdish perspective, is that they are out from under the destructive umbrella of the Sadam-led unified "Iraq" and have achieved their own polity—fed, in part, by the substantial petroleum deposits inhabiting the area beneath the earth under their control.

202 Ethnically, the Kurds are related to the Persians (today's Iranians); their language is related to the Persian branch of the Indo-Iranian branch of the Indo-European family tree of languages (of which English—and French, German, Russian, and Greek, among others—is part). Their presence in the same region from antiquity is attested by the very naming of Book Three in the early fourth-century BCE Greek writer Xenophon's work, *The Anabasis*, as "The March to Kurdistan."

203 That area was in any case promised to the French according to the dictates of the Sykes-Picot agreement, but it seems that the British hoped to get away with not honoring that part of the 1916 accord.

204 For more details, see Eugene M. Fisher and M. Cherif Bassouni, *Storm Over the Arab World: A People in Revolution*.

205 This would not have been bizarre at all a few years earlier since the Shah's Iran was on good terms with Israel, but for the Ayatollah's Iran—which had eliminated the Israeli Embassy and consistently spouted heavy anti-Israel rhetoric—to have been saved from Iraq by means of American arms and Israeli intermediation would be remarkable were the Middle East not so consistently unpredictable.

206 This is quoted by Pierre Salinger and Eric Laurent in their *Secret Dossier: The Hidden Agenda Behind the Gulf War*, 65.

207 See above, 89. In antiquity, what is now Iraq was variously part of the
     Assyrian and Babylonian Empires, swallowed up by the Medo-Persian
     Empire and Alexander the Great in turn, and subsequently part of
     the renascent Parthian and Sassanian Empires respectively. Its general
     topographic contours were what defined it for the Greeks, who called
     it Mesopotamia (meaning "between the Rivers") due to the dominating
     role played by the Tigris and Euphrates Rivers in its life. By the seventh
     century CE, it was dominated by the Arab Muslims and became the seat
     of the Abbasid Empire for five centuries; it was swallowed up by the
     Persians again and then became part of the Ottoman Empire, which it
     remained until the British took over.

208 Salinger and Laurent, 113.

209 Ibid, 136.

210 I am deliberately ignoring two issues here. One is that the alliance in the
     end failed because the attempt to bring in a third monarch, Muhammad
     V of Morocco, failed, and the other two apparently chose not to go it
     alone. Two, that there is an unhappy irony in a meeting in the US capital,
     named for the leader of the American revolt against a monarch, in which
     American support was being offered to two monarchs against the revolt
     of a people whose situation in 1957 might be said to have mirrored the
     American situation in 1776. This irony leads us to the question I shall
     raise at the end of this chapter: what *are* we Americans as we move about
     the world diplomatically, politically, and militarily?

211 Salinger and Laurent, 204–5.

212 Ibid, 210.

213 There is a growing library of articles on this issue. One particularly inter-
     esting one, tackling a slightly different aspect of the matter, is by Stephen
     Zunes, "The US Role in Iraqs [*sic*] Sectarian Violence," in *Foreign Policy
     in Focus*, March 6, 2006.

214 Petraeus was, among other things, Commanding General for the
     Multi-National Force in Iraq from February 10, 2007, to September 16,
     2008—in which capacity he oversaw all coalition forces—and subse-
     quently Commander, US Central Command, from October 13, 2008, to
     June 30, 2010; and Commander of the International Security Assistance
     Force and of US Forces in Afghanistan from July 4, 2010, to July 18,
     2011. Audio tapes of the lecture—actually a public dialogue with author
     and former soldier Wes Moore—may be obtained from Chautauqua
     Institution.

215 For more detail, see the article in the February 16, 2015, issue of *The
     Guardian* by Chris Stephen, "Libya's Arab Spring: The Revolution that

ate its children," and also Peter Cole & Brian McQuinn, eds., *The Libyan Revolution and Its Aftermath* (London: Hurst Publishers, 2014).

216   For a further discussion of Egypt in the context of the "Arab Spring," see Appendix 1.

Chapter 14

217   "Ira-" is cognate with the Greek root, "*ari-*." Thus "aristocracy" is "rule/power of/by the best [citizens]."

218   An Iranian friend of mine reported how his grandfather regaled him with stories of performances in which the actors playing the Umayyad villain would have to flee the performance space; the audience would get so emotionally riled up that, forgetting in, say, the year 1900, that the story being conveyed was more than 1,200 years past, some of its members would rush the stage to assault the villain.

219   It might be noted here that the Saudis offer a particularly intense example of the paradoxic manner in which so much of the Middle Eastern region operates. They are not only concerned, of course, about the Iranians but also more broadly about the sort of terrorism that can threaten their regime as much as anyone's and thus make them allies of not only Israel and the United States but of other nations fighting the so-called war on Terror. But they are at the same time among the more significant funders of groups whose ideology—*jihadism* in the common-parlance sense of that term, articulated specifically by an ossified version of Wahhabism—promotes and practices terrorism. See the very thorough article by Scott Shane on the front page of the August 26, 2016, issue of *The New York Times*.

There is more, as an even more disturbing article by Simon Henderson in the July 18, 2016, issue of *Foreign Policy* suggests that now that the 2002 congressional investigation into 9/11 has become public, one can see clear (if not absolutely definitive) evidence that some of the hijackers "were in contact with, and received support and assistance from, individuals who may be connected to the Saudi government," that members of the royal family were funneling money to Islamic extremists, and that they were paying Usama Bin Ladin "to cause trouble elsewhere but not in the kingdom."

220   Among the negative reflections of even the hint at warming US-Iran relations was the February 25, 2009, paper by Clare M. Lopez, "Rise of the 'Iran Lobby': Tehran's front groups move on—and into—the Obama Administration," written for the Center for Security Policy. The CSP was founded in 1988 to expose what it perceives as "jihadist threats" to the United States. The organization was referred to by the Southern Poverty

Law Center in 2016 as a "conspiracy-oriented mouthpiece" and has faced strong criticism across the political spectrum for its expressed views.

221   This was reported in an October 2, 2011, article in *Arab News*, by Ramin Mostafavi.

222   See the April 15, 2015, front-page article by Jonathan Weisman and Peter Baker in *The New York Times* for details on Obama and Congress; and the article by Thomas Erdbrink in the July 22, 2015, issue (A4) for details on the *majlis*.

223   See the front-page article by David E. Sanger in the July 14, 2016, issue of *The New York Times*.

224   See the article by Trinta Parsi in the January 2006 issue of *Jane's Intelligence Review*.

225   See above, 45ff.

226   The alphabet reform reflects the perception that Turkish, as a vowel-heavy language, was ill served by the Arabic writing system in place for centuries under the Ottomans, since that system emphasizes consonants. Adopting the Latin alphabet, with some adaptations, serves the Turkish language more efficiently.

227   The Soviets saw this as a kind of first declaration of a Cold War.

228   Among other Egypt-centered complications, Morsi and the Muslim Brotherhood were at that point pulling back from Hamas and its policy of armed struggle against Israel, moderating the Brotherhood's own prior stance and seeking rapprochement with Fatah in order to function more effectively as an advocate to the Israelis for Palestinian statehood. The Brotherhood's shift would have placed it in a contrary motion to that of Erdogan vis-a-vis the Jewish State.

229   For a concise and eloquent summary of the Gezi Park debacle within the larger context of Erdogan's ascent/descent to demagoguery, see the brief article, "Ghosts of Gezi," by Raffi Khathadourian in *The New Yorker*, June 2, 2014, 56–9.

230   For more detail on Gülen and *hizmet*, see Ori Z. Soltes *Embracing the World: Fethullah Gülen's Thought and Its Relationship to Jalaluddin Rumi and Others*. (Clifton, NJ: Tughra Books, 2013). Since the time of that volume, I have interviewed some forty followers of Gülen in preparation for an intellectual biography of him.

231   The unprecedented numbers involved in Erdogan's purges of the soldiers, policemen, judges, school teachers, university deans, members of the Ministry of Education and the Ministry of Finance; and the closing of media outlets is graphically translated into the equivalents were such purges to happen in America in the August 2, 2016, on-line article, "The

Scale of Turkey's Purge Is Nearly Unprecedented," by Josh Keller, Iaryna Mykhyalyshyn and Safak Timur.

232   See Appendix 2 for a slightly more detailed analysis of the July 15, 2016, "coup." For evidence to support my conclusions regarding Erdogan's desperate situation and what he might have done to relieve that situation, see in particular Sabrina Tavernise, "Turkish Leader Makes New foes and Vexes Allies," on the front page of *The New York Times*, July 5, 2016.

233   See, for example, Robert Parry, "A Blind Eye Toward Turkey's Crimes," in *Consortium News*, December 18, 2015. Among other things, Parry notes the "growing allegations that [Erdogan] tolerated the Islamic State's lucrative smuggling of oil from wells in Syria through border crossings in Turkey," and that "Erdogan's 34-year-old-son, Bilal [the same son overheard in the corruption scandal asking his father where to stash the cash], of profiting off the Islamic State's oil trade, an allegation that he denied."

234   The expulsion of Palestinians is not so surprising when one keeps in mind that Yassir Arafat, as leader of the Palestinians, had openly supported Saddam Hussein in 1990 in the latter's decision (and follow-up!) to invade Kuwait.

235   See the detailed discussion of this issue in the June 3, 2013, front-page article in *The New York Times* by Tim Arango and Clifford Krauss. Early on, they quote Michael Makovsky, who was a Defense Department official under the younger Bush: "The Chinese had nothing to do with the war, but from an economic standpoint they are benefitting from it, and our Fifth Fleet and air forces are helping to assure their supply."

236   The lecture was delivered at Chautauqua Institution, Chautauqua, New York, on Wednesday, August 18, 2004. Tapes of that lecture are available from Chautauqua Institution.

Chapter 15

237   The first quote comes from *Windows'* mission statement; the second from the first page of their newsletter, *Open Window* (September 2003/ Issue 7). The organization, appropriately enough, has two addresses: 35 Trumpeldor Street, PO Box 56096, Tel Aviv-Jaffa; and Near Jamal Abdul Nassir Center, PO Box 104, Tul Karem.

238   The two articles appeared on June I and June 2 respectively, on the front page of the Arts Section. The first is entitled "Minuets, Sonatas and Politics in the West Bank," and the second, "In the West Bank Turmoil, the Pull of Strings."

239 This is the same issue of *Moment* to which I called attention above: March/April 2009, 16.

240 It is directed by Dror Zahavi and written by Ido Dror.

241 Directed by Eran Riklis and cowritten by him with Suha Arraf. Arraf also cowrote *The Syrian Bride.*

242 He is quoted in a small article on page 12 of the April 23, 2009, issue of the *Washington Jewish Week.*

243 See above, 136–40.

244 See above, 72–3.

245 *Seeds of Peace* focuses more broadly on kids on different sides of any number of problem spots across the planet than on the Middle East, but in recent years the Israeli-Palestinian and larger Israeli-Arab issue has been its most consistent and steady focus.

246 Quoted in an Internet article, http://www.jewishtoronto.com.

247 One ought to recall the proposition by Daniel Gavron that the Israeli Arab population is a key potential factor in making the peace process work. See above, 139–40 and fnn 118 and 125.

248 *Ibid.* The words were spoken by Muhammad Darwashe, a prominent Israeli Arab, who was present at the soccer game.

249 Daniel Pipes, "The Real New Middle East," *Commentary.* (November, 1998, Vol 106. No. 5), 25–29.

250 *Ibid*, 26.

251 *Ibid*, 27.

252 Indeed, the shifting of the sands of coalition relationships among the various Muslim and Arab states continues and will continue into the foreseeable future, based on "resistance" to the West and the United States (most obviously at this writing, Iran, Syria, and Palestine) versus politically friendly to the United States. But within some states friendly to the United States (Israel, Jordan, Cyprus, Turkey, Egypt, Saudi Arabia, Yemen, the Gulf States, and Pakistan), there are strong political opposition parties that are part of the axis of "resistance" (Egypt, Yemen, Jordan, and Pakistan).

253 An excellent summary of the role of Syria—from the beginning of its civil war and the various groups playing proxy roles on behalf of Iran and Saudi Arabia, to the development of ISIS/ISIL—in Israeli-Turkish relations of the past decade may be found in the article by Moran Stern and Denis Ross, "The role of Syria in Israeli-Turkish Relations," in the Summer/Fall 2013 issue of the *Georgetown Journal of International Affairs.*

254 See the article by Tim Arango in *The New York Times*, November 2, 2015, A-8.

255   Joseph Braude, *The New Iraq: Rebuilding the Country for Its People, the Middle East, and the World.*

256   *Ibid*, x.

257   See the article by Anne Barnard in the August 23, 2016, *New York Times*: "Kurds Close to Control of Northeast Syria Province, Portending a Shift in the War," for a good summary of this development.

Afterword

258   Gilad Shalit was captured by *Hamas* and after being held prisoner for more than five years, he was released to the Israelis in a prisoner exchange on October 18, 2011. Ehud Goldwasser and Eldad Regev were captured by *Hizb'Allah* and either died during the attack in which they were taken captive or were killed later. The remains of their bodies were sent back to Israel in July 2008 in exchange for five *Hizb'Allah* prisoners and the remains of 199 Lebanese and Palestinian soldiers. The so-called "Second Lebanon War" that resulted from the two northern kidnappings lasted over a month, yielding about one thousand dead, most of them Lebanese civilians.

259   Turkey's Erdogan, in fact, claimed that through his influence on Assad, the Syrians were close to coming to an agreement with Israel in winter 2008, but that Israel's launching of Operation Cast Lead against *Hamas* in Gaza that December led to a collapse of negotiations, in part because of Turkey's anger over the Israeli military venture. Interestingly, Ehud Olmert asserted in his memoirs published in early 2011 that he and Abbas were near a deal in 2008 that was scutted due to Abbas's hesitancy, his (Olmert's) legal troubles and the Gaza conflict. Abbas, interviewed for a January 28, 2011, *New York Times* article by Ethan Bronner, essentially confirmed this account. Olmert didn't mention Erdogan.

260   Khalidi, *The Iron Cage*, XVI.

261   See above, 199–200 and fnn 195, 197, and the references to *J Street* and to Gershom Gorenberg's *Moment* magazine article, for two examples of the latter.

262   See Appendix 1 for a brief analysis of Egypt within the Arab Spring.

263   An important filament tangled within the little thread of Bahrain, which sustained the most unrest among the Persian Gulf countries during and after the Arab Spring: by July 2013, the US Navy, whose Fifth Fleet is based in Manama, Bahrain's capital, with its deep-draft port—about fifteen thousand Americans (including servicemen and their families) occupy the base—was considering alternative sites, or it was asserted that we should in a report by Navy Commander Richard McDaniel. He suggested considering the possibilities offered by Doha, in Qatar, or

Shuaiba, in Kuwait. Not everyone agrees, but the point was to put pressure on the Bahrainian royal family to take seriously the need to work with, not against their Shi'i majority.

264 He kept that promise. In 2015, for the first time in its history, the Kingdom of Saudi Arabia permitted female candidates and voters in the municipal elections and there were female victors. Municipal councils have very limited, localized responsibilities, dealing with garbage collection and street maintenance—but it is arguably a beginning.

265 Yet another intriguing observation with regard to the shifting sands of alliances came forth in an early November 2006 article by Alon Ben-Meir in *The Globalist* (November 10). Ben-Meir suggests that the threat of a Shi'i alliance between Iran and the Shi'is of Iraq (*both* steadily re-empowered by the United States' incursion into Iraq "during the past three years," at the time of his writing) could cause moderate Sunni states, in particular Saudi Arabia, to seek an alliance with Israel, as the only regional power with the capacity to stand up militarily to Iran's growing bellicosity. Syria could and would be part of that alliance, which, would seek to undermine Iranian support of Palestinian extremists while supporting the Palestinian moderates and Israelis to ally themselves with each other against the extremists—together with Egypt and Jordan, of course, and with a Syria returned to the Peace Table with Israel. Consider the implications of Ben-Meir's suggestion for the web we have been unraveling: the Shi'i identity in the first case is seen to trump the Arab/non-Arab identity that otherwise should (and has, in the past) made Iraq and Iran simple antagonists. In the second case, Sunni identity also trumps Arab/non-Arab identity. Moreover, Muslim identity as well as Arab identity would be trumped by concluding an alliance with Israel, because in the larger scheme of the region's complications, Israel is less of a threat to the survival even of Syria and certainly of Saudi Arabia than Iran has become in combination with Shi'i Iraqis. Thus, the issue for us is not only one of common enemies producing a new configuration of (potential) allies, but of being reminded of the expansive geopolitical terms in which one must consider the region encompassed by our tangled web.

Appendices

266 Appendix 1 was written as an opinion piece shortly after the second phase of the Egyptian revolution that brought down Mubarak in 2011; Appendix 2 was written as an opinion piece a few weeks after the Turkish "coup" of July 15, 2015.

Bibliography

267   Two things should be noted with regard to this bibliography. The first is
that it is far from comprehensive, and perhaps not even weighted with
regard to perspectives on the varied matter encompassed by it, but it
consists of books that I have found useful in achieving a better-rounded
understanding of the tangled web. The second is that any number of
works cited here is significantly skewed one way or another, so that the
fact that they are listed here should not be interpreted as an endorsement
of their contents and/or points of view. It simply means that they offer
information that is useful one way or another.